PROFESSIONAL DAY TRADING

E=MC^2 TRADING APPROACH©
"The Theory of Relative Timeframes"

APPLIED TO THE
S&P E-MINI MARKET

A ROADMAP TO DAY TRADING SUCCESS

Steven Nussbaum

Copyright © 2010 by Steve Nussbaum
Skyline Publications
Dallas Texas
Contact: tradingcreations@tx.rr.com
Website: www.tradingcreations.com

Printed in the United States of America
First edition printing September, 2010

ISBN-13: 978-0-945272-50-2

Library of Congress Control Number: 2010913756

RISK DISCLAIMER:

TABLE OF CONTENTS

SECTION 7 – CASE STUDY EXAMPLES

SECTION 8 – DETAILS

SECTION 9 - PUTTING IT ALL TOGETHER (CONTEXT)

PROFESSIONAL DAY TRADING

Welcome to the E=MC2 Day Trading approach. This is the exact approach I use to trade the ES market every day.

E=MC2 is designed to take advantage of one basic trading concept that clearly has had the biggest positive impact on my trading: "You don't have to overcomplicate trading!"

For instance, don't dismiss the power of observing price action with two moving averages as a meaningful way to define trend and trade opportunities.

My goal in trading is not to be in the market at all times, or to catch every price move in perfect fashion, or even to necessarily understand why price moves the way it does.

Instead, I simply am looking to establish a trading edge over a large number of trades which means (1) Come up with a consistent way to define trend (choosing whatever definition of trend you feel comfortable with) (2) Trade in the direction of this trend most of the time with consistent trade setups (whatever they may be), over and over again (3) Build a trading edge over time by placing consistent trade setups into a bigger picture context of what is unfolding in the market.

I have found this three phase approach to trading means you need to focus on trading differently than most traders do- or from the top-down versus from the bottom-up, which means big picture perspective comes first, and trade setups come last.

Therefore, the core of the E=MC2 trading approach presented in this book grows exponentially more significant the further you move along through the material!

Professional Day Trading means that before you can consider a trading set up you must first learn to read the market and develop expectations for where price is trying to go in relation to a host of different market structure conditions (Trend days, Intra-day chop, Price moving inside or outside a balance area, Volume confirmation etc.).

For my own trading, this means I spend 90% of my time analyzing big picture structure above all else. I always know where price action is located relative to current buyer-seller balance. I'm always trying to define what type of intra-day structure is unfolding.

A big picture structure first mentality has been the key to my trading success.

I believe a lack big picture focus is the main reason for the high trading failure rate you often hear about, and ultimately I feel trading from the top-down rather than from the bottom-up separates the Professional Day Trader from the Amateur Day Trader.

Section 1 - Overview

<u>ACKNOWLEDGEMENTS</u>

I dedicate this book to all aspiring traders, and I am especially grateful to those of you who have written to let me know how much this material has positively contributed to your trading efforts.

This is why I wrote this book.

I know how much a book of this nature would have helped me out when I first started my trading journey, and I hope this book helps everyone in the same way it has helped these traders:

"I hope you are doing well. I wanted to say hello and let you know my reaction so far to the method. I am reading it twice in two stages. I am up to the case studies. Steve, I can see that a lot of cerebral matter went into formulating and refining the E=mc2 approach, which leads me to believe that over the years, you may have tried as many commercial methods and so called "systems" as I did before you conceived of this great approach. Of all the systems/methods I have bought, and believe me there have been many, this is the most well thought out method I have seen. <u>Your book really does teach a "way to trade" instead of a set of rules that you just mimic.</u> Amazingly, you have even taken into account the possibility of having to adjust indicator settings should developing market behavior change by your technique of applying congruence between a 233 tick chart and a 1500 volume chart. You sir are a pioneer!"

"Thanks for the extra info. It's helpful. One thing I'm liking a lot about the book so far is that you start from the high time frames and work your way down to the trade. Exactly the opposite of what most of us do, finding an interesting idea on the trading time frame and then looking for other things to confirm."

"Finished the book, and If I never make a trade using your method, the stuff you presented is great... You have a good handle on trading... Have never seen the market as clearly as I do now. Today is another great day. Wow, the thought that I might have stumbled onto a method that I could literally do for a living makes me the happiest senior citizen in the country!"

"Charts with your comments are excellent. I would write more often to tell you how well I'm doing...both in capturing profits and duplicating the trades later when you post them. But your are busy and should know (as you have written) that those of us who do our homework and then ingrain what you have written on EMC2 is all a trader needs!! It is just true. Sure I'm not at the computer all hours, but man, what a logical approach to the market. Becoming 2nd nature each day to "evaluate" the market and the trends and setups as they invariably develop. And today I realized the choppiness early on and how important was that. Keep up the good work. From one of your happiest followers!"

"Just a quick note to let you know I'm really starting to see how the system works... kind of seeing the forest for the trees... (still paper trading to get myself real comfortable) but the trades are coming more and more effortlessly. Again, like I mentioned to you in our first Email I had been through a few courses and systems and I can unequivocally say yours makes the most sense in both a practical and intuitive sense..."

"The manual arrived on Friday. What can I say? I'm impressed! What impresses me about the system is how you have combined one simple screen full of charts to consistently and effectively build a framework of dynamic context within which to assess unfolding market conditions. I consider myself a discerning, yet open, person. I'm very happy to find that I'm already confident enough in the theory behind the system that I want to give myself over to it. That is to say, follow it to a tee! I also received your addendums that explain your recommendations for the ideal setups to be traded initially, and perhaps forever. I will follow your advice on all of these points. As I progress through the motions of learning and applying the information, I will stay in touch. Right now, I don't have any specific questions thanks to your thorough and clear writing style."

"My account is up well over 30% since I began trading futures with your method. Thanks again and again. The fund I manage is also able to control risk better using your methods and trading SPY."

FOREWORD

The material presented here represents a framework to successfully trade the ES stock index futures market.

Success simply means that when you stay within the confines of this framework, the net results from winning trades vs. losing trades over time will result in an increasing equity curve week to week, month to month, that can fulfill realistic trading goals and expectations in line with the size of your trading account.

You will never be a perfect trader. You will make trading mistakes. You will make good trading decisions and bad trading decisions.

But, in the end, factoring in all the ups and downs, this framework provides plenty of good trading opportunities to allow you to achieve realistic trading goals.

This framework is not the only way to successfully trade, or even necessarily the "best" way to trade, but after years of experimenting with virtually every type of trading approach out there, and experiencing every type of trading up and down imaginable, the material presented here will bring any trader closer to his or her goal to trade successfully.

By the time you finish reading this material, your eyes will hopefully open to a "common sense" way to view day trading.

The road to successful trading isn't easy.

If you are expecting to find a simple 1-2-3 formula for trading success, I am of the opinion that you have misconceptions about what successful trading is all about.

Unfortunately, most marketing efforts in the trading arena are designed to lead you to believe that trading is easy.

Common sense should tell you otherwise. Not only do most traders fail, but even the best traders in the world point out that in many cases it took them years of ups and downs, and mistakes, to finally break through to the winning side.

It is important to set a realistic tone right from the start, and this is what makes this material different from other discourses on trading.

In my opinion, most people go about learning to trade the wrong way.

Most traders try following the advice of trading books that say trading is simple and psychology and discipline are the main keys to trading success.

Therefore, most traders search for set-ups that "work all of the time" in order to take the analytical side out of trading.

Most traders want "discipline" to mean that there are simple rules to guide all of their trading decisions, but there are problems with this mindset.

First, while psychology and discipline are important, they are not everything, and the discipline side of trading doesn't mean you must try to do the same exact thing each and every time a valid trading setup is triggered.

For instance, the E=MC2 trading approach only looks at THREE MAIN TRADING SETUPS, which on the surface sounds very easy and simple.

However, these setups can develop before, during, or after the market has made a clear directional move, and each condition may or may not be better than the other to enter and/or manage a trade.

While trading is about some fairly simple principles, actually finding an edge in trading is NOT simple.

In reality, successful trading is about being okay with ambiguity. It's about tolerating confusion. It's about sitting with discomfort and being at peace with it. It's about not having an exact script of when to trade, or when not to trade, or what really is a high odds trade or not, and being okay with that. It's about exceptions to the rules. It's about contradiction. It's about uncertainty.

And yet traders want to keep things simple all the time. They want to reduce trading to a few standard rules to trade with discipline. And yet the market is not simple. The market is filled with uncertainty, complexity, and ambiguity. Standard rules all the time could never capture this, and will never give you a true lasting edge.

So what's the solution? Is the problem trying to develop simple rules themselves?

No, the problem is how simple rules are being used.

The bottom line is, every trader needs to learn how to "READ" the markets. This means that simple rules on their own, used in a vacuum, will not work.

There has to be a synthesis of different elements together- price action, indicators, intra-day structure formation, big picture context, etc. and real-time interpretation must factor all these elements together at the moment of the trading decision.

Trading has to be about CONTEXT. Once you can read the markets (at times easy, at times complex), then you can choose to employ an overall "simple framework" to enter and exit trades.

But the real work will be to interpret a variety of market factors simultaneously to see how a particular set-up falls into a bigger picture context. Seeing a possible reversal near a support area means nothing unless you've identified the broader picture of what seems to be developing which leads to a sense of what tactics you should use to manage your trade.

Most trader's main focus is just on set-ups alone, and not on reading the market on a minute to minute, hour to hour, day to day basis to help figure out the probabilities of price doing this or doing that, which allows you to adapt dynamically, and think of trading decisions from a variety of angles at the same time.

Of course this requires thinking and synthesizing a variety of thoughts together which goes beyond the notion of waiting for a simple rule to pop up to trade. It's easy to look for a certain setup over and over again.

But who ever said "easy" makes you money?

What I have learned in my years of trading is that the market rewards what is hard to do. It's hard to embrace ambiguity regarding the market. It's hard being uncertain. It's hard dealing with competing and sometimes conflicting signals.

And yet, this is what the road to successful trading is all about as well as realizing you will never get everything right all of the time.

You have to stop trying to avoid ambiguity in an effort to have everything so clear cut.

So, the conflict becomes "How can you truly be "disciplined" when there's so much uncertainty and ambiguity about the right trade to make, especially when you are told rule number one is you must be disciplined to trade successfully?"

Therefore, instead of trying to avoid uncertainty, and maintain discipline by looking for straight-forward "trading rules" all of the time, you need to train your mind to deal with, and embrace uncertainty, and put discipline to use in a unique way.

As for the learning process of how to go about doing this, it's all about being constantly being engaged with the markets on a number of levels at the same time, and then learning from experience over time.

It's about watching market action day after day, minute after minute, over and over again. It's all about perception and interpretation. It's all about making mistakes and wrong decisions, and at times being conflicted as to what is going on.

It's about not knowing if market interpretations will end up correct or not, and yet gaining experience from every interpretation, every trade, no matter what the outcome, as you continue to learn and grow as a trader.

It's about continuously viewing charts and combinations of charts, and noting certain behaviors and patterns. For instance, trend days are completely different from range days. Therefore, you need to define trend days vs. range days and notice what characteristics trend days have in common so you can pick up on these characteristics in real time.

You need to understand the basics of support and resistance, congestion areas, breakout scenarios, etc. to provide context for trading setups.

You need to develop a sense for different types of price action- solid momentum movement vs. more random price swing behavior.

Over time, these factors together provide you with a "feel for the markets," and an understanding of how certain days differ from other days and provide different types of trading opportunities, while alerting you to various subtle signs that differentiate one type of trading environment from another, which provides overall context for your trading decisions.

With all this as a backdrop, you should begin to see how a static set of predefined rules and setups to follow all the time, and in every condition, will not work.

Of course you will need an overall simple framework to look to enter and exit trades, but exits and entries will never exactly develop the same way all the time, nor should you expect them to.

Your goal in trading is to get in a trade with good trade location relative to unfolding big picture price structure, and this "art of execution" requires patience, and is never completely straight forward.

For instance, in some environments it's best to wait for deeper pullbacks to enter, and in others environments you will need to get into a price move fairly quickly or you'll be left behind.

In the end, you will became consistently profitable when you realize the market, and trading, is dynamic.

In time, everyone develops their own style of trading and their own trading personality. Some traders will be more discretionary than others and that's fine, but even purely mechanical traders still are very adept at reading the market, and are very aware of all of the complexities and ambiguities that are thrown into the mix.

A mechanical trading approach may end up being simple, but it will also align with a thorough, and deep, and complex understanding of market, and a good trading approach will always take market environment (i.e. context) into account. It will not just be a series of mindless set-ups thrown together.

This means you will need to develop a somewhat complex mental map when you trade, and you will never develop this mental map if you spend all your trading efforts focused on finding the single, perfect set-up that will lead to uncovering the "Holy grail of trading." The Holy grail of trading doesn't exist!

Most trader's learning curves becomes stagnant because they are not studying the markets, and instead are looking for the easy way out.

Time is wasted searching for something that will unlock the key to grab every single price move, and most traders are not properly focused on developing the intuition to read what the market is doing in the present tense by bridging together multi-dimensional factors, and then determining how to best handle each unique development that unfolds through a keen sense of observation and multi-layered analysis.

Also, because there is a fear of loss (psychological), most traders aren't willing to experiment. This means most traders are hesitant to act, and therefore aren't making the mistakes that are an important part of the learning process.

In conclusion, it is my opinion that most traders need to make a significant mental shift with regard to their focus and trading approach.

The "learning to trade" journey is not an easy one, but it can be a very rewarding one in the end. You will need to embrace uncertainty and ambiguity like never before. But this needn't be scary. Instead, it should be exciting, because this is what successful trading is all about.

You will need to embrace trading as an "quasi-art form." When you embrace trading as "ART," then everything, including trading success, becomes possible instead of just a distant dream that keeps appearing to be so close, yet remains so far away.

If you happen to be a struggling trader, you'll need to develop a new thought process, study the markets in a new way, develop new market instincts, and then start to trade.

Take losses. Make mistakes. Be uncertain, and don't be afraid of it. It's all okay, and it's the only way you'll progress.

I'm sure this all sounds overwhelming and confusing.

The good news is that the material presented here will propel you years forward along the "learning curve of trading."

When you finish this material you will be situated at the "trading starting line" with a very good chance to succeed if you continue to forge ahead, apply this material in your own unique way, have realistic trading goals and expectations, and then always maintain an open mind to adapt and grow with each new trading experience.

INTRODUCTION

What are you trying to accomplish day trading the ES market?

If you don't know the answer to this question, you need to think long and hard before you start to trade.

Day trading really boils down to a few main areas.

(1) Having the fearlessness to take good trade setups when they develop (2) Managing the trade in accordance with eliminating risk as soon as possible in one form or another (3) Maximizing winning trades according to unfolding price action after the trade is entered (4) Understanding how all the wins and losses in the trading game come together to make money in the end.

Fearlessness to take trades – You will only successfully trade this method (or any other method) when you learn to accept that losses will occur in trading, and you know that every trade is part of a much bigger probability puzzle in line with what you are trying to accomplish.

We intuitively know we <u>must take small losses vs. large losses</u> to trade successfully.

Most traders have taken large losses before, and have seen how difficult it is to recover from such large losses.

If you take a large loss and continue to stick with your trading plan, it takes you a long, long time to catch up.

Because it takes a long time to catch up, this often leads to breaking the trading plan on subsequent trades – either by taking overly aggressive trades, or just by taking completely random trades with a sense of panic to "get losses back quick," or push the envelope on winning trades way too far in terms of going for the "homerun" in an effort to win back losses when you should be chipping away with moderate gains instead.

So, from a mathematical, and psychological standpoint, big losses kill you!

<u>But no one ever talks about the psychological difficulties of taking proper small losses!</u>

For example, even when you take a proper small "1-point loss," according to all your rules, there is a feeling that kicks in which says: "I've done something wrong, I've failed on the trade, the approach doesn't work anymore, there has to be a better way to avoid this loss in the future, etc."

The danger of this normal and very natural reaction is that **<u>THIS WILL INSTILL "FEAR" IN YOU TO TAKE THE NEXT GOOD TRADE!</u>**

Hopefully the material in this book will alleviate some of this fear, but in all candor, this fear never truly goes away, and you need to understand where this fear comes from. <u>It comes from following your plan, and taking proper small losses!</u>

I don't think I've ever heard it explained this way before.

Even if you are doing everything right, the human brain is still ingrained with a sense of "losing is bad" and "winning is good," and this basic natural instinct makes trading very difficult to master no matter who you are, no matter how smart you are, or no matter how much you may intuitively understand what it takes to trade successfully- **BECAUSE NO ONE LIKES TO TAKE A LOSS!**

I don't think you can ever learn to "feel good" about taking a loss, but you must do everything in your power to accept small losses when a trade doesn't work out, and move on.

I will simply say this: "It is easier said than done," because there is no easy answer on how to make a loss feel good, or normal. <u>A losing trade simply never creates a positive feeling or experience!"</u>

All I know is that you cannot succeed in trading if you don't learn to accept small losses, treat small losses as part of the game where many good winning trades are always right around the corner, and not let small losses destroy your confidence to take future good trades.

Trading is a probability game – Perhaps the best way to learn to accept small losses and maintain steadfast confidence in your trading plan is to set up a complete trading plan ahead of time with <u>realistic trading goals and expectations</u>.

The goal and expectation side of trading often gets "completely distorted and blown out of proportion."

This stems from the winning side of trading- where you can put down your original bet, and win way more than your original bet if everything goes right.

<u>Such positive, "feel good" outcomes, completely distorts the reality of trading expectations for many traders!</u>

Not only do many traders expect such positive outcomes on **every trade**, but they also subconsciously set their trading goals to fall in line with a "homerun" mentality regarding how much money they should make on every trade.

Many traders feel like they can take a $5000 account and double, triple, or even quadruple this account in a short period of time because certain trades provide a $500 gain in a matter of minutes.

This distorted view is so far from reality that you must take a step back and really understand what realistic trading goals and expectations are all about.

Trading expectations need to be about most winning trades providing moderate gains, a few trades providing large gains, and in the end you will end up with a slight "net edge" over your small losing trades.

If you can establish realistic trading expectations from the start, then the difficult aspects of trading can be better managed and handled, and in the end, you can become a successful trader in line with realistic goals and expectations.

Realistic trading goals and expectations - You must establish some type of trading plan ahead of time, before you start to trade.

You need every trade you take to be viewed as nothing more than a single piece of a much bigger trading probability puzzle that is set in place from the start.

Do you think a casino puts out a slot machine that provides all kinds of random outcomes? Of course they don't. The entire payout of a slot machine is set up ahead of time. So too should your trading plan be completely set up ahead of time.

To repeat: "Having a trading plan, fearless trade execution, accepting small losses, riding winners to at least logical extension points, and understanding how a series of winning and losing trades come together in the end to make money is what the trading game is all about.

Right now I know most of you are probably focused on the "method" side of trading, and can't wait to learn the setups to enter and exit trades.

This is fine, but it is not nearly as important as understanding how all this falls into your trading plan, and more importantly, understanding how you don't always have to be perfect in your trading.

You must feel comfortable that losing trades are a part of the game.

In addition, I will show all kinds of numbers that provide for missing good trades, and still doing very well.

I even show how a trading plan can miss "the very best trade each day" and still come out nicely ahead when you have realistic trading expectations.

You don't have to be perfect with regard to catching every good trade, or every market move, or never taking a loss!

When you set up a realistic trading plan ahead of time, you come to realize that trading is nothing more than a probability game, and the probability view of trading will allow you to develop confidence to trade your method, and this ultimately this will lead to your trading success.

Building up contract size – The realistic way to succeed, and even "make a living" trading is to start small, develop consistency, and increase your contract size over time.

You are NOT going to be able to make a living trading 1-contract on a $5000 account!

In fact, trying to do so will likely cause you to blow this account up for trying to reach way beyond what a small account can reasonably offer. The first part of your trading plan needs to account for starting out small and building up your contract size as you gain confidence and consistency.

I will show how you can do very well if you can develop consistency regarding a series of average winning and losing trades and eventually build your account up to trading 5, or perhaps 10 or more contracts at a time.

This will require close to $30,000 (10 contracts) account vs. a $5000 account (1 contract), but even if $30,000 is a reasonable account size for you to start with, you should still start much smaller, and let your trading profits, and trading consistency, allow you to add more contracts over time.

Start with a $5000 account, trade only 1-contract to start, and develop a long term plan that eventually allows you to "trade for a living" with 10-contracts.

Or, as you master trading over time, and see how very modest goals to start can be surpassed, you may need to trade 5-contracts at a time.

UNREALISTIC TRADER - Let's say you plan to be a very active trader, take 10-12 trades a day, and hope to average 10-points a day trading 1-contract.

Total outcome - The results for such a plan may produce 243 trades a month netting 197 points. 197 X 50 = $9850. Commissions = 243 X 5 = $1215. Nets results for month = $ 8,635 per contract.

I guess you should go open up a $30,000 account, trade 10 contracts at a time, and start earning $86,350 per month!

EXPECTING TO MAKE 10-POINTS A DAY FROM 10-12 TRADES IS EXTREMELY UNREALISTIC AND WILL LIKLEY CAUSE YOU TO BLOW UP YOUR ACCOUNT BY STRETCHING EACH TRADE WAY BEYOND WHAT EACH TRADE CAN REASONABLY EXPECT TO OFFER!

Therefore, start by developing a trading plan that severely curtails these expectations and develops much more realistic expectations for results.

Let's make some very important and realistic assumptions:

1. You will make trading mistakes.
2. You will take larger than expected losses.
3. You will miss good trades.
4. You will make errors in judgment reading the market.
5. You will over-trade.
6. You will exit winning trades too early.

Unfortunately, all of these negative outcomes happen even with a very good trading framework such as the one outlined in this material.

You should never expect to be perfect with your trading, and your trading plan needs to build in a margin of error for your mistakes.

Sure, you will do many things right if you stick to the guidelines of your trading framework, but good will be offset by bad, and in the end, your goal is to simply have a slight positive edge in place when the good and bad are combined together.

I know you can make 5-10 points on many trades. I know the ES provides wide price ranges of 20-points per day.

These extraordinary outcome possibilities simply means you have a market that is very good for day trading, but also skew expectations regarding how many points you can expect to make each day.

Let's say you take two, 2-point losses in a row. You start out the day down 4-points and may be clawing and scratching your way back to break even for the day. You may even end up with a small loss for the day.

Other days may start out strong, and put you up 4-5 points early. Do you stop trading? Continue trading?

What if you continue to trade, give back 2-3 points, and only end up 1-point for the day?

Or, what if you continue to trade all day long, do a very good job with trade selectivity, and end up the day 10-points?

The main point is that trading results are scattered, and random. You never know the outcome from one trade to the next.

With the ES day trading framework presented here, there are plenty of good risk/reward trade opportunities that arise over and over again each trading session.

Therefore, you can be confident knowing that you have a framework in place to provide you with net positive edge over time, even with a variety of trading options and decisions you will have to make along the way.

You don't have to catch every market move in order to come out ahead. Trading is all about waiting for setups to develop your way, and your way only. As long as enough of these setups develop over and over again, who cares if the market makes a 10-pt move and you are not in it.

We simply want a trading plan that provides enough good risk-reward opportunities day to day, that have a slight positive edge built in.

In the end, a net positive edge has to be realistic factoring in good and bad decisions.

Realistic expectations go back to the concept introduced early on in the material- you have to be comfortable embracing uncertainty, ambiguity, and random outcomes scattered over time.

In terms of trading results, this means you can't measure results trade to trade, or even day to day, but rather week to week, or month to month.

Therefore, your goal at the end of each week, or even at the end of each month, is to simply reach a net realistic trading profit when daily results are averaged together.

Then once a very realistic goal is in place to start, you will actually have room to surpass this goal as your trading experience, and trading mastery grows over time.

1-POINT NET PER DAY TRADING GOAL:

When day trading ES, a 1-point per day (net) trading goal average is all you need to "succeed" in your trading.

I'm sure the thought of 1-measly point per day seems ludicrous to many of you, especially given the wide range of price movement that takes place in the ES each day, as well as what you were hoping for relative to all the time and effort you plan to put into your trading.

If you are initially offended by what seems like such a "small trading goal," I suggest you think more deeply about the topic of trading expectations.

A 1-pt per day average doesn't mean you stop trading each day when you are up 1-point. This puts too much pressure to make 1-point every single day.

You will have losing days trading. Accept this reality right now.

Therefore, a 1-pt per day average really means that you strive to make as much per day as possible by maximizing the results for each trade setup, while understanding that you may have a month where you end up on average winning 3-points a day for 3 weeks (15 days), and losing 3-pts a day for 1 week (5 days).

Furthermore, these outcomes will likely be scattered, where you will make 8 points on some days, lose 2 points on other days, etc., etc.

This realistic, scattered view of trading outcomes becomes your starting point to view average trading results over time.

Therefore, if you lose money on some days, and keep overall expectations conservative and realistic, you can average 30 pts per month gross with approximately 6 trades per day, winning 15 days on average, and losing on 5 days on average as follows:

$15(3) - 5(3) = 30$ x $50 = \$1,500$. Commissions = 120 X $5 = \$600$ (6 trades a day average), or a net of \$900, or slightly less than 1-point a day net (\$1,000 per month per contract traded)

If you trade 10 contracts, this would result in \$9,000 per month, net.

Over time, the notion of netting 1-point per day is somewhat limiting.

With a large variety of trading options and outcomes available each day, I feel you should start with a realistic ES day-trading goal of trying to make approximately 30 points per month/per contract, knowing that if volatility is very high for a given month, greater returns are possible, and if volatility is low for the month, lower outcomes can result.

But 30-points per month, per contract, is a realistic starting level to strive for and expect.

DAY- TO- DAY DECISIONS – On the way to 30-points per month there will be a variety of daily trading decisions to make.

One of the most difficult things to teach in trading is to describe how much to trade each day, i.e. when to continue trading, and when to stop trading relative to the open ended environment you are in, including the trading goals you have in place.

The best I can do is share with you what I find works best. Much of this you will simply have to experience on your own to truly understand.

I have found the best way to meet weekly and monthly goals is to stop trading at some point when you are ahead on the day, continue trading when you are behind on the day in an effort to get to some small win or loss on the day, and continue trading aggressively when ahead on the day and when big picture conditions scream out for you to continue.

So, there are many days to stop trading if you are nicely ahead and can sense price has worked much of the way from Point A to Point B for developing intra-day structure, or other favorable big picture conditions such as trend days and breakouts aren't in place.

Unless you see something very obvious form later on, it is almost always best to preserve any good trading gains you make early on, **and not risk giving them back**!

If you start out up 5-points and stop, and if 12-points on the day were possible, you should be thrilled for the 5-points early, and an easy day of trading!

Next, are trend days and breakout day conditions. Always look for these conditions to stay aggressive and try for big gains. These days by themselves offer the best trading opportunities for the month and you should try to stay very aggressive trading on these days in one form or another.

Finally, there are just bad trading days. You try to do everything possible to avoid these days (avoiding trades in conflict with the big picture or open, avoid dubious setups in choppy conditions, etc) but it is simply impossible to avoid poor trading days/decisions altogether, and sometimes you can do everything right and price action just isn't in sync with the trading timeframe you are looking to exploit.

When you start out with a poor trading day, accept that these days are inevitable and try to minimize the damage on these days as much as possible.

This means if you are down 4 points early, be very happy to end the day down 2 points.

If you can "eek out a small gain" after being down to start, have the discipline to stop trading and walk away thrilled.

Don't stop trading when down. In fact, it important to stay aggressive because you need to have faith that the next good trade set up will bring you back at some point.

Just know not to expect large gains on these days. I know walking away with a small loss on some days is not a pleasant thought, but this is fine when put into the bigger picture context of trading goals.

Remember, we actually have allowed for 5-losing trading days per month, or 25% of the time. Never forget that trading outcomes are random, scattered, and widely dispersed in terms of scope and size.

One of the biggest learning curve elements you will work to develop over time, is gaining a feel for the **time to stop trading on days when you have gains**, or at least protect as much of these gains as possible, and take very limited risk going forward.

There are times to stay aggressive trading, and these times almost always relate to big picture conditions (Trend days, Breakouts, First new intra-day trends, etc.)

Finally, you just have to accept that not every day can, or will be profitable.

Do your best to keep losses small on these days, wipe the slate clean, and come back strong the next day.

As long as you keep losses on each trade relatively small, there will always be great trade setups/trading conditions right around the corner, and in the end trading is a marathon much more so than a sprint, so where you end up at the end of the month is much more important than where you end up at the end of each day.

At the very least, I hope the information presented in this section sets you on the path to understanding realistic goals and expectations when trading, and shows you the importance of setting up a very specific trading plan ahead of time, before you ever start to trade for real.

Only with such a plan will you have the <u>confidence to trade with the consistency required</u> to succeed at game that is all about uncertainty, random outcomes, and probabilities in the long run.

You will do very well trading if you start out with realistic trading goals that account for and permit errors and mistakes, etc., and still provides a nice cushion to come out ahead.

Many traders never take the time to establish realistic trading goals, or take the time to understand how their trading plan fits within their trading goals (assuming they have a solid trading plan to begin with).

Without trading goals, or a trading plan, traders develop a distorted view of trading reality, which often leads to a host of distorted trading decisions.

If you can start out with a realistic view that successful trading is all about overall probabilities in a very random environment, then you start out with an excellent chance to succeed if you can develop the confidence to apply the rules of a solid trading plan over and over again.

WHAT IS THE E=MC2 TRADING APPROACH?

The E=MC^2 trading approach seeks to capitalize on a variety of consistent price movements that take place in the ES E-Mini Stock index futures market.

E=MC^2 defines a unique price roadmap for each E- Mini trading session - then specifies the best moments to execute trades in an effort to realize the incredible profit potential the ES E-Mini stock index market has to offer.

E=MC^2 does not apply Einstein's "Theory of Relativity" but instead focuses on a unique "Theory of Relative Timeframes."

E=MC^2 means:

(E) mini displays **(M)** omentum that either **(C)** ontinues or **(C)** onsolidates.

Momentum continuation and momentum consolidation are always "**RELATIVE**" to a variety of timeframes influencing price at any moment in time.

This means momentum in a short timeframe may be nothing more than a normal pullback in a long timeframe.

Don't worry. Multiple timeframes may seem confusing at first, but the E=MC^2 trading approach keeps it very simple.

It is assumed you possess basic knowledge of the ES E-Mini stock index market, including the structure of the market (i.e. each tick = $12.50, etc.), and especially the risks and rewards inherent to trading the E-Mini market.

If not, there is plenty of material available (beyond the scope of this book) for you to gather such information before you start to trade.

We use the "**Tradestation**" platform to plot all charts and indicators.

These same charts and indicators can be found in almost all other charting packages, but as of this writing, Tradestation is considered the Cadillac of the industry when it comes to data and charting.

E=MC^2 is a strictly a day trading method. All positions are entered and eventually closed by the end the day. No positions are executed, or carried over into the after-market (Globex) trading session. At present, the day session is 8:30-3:15 CST.

This book wastes no time in presenting the "nuts and bolts" of how to trade using the E=MC^2 approach, but always keep in mind the following:

THE $E=MC^2$ TRADING APPROACH IS THE RESULT AND OUTCOME OF MANY YEARS OF STUDYING AND TRADING THE ES MARKET, WORKING WITH JUST ABOUT EVERY STANDARD APPROACH TO TRADING THERE IS.

EVERY RULE AND NUANCE OF $E=MC^2$ IS DEEPLY ROOTED IN A SENSE OF SOUND MARKET AND TRADING LOGIC, INCLUDING:

- IDENTIFICATION OF MOMENTUM CONTINUATION AND CONSOLIDATION PATTERNS RELATIVE TO MULTIPLE TIMEFRAMES.
- THE AVOIDANCE OF OVERTRADING BY KNOWING WHEN TO TRADE AND WHEN NOT TO TRADE.
- ANALYZING BIG PICTURE MARKET STRUCTURE TO HELP CONFIRM DEVELOPING INTRADAY MARKET STRUCTURE .
- OPTIMAL TRADE MANAGEMENT TO MINIMIZE LOSSES AND MAXIMIZE GAINS (STOPS, BREAKEVEN, RIDING WINNERS, POSITION SIZE, ETC.)
- THE IMPORTANCE OF TRADE LOCATION RELATIVE TO DEVELOPING MARKET STRUCTURE.
- USING VOLUME TO CONFIRM MARKET STRUCTURE ANALYSIS.

If you are an experienced trader you understand the importance of these concepts. If you are new to trading, I hope you will appreciate **that this approach is the outcome of every type of trading success and failure you can imagine** in trying to arrive at a sound way to profit from price movements that take place in the ES E-Mini market.

Remember, there is no "one best way" to trade. Nothing works all the time. In order to trade successfully, you must combine two things - **a sound trading plan that provides some type of "edge," and the ability to execute such a plan consistently over time.**

Most traders never combine these two conditions together in the proper way.

$E=MC^2$ provides a sound way to do this.

The numerous chart examples in this manual, along with your own back and forward testing, will confirm the soundness of the $E=MC^2$ approach to you.

Once you are comfortable with the nuances of $E=MC^2$, it is my strong hope that you will have the fortitude necessary to consistently execute this approach and succeed in your trading endeavors.

DAY TRADING AND THE E-MINI MARKET

A day trading revolution has been upon us for quite some time. Information is available to the individual trader like never before. High-speed trade execution is within the reach of every individual who has access to a computer. Transaction (commission) costs are a fraction of what they were just years ago.

There are many advantages to day trading including: (1) No overnight exposure (2) Small risk per trade (3) Money can be multiplied many times over.

With so many day trading options available, confusion often sets in regarding which direction to go. Should the focus be on Stocks? Options? Futures? How many markets should be followed? How often should one trade during the day? These questions (and many others) confront the aspiring trader as he or she sets out to formulate a trading plan.

If you plan to day trade, you need nothing more than the S&P (ES) E-Mini market to succeed.

The ES E-Mini market has exploded in popularity, and for good reason.

Stock trading has been around forever, but it is not the most efficient vehicle when it comes to trading. First, considerable research is required to select the best stocks to trade. Second, it is hard to choose the right stocks to trade at the right time. Volatility can be low for periods at a time, and a considerable dollar investment is required (even with day trading margins). Also, rules such as the "up-tick rule," make it more difficult to execute short, as well as long positions.

Option trading also has been around a long time. The lure of high leverage and big profits seems very appealing, but in practice the task is quite difficult. The option buyer not only has to guess what price the underlying issue will reach, but also must be correct with respect to what time it will do so before time decay of option premiums sets in.

The option seller increases his/her odds of success, but with limited gains and potential unlimited losses. Also, options often do not provide the liquidity of other trading instruments, and wide bid/ask spreads can adversely affect desired trade execution.

Future trading is a lot more "pure" than either stock or option trading, and "Stock Index Futures" offers everything a trader can ask for, namely- **volatility, liquidity, leverage, and ease of execution.**

Markets like the ES E-Mini stock index futures are 100% electronically traded, so there is no physical broker effecting trade execution. Buys and Sells take place within a fraction of a second!

Stock index trading is also truly bi-directional, without an up-tick rule. You can just as easily go long or short, make money as price moves up or down, and reverse positions in an instant if you choose.

Stock index futures trading carries tax advantages over stock trading, and since the S&P E-Mini is a 500 company index, you eliminate the guesswork of selecting individual stocks, as well as the worry of surprise announcements that may adversely impact individual stock prices. (Although you always need to be aware when Economic Reports and/or Federal Reserve announcements are released, to decide how you want to handle the volatility that will almost always ensue afterwards).

The $E=MC^2$ approach is the result of many years of actual, hands-on trading experience, working with just about every type of trading approach there is.

$E=MC^2$ eliminates the three most common problems most traders face:

1. The trader watches price move up and down each day with many opportunities to make excellent profits, yet sits idly by on the sidelines, unable to recognize or take advantage of such opportunities until after they have passed.

2. The trader fails to grasp the "big picture" of what is happening in the market each day, and is unaware of the repetitive opportunities offered by the market, day in and day out.

3. The trader experiences losing trades far more often than desirable or affordable, and also finds it difficult to know when and how to exit winning positions as well.

In short, $E=MC^2$ goes far beyond the notion of whether just to buy or sell.

$E=MC^2$ provides a guideline for how the markets repetitively move, and therefore provides the trader with a "probability edge" in the long run if good trade setups are consistently entered over and over again.

The best chance for trading success comes from a trading plan that is based on <u>**consistent execution at points where the probability of at least some continued price movement in the direction of the trade is greatest.**</u>

Some trades move strongly your way right after entry. Other trades pull back after entry before continuing in your desired direction. Still, other trades never move your way, and you must take a small loss.

The key, however, is you just need slight favorable price movement in the trade direction soon after entry to allow you to manage your trades effectively. This makes the timing of entry very important.

Do not confuse $E=MC^2$ with "mechanical systems" that are out there.

Such systems are in conflict with the dynamics of market behavior. They are based on the premise that price movement will repeat past history <u>in the exact way</u>, over and over again. This, of course, is in conflict with the wisdom that price movement is dynamic and never quite moves the same way all of the time.

For price to move the same way each time means the exact same market participants must be present and act the same exact way as before. This never happens.

There is a big distinction between price predictability and consistent execution with high price probability- the former being almost impossible to achieve, the latter being the key to trading success!

Trading is a probability game.

With $E=MC^2$, we are like the "house" in a casino. We don't win every time, but in the long run, by playing the game, the odds are in our favor to win.

$E=MC^2$ treats price movement as nothing more than a "random variable" in the trading equation, and places far more emphasis on the **constants** of "execution, timeframe, and trade management" as the means to monitor, measure, and ultimately trade such price movement successfully.

I recommend that you monitor $E=MC^2$ trades for a period of time before you ever begin to trade for real.

Forget about past performance (as good as it has been).

As you monitor the forward results for $E=MC^2$, day after day, week after week, you will begin to see the benefits of a trading with an approach that flows naturally with price movement in a market.

You will see a variety of trades that win, and a variety of trades that lose.

You will not make money on every trade (no traders do). You will make money most days but not every day (this too is impossible). You should easily make money every week if you are patient and disciplined with your approach.

The understanding of "trading as a probability game" will provide you with the confidence to trade $E=MC^2$ <u>knowing that this approach will work over a continued series of trades if you stick with it.</u>

We all have our own trading styles and personalities. Some traders sit patiently and try to execute just a few trades a day. The risk is that you may miss some of the best trades that set up.

Other traders like to click the buy/sell button all day long. I have always found a direct correlation between "over-trading and losing money."

Execution costs are high, and there are only so many high probability entry points during a trading session no matter how small your timeframe.

$E=MC^2$ provides a perfect mix for those looking to day trade- a great balance between isolating a healthy number of very good trade opportunities, combined with high profit potential from the opportunities that set up.

ROADMAP APPROACH

In order to categorize price movement, $E=MC^2$ applies a "Roadmap Approach" to the trading session.

This means that each trade is based on a logical big picture market structure that continuously unfolds as time goes on.

<u>Profits and losses from each trade are not as important as executing the logical set ups that develop within the trading roadmap</u>, and each trade is analogous to green and red lights along the road to trading success.

Since there is no hurry to reach the final destination, it doesn't matter how many red and green lights you encounter. The key is to simply take the correct trades over and over again based on the roadmap that forms in front of you.

$E=MC^2$ goes with the natural market flow, and patiently waits to capture momentum "continuation and consolidation" price movements that repetitively develop in the ES E-Mini market.

Therefore, to repeat - <u>It is far more important to consistently execute each trade as it develops rather than worry about, or predict how each trade will turn out.</u>

<u>This is the only way to capture profits and succeed using $E=MC^2$ (or any other trading program for that matter).</u>

MULTIPLE TIMEFRAMES

Price movement is fractal in nature. This means price movement in one timeframe is the cumulative result of price movements in many other smaller timeframes that make up the larger timeframe.

Within any timeframe (1 minute, 3 minute, 30 minute-60 minute, daily, weekly, etc.), there are only two directional movements that can be force – up or down.

The market is always moving directionally in a given timeframe. Sometimes it consolidates along the way, and sometimes it changes direction.

One can never predict ahead of time, which directional frameworks will form, how far directional moves will go, or how long directional moves will last.

No market ever moves in a straight line for long because buyers and sellers of different timeframes are always fighting for control.

The best we can do as traders is monitor a variety of timeframes together, and see how these timeframes relate to one another.

A key premise of $E=MC^2$ is that it never looks to pick a top or bottom in the major timeframe!

I can write an entire book about how picking tops and bottoms is the fastest way to the poorhouse in trading.

Of course, tops and bottoms are always <u>relative</u> to a timeframe.

There are many trading approaches that will attempt to buy bottoms/sell tops in a shorter timeframe relative to the direction of a longer timeframe.

These approaches try to buy at specific "pullback" levels (Fibonacci Retracement Levels, Support/Resistance levels etc.)

These approaches contain merit, and $E=MC^2$ puts this principle to use too, but in a much different way than by just focusing on specific pullback levels to buy or sell.

Attempting to trade pullbacks at key price points can be very frustrating.

You miss trades that don't pull back to what you think are key levels. You enter trades at key levels that never turn back around in your trade direction.

$E=MC^2$ combines multiple timeframes to make trading decisions in accordance with the fractal nature of price movement, and lets the market determine the type of pullback to enter into.

If price is moving up, we only look to buy. If price is moving down, we only look to sell.

A directional move in a smaller timeframe must precede the same directional move in the larger timeframe.

Therefore, there is never a need to try to pick a top or bottom relative to the smaller timeframe.

Small timeframes can therefore be used for optimal trade location relative to long timeframe price behavior.

Good trade location relative to overall risk/reward is the first key to putting trading probabilities in your favor.

When you combine big picture price direction with small picture trade location and sound trade management, the overall probabilities will always be in your favor.

The reason successful trading is so difficult for so many is that three things must always be in place, and you can't get any of these wrong - proper entry, exit, and stop.

A good entry from a risk/reward standpoint always takes into account trade location relative to multiple timeframes.

Good trade location always takes place on the smaller timeframe relative to the larger timeframe.

Finally, exits fall into place in accordance to subsequent unfolding price action starting with the small timeframe and evolving into the large timeframe price structure.

From a risk/reward angle we can take small losses based on the small timeframe, and large wins based on the large timeframe.

THE BENEFITS OF DAY TRADING

Nothing beats the day timeframe in the E-Mini market for taking advantage of directional price movement.

Momentum price movements take place quite often during the day timeframe because this is when all market participants are most active, and balance of force between buyer and seller is greatest, with one set of participants often overpowering the other.

Continuation, consolidation and even counter-trend moves set up in consistent ways relative to the big picture over and over again, and $E=MC^2$ looks to exploit this price action as it unfolds.

The day timeframe is perfect. There are many trade opportunities with appropriate volatility to more than offset the negative effects of slippage, poor execution, and trading mistakes that are bound to occur.

The primary goal of $E=MC^2$ is to exploit both new and continuing momentum price movements when they occur.

Such price developments occur over and over again in the day timeframe in the ES E-Mini market.

It does not matter when momentum occurs, or how momentum occurs. It only matters that we recognize good points in developing market structure to give us an edge to enter trades that lead to directional price momentum more times than not.

If we can't predict ahead of time how or when directional price moves will occur, there is only one way to exploit these moves - apply a consistent form of execution to all trades, within a consistent multiple timeframe structure.

In this way we can naturally capture many of the strong directional price outcomes when they develop.

<u>TRADING LOGIC</u>

The following list highlights the key trading axioms embedded in the **E=MC²** trading approach.

1. <u>Eliminate Over-Trading</u> – In trading there is a direct correlation between fewer trades and greater profits. **E=MC²** Is patient to wait for the best trade set ups according to market structure.

2. <u>Market is always right</u> – **E=MC²** uses the markets natural price behavior as a basis for trading decisions rather than self imposed rules that may or may not be in sync with current market conditions.

3. <u>Trade location is critical</u> – **E=MC²** analyzes major/minor market structure to dictate trade location. **E=MC²** patiently waits to take trades that are likely to follow through in the intended trade direction.

4. <u>Trend</u> - **E=MC²** applies a consistent, constant roadmap approach to determine price structure. You will primarily be trading with the main trend, and know when to look for counter-trend set ups.

5. <u>Profits/ losses are dynamic</u> – **E=MC²** does not set fixed stop loss or profit targets with each trade. The market is too dynamic for this type of trading approach. Risk is always the key factor for every trade. The trader always needs to have some maximum stop loss amount they are comfortable with, or the trade is bypassed. Risk is always taken out of the trade as soon as reasonably possible, but you still always must trade according to market structure and price action. <u>We never place a target for profits</u>. Every winning trade uses market action to exit in an attempt to maximize profits when strong momentum price movement develops.

TRADING IS BOTH ART AND SCIENCE

$E=MC^2$ is not another mechanical system developed from computer optimized back tested data.

Such mechanical systems are very good in the sense that they offer consistent execution, but they often suffer performance-wise because they do not adapt well to changing market environments.

$E=MC^2$ realizes the best of both worlds by offering "consistent execution that also factors in changing market conditions."

This combines the "scientific" strengths of mechanical systems with the "art" strengths of <u>learning how read the market and trade</u>, and makes trading more dynamic because each day brings a unique set of trading circumstances to the table.

Although $E=MC^2$ market structure interpretations and trading decisions are quite straightforward, no two traders will trade $E=MC^2$ exactly the same.

The real world of trading means trading is as much art as science.

You need to get used to the fact that you will make good trading decisions, poor trading decisions, and every other trading decision in between.

You will miss good trades. You will exit trades too early. You will misinterpret market structure. All of these "errors" must be factored into your trading plan.

That said, as long as you control risk (more on this very important topic later), you will do very well if you stay consistent and follow the $E=MC^2$ trading plan.

This means taking proper trades in accordance to market structure over and over again, and managing trades according to price action.

Remember, $E=MC^2$ is a "framework" for you to succeed at trading. It is a framework that is generally very straightforward, but you will always have decisions to make.

With experience you will master most of these decisions as you "learn to trade."

You will learn from mistakes. Trading mastery is no different from any other endeavor you wish to master. It takes time.

Rest assured that as you gain experience watching price movement, you will make proper decisions with respect to the "artful" areas of trading more often than not, and you will master your trading skills.

PHILOSOPHY OF E=MC^2 METHOD

You must understand and accept the philosophy of E=MC^2 in order to have the confidence to trade the approach successfully.

The general philosophy of E=MC^2 is (1) We don't look to capture every single move that takes place in the market (2) We only wait for the best trade setups according to developing market structure, (3) We never try to pick tops or bottoms against current price momentum.

Also, we are quick to reduce risk, but patient enough to ride winning trades as far as possible when they develop.

There is one word to describe the main ingredient necessary to trade E=MC^2 successfully - "Patience."

While E=MC^2 is a "day trading" method, you should not be clicking the buy/sell button all day long, and you will not be making money on every trade. You may not make money on every trading day. This is the bad news.

The good news is that there are so many good repetitive trade opportunities that setup, and in the end, if you stay consistent and patient, you should easily be able to achieve your weekly, and long-term trading goals.

This is a very hard concept to accept because the words **TRADING** and **PATIENCE** do not go hand in hand.

Human nature dictates the need for instant gratification - especially in the world of trading, where there is a strong psychological desire to "always be in the market," and "always win on every trade."

Remember, the vast majority of traders lose money! Common sense tells us most traders must be making the same types of trading mistakes. In contrast, note all the good trading opportunities E=MC^2 offers. If you stay the course, E=MC^2 works.

BUT PLEASE UNDERSTAND TRADING IS NOTHING MORE THAN A PROBABALITY GAME.

Of course you will feel like every trade should win, because you are entering on price/volume patterns that are successful a majority of the time.

But you still must realize, that while these patterns have a high probability of success in the long run (the edge for you as the trader), not every single market participant is the exactly the same for every identical pattern that sets up.

Therefore, the exact same outcome cannot be expected each time a repetitive pattern forms.

With the exact same pattern, some trades will provide much larger gains than a previous similar pattern.

Other trades will pull back further than the pullback that occurred with a previous pattern. Other trades will pull back very far and stop you out for a loss.

You never know. All you know is that you are taking trades that have a high probability of turning into price momentum, and this gives you an edge in the long run.

With each new trade, there are new participants than before so the outcomes are always random. $E=MC^2$ doesn't look to capture small moves in the market, although many trades end up either as either small winners, or break even trades after commissions.

$E=MC^2$ builds its foundation around the premise that capturing bigger moves in the market will prove to be significantly more profitable in the long run, than trying to capture smaller moves.

Here is why. Trading to capture small profits leaves virtually <u>no room for error</u>, and errors come in all shapes and forms in the world of trading.

Trading is one of the most psychologically demanding ventures there is - from entering trades, to exiting trades, to trying to follow your trading plan, to everything in between.

If your trading plan carries ambiguities of any kind, these issues become especially difficult to deal with.

Also, when your trading plan is set up to capture small profits, **market imposed costs** are magnified, and have a much greater chance to negatively impact your bottom line.

These costs include everything from commission costs, to execution costs, to costs of operating in a fast market - and even include costs such as computer tie-ups, phone delays, or anything else outside your direct control.

Trading successfully is difficult no matter which method you choose.

Trading $E=MC^2$ will pose difficulties too, in part because there are just so many mental hurdles that very few traders are ever able to master.

It is hard to execute trades even when you know you must. It is hard to stick with a trading plan even though you know it is sound. It is hard to remain consistent when you encounter a series of trades that do not go your way, and it is easy to make many other trading mistakes in the face of all of the emotional obstacles you are faced with each day as you watch price move up and down.

When you factor all these variables into the trading equation, the best chance for success comes from a trading method that <u>attempts</u> to capture big price moves and large profits rather than small moves and small profits.

Gunning for big price moves will offset the variety of trading costs that are always present.

With $E=MC^2$, trading costs won't destroy your bottom line, and in time, as you see your bottom line continue to grow, you will be filled with the confidence to consistently execute this method day after day, even in the face of all of the emotional hurdles thrown your way.

Section 2 - Market Structure

PRICE CHARTS AND TECHNICAL STUDIES

$E=MC^2$ analyzes market structure and trade opportunities through use of price bars, moving averages, and volume, all in the context of multiple timeframes. These tools provide us with very powerful combinations.

By analyzing price action in three timeframes simultaneously, we effectively are able to take advantage of the fractal nature of price movement, which means short-timeframe price movements are viewed as a piece of long-timeframe price movements.

Price moves directionally in all timeframes, but rarely moves in a straight line due to the fact participants in a variety of timeframes exert influence on price all at the same time. This is what causes back and forth price swings to develop.

By smoothing price data with moving averages we are able to better isolate true directional price movement in a given time frame without being distracted by the variety of up and down price swings, or "waves" that develop along the way.

Finally, we can gain additional information about price direction if price movement is supported by up volume or down volume. Price direction is important, but volume is always the fuel that keeps price direction going.

We confirm the validity of long positions when swing lows hold, and up price direction is supported by strong and maintained up volume.

We confirm the validity of short positions when swing highs hold and down price action is supported by strong and maintained down volume.

E=MC2 Price charts:

Bar charts - A bar chart is a visual representation of price, and shows the open, high, low and close of price for a chosen period.

There are standard bar charts, and candlestick bar charts.

The E=MC2 approach can use either type of bar chart, but doesn't use standard candlestick analysis to make trading decisions.

Instead, we use paint bar studies to "color" bars based on price being greater than or less than an average price over "X" bars, and this analysis helps us to identify valid pullbacks to best time entries, etc.

All price bars show the open, high, low and closing price relative to the way the bar is constructed.

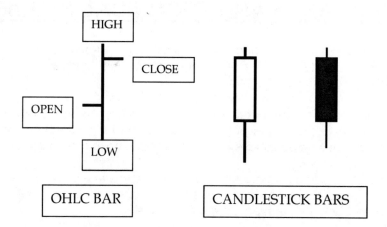

As you can see, standard OHLC (Open, High, Low, Close) bars are represented with a single line that include two dashes representing the opening price on the left, and the closing price on the right.

Candlestick bars show the same open, high, low, and close but the open and close are represented with a "body" between them, and the body is open when the close is above the open (strength), or colored in when the close is below the open (weakness).

Price bars can be constructed on the basis of <u>time, ticks, volume, or range</u>.

For E=MC^2, tick and volume price bars work best because they effectively speed up and slow down as market activity speeds up or slows down.

This is especially important when price action speeds up (price momentum) and we need faster ways to take advantage of such activity.

<u>Tick Bars</u> are constructed on the basis of the number of up and down price ticks that take place. A 55-tick bar will finish plotting after 55-price ticks, and plot much faster, and more often than a 300-tick bar, and depending upon volatility, can have many bars plotted in a given timeframe interval.

<u>Volume share bars</u> are constructed on the basis of number of contracts traded.

A 1500-volume share bar will plot after 1500-contracts are traded.

Again, volume based price bars speed up or slow down according to market activity and are very useful to take advantage of momentum price movement.

We use <u>time bars</u> (the most common) only for big picture analysis, and not for executing entries and exits.

<u>Range bars</u> are new to the trading scene and are constructed on the basis of price range movement. E=MC2 does not use range bars at this time.

Tick and volume bars:

Although constructed differently, tick and volume price bar charts are closely related in the sense that they speed up and slow down based on market volatility.

If you play around with the input values for these two types of bars you can find an appropriate tick bar interval that "matches up" almost perfectly with a volume share bar interval.

$E=MC^2$ uses the following tick and volume bar charts intervals for short, medium, and long multiple timeframe price analysis.

1. Short – 55 tick price bar
2. Medium -1500 volume price bar
3. Long term – 5000 volume price bar
4. Big Picture – 5 minute bar (day only)

These timeframes generally step up 5X from each other.

The $E=MC^2$ method only executes trades between 8:30 –3:15 CST. This is considered the "day session."

Price bars continuously form over a longer overnight "Globex" session as well.

We plot all price bars and studies with overnight data included, even though we only start trading at 8:30 CST

In Tradestation, we use the @ES symbol for all tick and volume charts, which represents the most actively traded ES futures contract.

We use day session data (@ES.D) for only the 5-minute chart because it provides a more clear depiction of long-term price activity, including "gaps" etc., from previous days.

<u>TECHNICAL STUDIES</u> - Price action can be measured and analyzed in many ways. One way to analyze price data is by observing price patterns that form.

Another way to analyze price data is by applying mathematical formulas to price data in an effort to define price activity.

Such mathematical applications are called technical studies, and include indicators such as moving averages, relative strength index's, overbought/oversold oscillators etc.

$E=MC^2$ uses the following technical studies – **Moving Averages, Volume Ratio, and Paint Bars.**

Moving Averages - As stated, moving averages smooth price data, and we plot a variety of moving averages on the charts.

1. Medium term 1500-volume chart- 13,34,89 simple moving averages.
2. Long term 5000 volume share chart – 18 and 89 simple moving averages
3. Big Picture 5 minute chart- 18 simple moving average.

Volume Ratio- The Volume Ratio indicator calculates an exponential moving average of the ratio between up and down volume. The exponential moving average is then plotted as an oscillator around a zero line.

Volume provides insight into the strength or weakness of a price move.

The $E=MC^2$ method keys on whether the Volume Ratio indicator is above or below the zero line, rising or falling substantially beyond +/- 5, and especially keys on when this indicator crosses the zero line - either down to up, or up to down.

We plot volume ratio as follows:

> 1. Short term 55-tick chart – 89,5,-5,5 values
> 2. Medium term 1500-volume chart – 89,5,-5,5 values.

Paint Bars, Bar Styles and Colors – Paint bars are helpful to visualize pullbacks in price direction. We rely on pullbacks to look for trade setups on the long and medium timeframe charts

We rely on identifying the "groupings" of pullbacks to enter trades on the short timeframe chart.

5000 and 55 charts - We apply a "price greater than average," and "price less than average" paint bar to each of these charts. We set the value to 8 in all cases.

We set the style for the "price greater than average" bars thicker than the "price less than average" bars. This allows us to clearly separate the two (Of course you can set them to different colors as well)

The $E=MC^2$ method enters trades after pullbacks on the 5000 chart.

The change in bar styles/colors using the price greater than/less than paint bar study helps tremendously with getting a feel for the strength and duration of a pullback.

<u>5000 Chart Pullback example</u> – During the downtrend below note how (1) Price moves below a falling 18-ma (thick line) (2) Normal pullbacks in a down trend are represented by thicker, "price greater than average" paint bars moving up (arrows).

THE IDEAL SCREEN LAYOUT

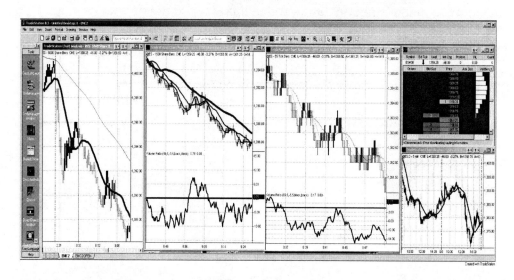

It is highly recommended that you trade with a computer that has at least two screens side by side. This allows you to best space your charts, and include all charts on the screen at the same time. If you don't have two screens you will create the left side as one workspace (setup) and the right side as another workspace (execution) and flip back and forth between the two.

From left to right:

1. @ES 5000 Volume Share Bar
2. @ES 1500 Volume Share Bar (w/Volume Ratio Study)
3. @ES 55 Tick (w/Volume Ratio Study)
4. Order Matrix (ESHO8) (top)
5. @ES.D 5 minute (bottom)
(**In Tradestation, select dialogue box Trade Volume, not Tick Count)

(Note- For the order matrix you cannot use @ES symbol. You must first create another chart with the most actively traded ES contract (March (H), June (M), Sep (U), or Dec (Z) plus the current year extension (08, 09, 10, etc.). Highlight this chart, click on the Matrix icon, and the matrix will appear. You can then delete the chart and keep the matrix.)

CHART STRUCTURE

The E=MC^2 method uses the long-timeframe 5000-volume bar chart and the medium timeframe 1500-volume bar chart to dictate all trade setups.

These charts are on the left hand side of the screen.

We start all analysis by determining if **LONG TIMEFRAME** 5000-price is moving up or down.

Once we determine if 5000-price is moving up or down, we next determine if 5000-price momentum is (1) Continuing- C1 (2) Consolidating- C2,C3.

There is "normal" consolidation (C2), and "chop" consolidation (C3).

UP AND DOWN – The pure definition of up means 5000 18-ma is above the 5000 89-ma. The pure definition of down means the 5000 18-ma is below the 5000 89-ma.

If the 18 and 89-ma are moving in the same direction we say price momentum is Continuing. If the 18-ma turns against the direction of the 89-ma we say price momentum is Consolidating.

Finally, if the 18-ma crosses the 89-ma, but the 89-ma is still moving in the direction of the trend, we say price momentum is Consolidating "with chop."

PRICE DIRECTION – The chart below isolates only the 5000 18 and 89-ma (no price). When the 18-ma is either above or below the 89-ma, direction is either up or down (arrows). In vertical line segment #2, the 18-ma is below a rising 89-ma. We call this "consolidation chop"

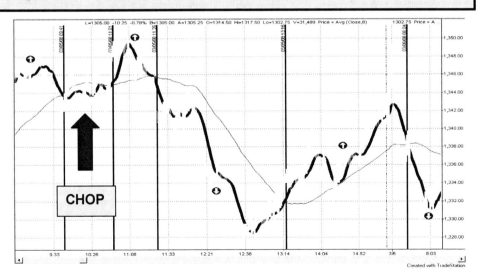

CONTINUATION vs. CONSOLIDATION –

Using the same chart, we further break up and down direction into (1) Continuation, or (2) Consolidation.

Continuation means the 18 and 89-ma are moving in the same direction (Down arrows, section 4).

Consolidation means the 18-ma is moving opposite the 89-ma (Up arrows, section 4)

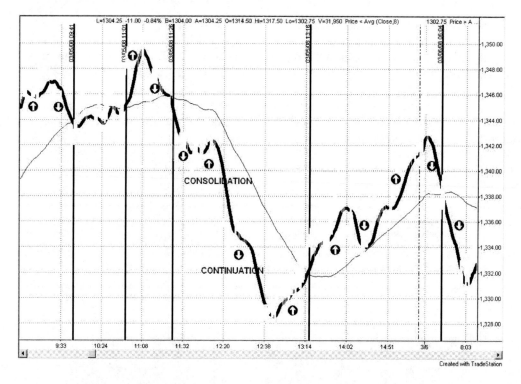

In section 5 above, we know price is in an uptrend (18 above 89). Further we see a flow of continuation, consolidation, continuation, consolidation, before direction ultimately turns down in section 6. (18 below 89)

CHOP CONSOLIDATION – **From section 1 to section 2, price goes from continuation, to normal consolidation, to chop consolidation (circle).**

Chop consolidation takes some getting used to. On one hand the 18-ma is crossing the 89-ma, which normally means direction change. On the other hand, the 89-ma is still moving in the main trend direction, which means no direction change yet.

We will show later on how big picture analysis solves this dilemma, and tells us what we need to do.

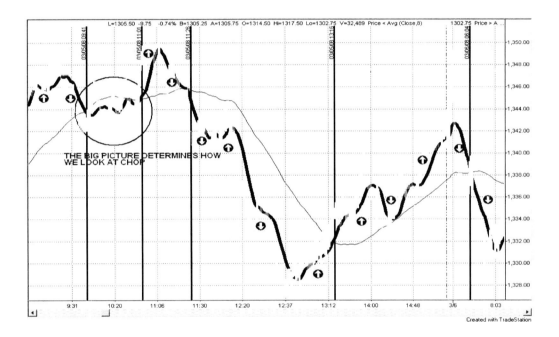

THE BIG PICTURE DETERMINES HOW WE LOOK AT CHOP

SUMMARY - PRICE DIRECTION

With $E=MC^2$, we always start by looking at the 5000-chart. We watch the 18 and 89-ma, and we note when the 18-ma crosses the 89-ma.

The astute trader is always on the lookout for healthy directional price movement vs. chop price movement.

Healthy direction price movement produces continuation and consolidation setups.

Chop price movement requires analysis of the big picture to resolve. Often, chop is just a deep pullback to a trend line support/resistance area in the big picture trend.

If chop continues for a while, and the 89-ma "rolls over" and changes direction, then chop consolidation turns into new price direction.

In addition to the 18/89-ma relationship we will explore (1) Volume analysis (2) 5-minute big picture structure to help support trading decisions with $E=MC^2$.

Five Examples of 5000 price direction classification:

The following five charts show examples of what you need to be looking at on the 5000 chart. Trend changes develop when the 18 crosses the 89, and the 89 either rolls over and/or turns.

These charts show the way the charts look at the "right edge of the screen" <u>in real time.</u>

Consolidation in Downtrend – 18 below 89, and 18 moving up.

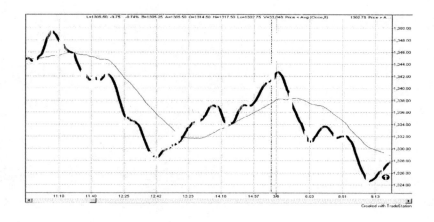

Continuation in Uptrend – 18 above 89, Both ma's moving up

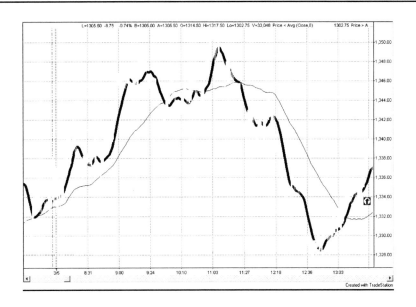

Chop Consolidation in Uptrend – 18 below 89, 89 still moving up.

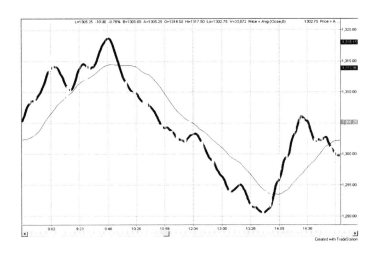

Continuation in Down trend – 18 below 89, both ma's moving down.

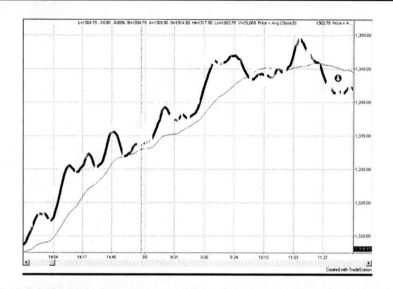

Continuation In Down trend – 18 below 89, Both ma's moving down.

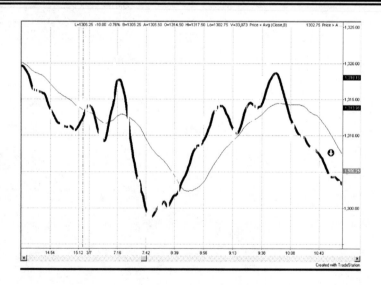

Section 3 – Trade Development

<u>TRADE SETUPS</u>

$E=MC^2$ looks to buy when the 5000 89-ma is moving up, or is in the process of turning up.

$E=MC^2$ looks to sell when the 5000 89-ma is moving down, or is in the process of turning down.

$E=MC^2$ enters all trades after a pullback on the long and medium timeframe. Price on an appropriate shorter timeframe is used for precise entry and exit timing.

There are three types of pullbacks on the long timeframe (5000), confirmed by price and volume activity on the medium timeframe (1500) - **(1)** Continuation pullback (C1), **(2)** Consolidation pullback -normal (C2), and **(3)** Consolidation pullback -chop (C3).

Although certain pullback trades have higher probabilities and greater potential than other pullback trades (dictated in part by big picture and volume analysis), you never know for sure how a given trade will turn out. Therefore, to play the probabilities correctly, you can take "all" setups that develop until a point where developments enter the picture that lower the probabilities- namely (1) More than two successful C1 continuation trades in a row (2) A C1 continuation trade that develops right after a significant volume divergence on the 1500 chart (3) C2/C3 Consolidation trades that form after a volume "breakout" in the opposite direction.

These three conditions lower the probabilities for price follow through.

Trends do not last forever.

Big picture analysis also helps to determine how many trades you may want to take during a trend. We will discuss the significance of avoiding the low probability setups mentioned above that develop near key macro areas such as (1) Key Bracket highs and lows (2) Key Retrace points, etc.

We put all trades in the context of trade management later on, but for now begin to think of a continuous cycle of price movement, where we look to enter on (1) The first set up after a trend change (2) Additional continuation and consolidation set ups that develop as the new trend unfolds, until (3) A new trend starts in the opposite direction, where the cycle starts over again.

Within this continuous cycle, you will learn how to exercise discretion, but you should always be able to look at the 5000-chart, and in an instant, determine what phase of the market you are in, and what trade setups are developing.

TYPE OF PULLBACK – There are three elements to look at with every pullback: (1) Relationship of the 5000 18-ma to the 89-ma (2) Relationship of 5000-price to the 18-ma. (3) Relationship of 1500-price to its' long term moving average.

<u>**Continuation Pullback (C1)**</u> - A continuation pullback setup always has the 18-ma beyond, and moving in the direction of the 89-ma. In most cases 5000-price will change paint bar style during the pullback.

Pullbacks in downtrends are thin bars that become thick bars. Pullbacks in up trends are thick bars that become thin bars.

The key, however, is that for a normal continuation pullback, 5000 price makes a <u>brief penetration of the 18-ma</u> which is moving in the trade direction. (i.e. - a continuation sell set up takes place when the 89 and 18-ma's are moving down, and price rises above the falling 18-ma). Note – If very strong or weak momentum is in force, price may just fall short of penetrating the 18-ma during a continuation pullback.

<u>**Continuation pullback in an uptrend**</u> **- 18-ma is above 89-ma. Both ma's are rising (or starting to rise). When 5000-price pulls back below a rising 18-ma in an uptrend (circles), this is considered a C1 continuation pullback.**

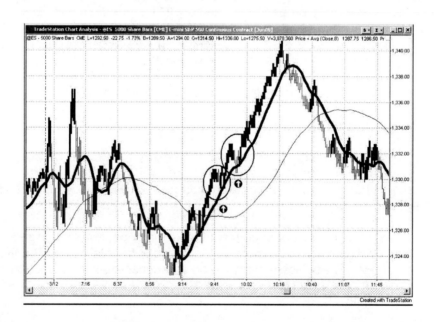

<u>Consolidation Pullback - Normal (C2)</u> – A continuation pullback turns into a consolidation pullback when the <u>18-ma turns opposite the 89-ma</u>. Also, in most cases 5000-price makes a zigzag, 1-2-3-pattern during the pullback (i.e. down-up-down or up-down-up).

As long as the 18-ma doesn't cross the 89-ma, we know the market is just "consolidating" in the direction of the 89-ma, even though the 18-ma has temporarily turned in the opposite direction.

> **<u>Consolidation pullback (normal) in an uptrend</u> - 18-ma is <u>falling</u> above a rising 89-ma. When price pulls back below the 18-ma, and the 18-ma turns down in an uptrend (circles), this is considered a normal C2 consolidation pullback.**

Consolidation Pullback – Chop (C3) – A normal consolidation pullback turns into a chop consolidation pullback, when the 18-ma crosses the 89-ma, but the 89-ma is still moving in the trend direction.

We call this "chop" because this is often an inflection point, and the market can go either way. If the 89-ma continues with the trend, we look for this pullback to resolve back in the trend direction. If the 89-ma starts to roll over in a new direction, a new trend will emerge.

To determine which way to go, we look at big picture analysis (5-minute chart), and volume analysis (1500 chart). In most cases these two areas will tell us if the current trend is still in force, or not.

There are three indications to look for if a trend change is taking place: (1) The 18-ma strongly crosses beyond the 89-ma (2) Price action moves strongly beyond a key trend line support/resistance area (3) Time goes by which allows the 89-ma to roll over in a new direction. Volume will also confirm.

We will go over many examples later on.

Consolidation pullback (chop) in an uptrend - 18-ma is <u>falling and below</u> 89-ma which is still rising. When the 18-ma crosses the 89-ma, and the 89-ma is still moving with the trend (circle), this is considered a chop consolidation pullback area.

Paint bars on the 5000 chart – On the 5000 chart below there are 12 pullbacks that change paint bar style (arrows).

Pullbacks in up trends are thick bars that become thin bars. Pullbacks in downtrends are thin bars that become thick bars.

If a pullback to the 18-ma either doesn't reach the 18-ma, or doesn't change paint bar style before resuming its trend (shallow pullback), then the market is either in a very strong, or very weak condition (i.e. - between arrows 3 and 4).

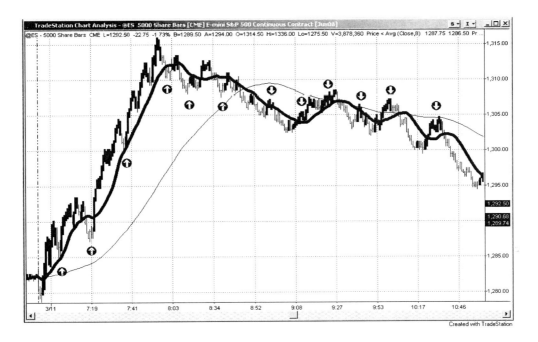

Note how "up pullbacks" take place when the 18-ma is above the 89-ma, and "down pullbacks" take place when the 18-ma is below the 89-ma.

From left to right, here are the types of pullbacks for each arrow: (1) Up Continuation, (2) Up Consolidation, (3) Up Continuation, (4) Up Continuation, (5) Up Consolidation, (6) Up Consolidation, (7) Down Continuation, (8) Down Consolidation, (9) Down Consolidation, (10) Down Continuation, (11) Down Consolidation, (12) Down Consolidation.

This represents a normal cycle of the way trades develop. Continuation trades move to Consolidation trades, and there can be several in a row of each.

Many trading approaches look to enter on pullbacks, but not all trading approaches dynamically allow the market to dictate the type of the pullback.

If you have ever tried to enter trades at Fibonacci pullback levels, or pre-determined support/resistance pullback levels, you know the frustration of either missing trades that never reach your predefined pullback level, or entering trades into strong price movement <u>against your trade direction</u> that never turns back around in the direction of your trade.

$E=MC^2$ works differently. Although certain market moves are missed, and certain trades lose, $E=MC^2$ uses the short and medium timeframe to dictate long timeframe entry, which puts us in great position to establish a very nice risk/reward criteria by allowing the market to tell us the best way to enter during a pullback.

Medium timeframe confirms Long timeframe

To confirm 5000-(long timeframe) pullbacks we also look at the 1500-medium timeframe chart. The 1500-chart contains 3-moving averages.

A pullback on the medium 1500-chart starts with price beyond all 3-averages. <u>Price then pulls back to either the short (13), medium (34), or long-term (89) moving average area.</u>

During strong momentum continuation pullbacks, price only pulls back to the 1500-short/medium moving average area (shallow pullback).

During normal continuation pullbacks, price pulls back to the 1500-long term moving average area (normal pullback).

If price, significantly crosses the 1500-long term 89 average on the medium timeframe chart (deep pullback), <u>then we want to see price eventually move back through the long term moving average in the direction of the trade before entering a trade.</u>

The key benefit of observing pullbacks on two timeframes at the same time is that it allows us to categorize shallow vs. normal vs. deep pullbacks in such a way that we can act appropriately aggressive during shallow pullbacks, and remain appropriately patient during deep pullbacks.

Continuation Pullback (C1) - During a 5000-long timeframe C1 continuation pullback (circle, left), 1500-medium timeframe pullbacks are contained within the 89 Long Term moving average area (circle, right). (<u>Note</u> - The 1500-long term moving average is not a "magical line," so price can briefly probe through the 89 long term average and still be exhibiting C1 continuation behavior.

Normal Consolidation Pullback (C2) - During a 5000-long timeframe consolidation pullback (circle, left), the 1500-medium timeframe pulls back beyond the 89-long term moving average area (circle, right).

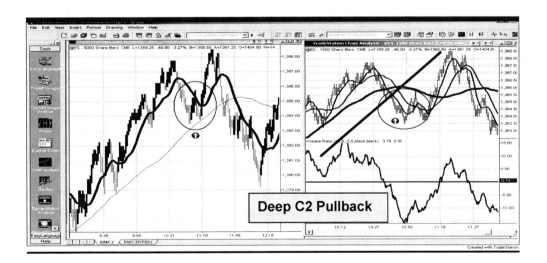

Shallow Pullback During Price Momentum - A shallow 5000 pullback (circle, left) barely makes it back to the 18-ma, may or may not change paint bar style, and is confirmed by 1500-price action that only pulls back to the short/medium term moving average area (circle, right)

(Note - These trades are best taken at the <u>beginning of a new 5000 18/89 trend</u>, or <u>after a consolidation breakout</u>, are more aggressive trades during an established trend, and are usually preceded by a strong breakout in price and/or volume).

<u>Deep Pullback</u> – Here is a real time (right edge of the screen) view of a normal, deep, C2 consolidation pullback.

18-ma is falling, and above a rising 89-ma. This means we have a C2 consolidation pullback in an uptrend (left).

1500-price goes way below long term moving average (right).

<u>A buy signal will develop in coordination with 1500-price moving back above the 89 long term moving average line.</u>

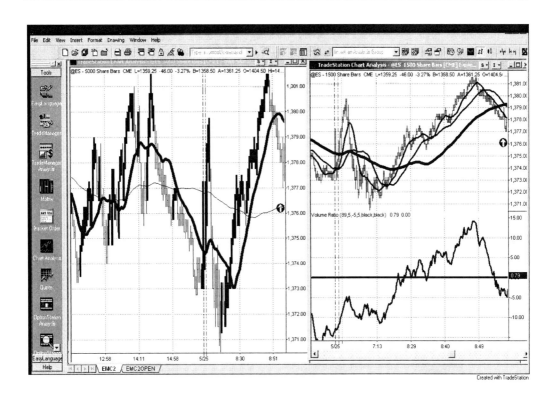

MEDIUM TERM CONFIRMS LONG TERM – 5000-price (arrow, left) pulls back in a downtrend. You may be wondering if this is a C1 continuation pullback (18 ma moving down), or a C2 consolidation pullback because of the choppy price action?

It's a close call, but the edge goes to a C1 continuation pullback. Why? As stated, 5000-price makes a zigzag "1-2-3" pullback (up-down-up). This is the normal characteristic of a C2 consolidation pullback (C1 pullbacks usually move with only one swing).

However, look at the 1500-price (arrow, right). Price pulls back right to the 89 long term-ma area. This is normal <u>C1 continuation</u> pullback action, especially confirmed by volume that can't make it back to the zero line.

Section 4 – Confirmation Tools

VOLUME CONFIRMATION

Volume Confirmation – Trading is a probability game. The E=MC^2 method places the trading odds in our favor by combining multiple timeframe analysis, consistent price setups, and good trade management. Probability is increased even further when volume confirmation is included.

You always want to trade in the direction of volume!

For example, if price is moving up and supported by increasing up volume, and volume pullbacks are shallow, the odds strongly favor continued up price movement at least long enough to effectively manage a trade.

Conversely, if price is moving up, and not supported by increasing up volume, then the move up is likely to pause in an existing trend, or can be nothing more than a pullback in a longer term down trend.

Volume confirmation is critical to any trading plan.

With the E=MC^2 method, the best trade set ups are always confirmed by volume.

This doesn't mean every trade must have volume confirmation in place immediately (although most trades will), but if not, we want to see volume confirmation enter the picture very shortly after the trade is underway, or else we become very cautious.

> **We use the medium term 1500-volume chart for our main volume confirmation. (55-Tick chart for secondary volume confirmations)**
>
> **1500- Buy Volume Confirmation** – 1500-volume ratio line crosses above zero, and rises strongly above +5.
>
> **1500- Sell Volume Confirmation** – 1500-volume ratio line crosses below zero, and falls strongly below –5.

1500-volume ratio confirms price action - Vertical lines show where the volume ratio indicator crosses zero.

Notice when the volume line moves strongly beyond +/- 5 after crossing zero, (sections 1,4,5) how strong directional price movement becomes.

When the indicator cannot move and hold past +/-5 (sections 2,3), price direction is more difficult to sustain.

If you look early in section 1, volume ratio moves up, but cannot cross zero. Also, 1500-price cannot move above the 3-moving averages. This is a classic continuation pullback.

Section 2 shows volume moving above zero temporarily but not strongly beyond +5. Therefore, this is likely a normal consolidation pullback in a downtrend, and is confirmed when price moves back below the long term moving average.

Price doesn't move strongly to new lows in section 3 (lows are just tested). Unsustainable price movement is confirmed by volume that cannot strongly move below –5.

Currently (right side of the chart, section 5) price is in a clear downtrend, and setting up for a great continuation sell if volume doesn't cross zero, and price stalls in the area of the long term moving average.

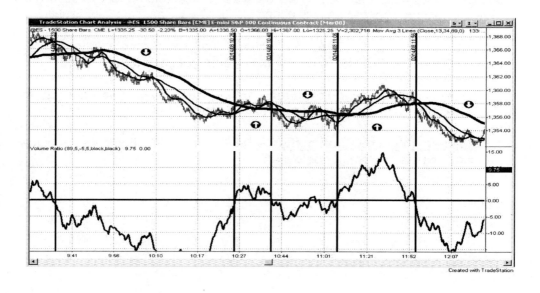

<u>Consolidation Pullback</u> (C2) - 5000-price pulls back in a downtrend turning the 18-ma up (circle, left). This is a C2 consolidation pullback.

Notice how volume never strongly crosses the +5 level during this pullback before turning back down (circle, right). This indicates the price move up doesn't contain volume support, and is likely a pullback in a downtrend.

This pullback area also happens to coincide with a "big picture" pullback to the 18-ma trend line/resistance area on the 5-minute chart (not shown, but explained later)

1500-price moves above the 3-ma's during the pullback, and a C2 consolidation sell is confirmed when price moves back down below the long term moving average (arrow, right.)

Created with TradeStation

Many times, a variety of factors come together at the same time - a pullback to a big picture resistance level, and a 5000-consolidation pullback without volume confirmation.

Not only does such combined action make you very wary of looking for long setups, but it also makes you that much more comfortable entering short setups when the down trend resumes.

Although not highlighted on the 1500-chart above, volume moves strongly below -5 on the next move down, and a strong, lengthy downtrend develops. (See 5000-chart after the circle, left).

When you see strong +/-5 volume action, you know to stick with existing trades for large gains, and you know that continuation and consolidation trades that develop have a high probability of success.

(**Note** - At times, +/-10 becomes the key volume range, and this will become clear when you examine the charts).

1500/55 Volume Ratio Relationship – When the 1500-volume ratio crosses zero and continues strongly past +/- 5, there is high probability that directional price action will continue for a period of time.

If you are in a trade at this point, the following analysis will help confirm normal pullbacks to ride through if you choose to stick with a trade for larger gains (i.e. Beyond the standard exit rules for this method).

If you are not in a trade, the following analysis will help confirm what a typical pullback looks like from a volume perspective as you look to enter fresh continuation and consolidation trades.

During a normal C1 continuation pullback, 1500-volume doesn't cross zero, and 55-volume briefly crosses zero, or gets right next to zero before turning back in the trade direction.

Often when you see 1500-volume hold zero, as 55-volume "brushes" zero, this represents the exact continuation pullback extreme area, so you need to get ready to enter a continuation trade dictated by 55-price action (to be discussed in trade entry section).

> **1500/55 Volume Setup 1**– The chart below shows a classic C1 continuation trade from a volume perspective. First, there is a 5000-continuation buy pullback setup where price dips below a rising 18-ma (circle, left).
>
> **1500**-price stays above long term-ma (arrow, middle), and volume stays above zero (circle, middle).
>
> **55**-volume pullback brushes the zero area (circle, right), which represents extreme area of price pullback before price heads higher.

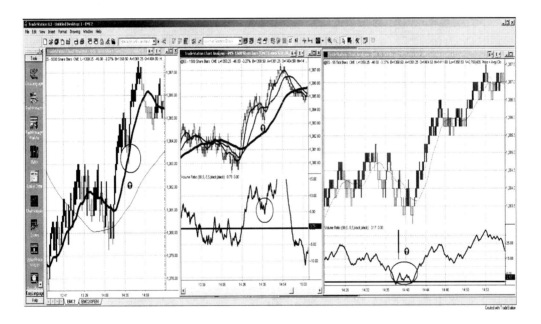

Therefore, when pullback trades setup on the 5000, always look to see if 1500 volume fails to cross the zero line as 55-volume reaches the zero line.

Time and time again the best C1 continuation trades setup in this manner.

Sometimes, 5000-pullbacks are deep, and 5000-price deeply penetrates the 18-ma during the pullback.

In these cases, the 1500-volume will usually briefly cross zero but not go beyond the +/- 5 area.

As long as the 5000 18/89-ma trend is still in place, very good "deep pullback" continuation/consolidation trades take place when 55-price turns back in the trade direction, confirmed by both volume and price action on the 1500. Also, 1500 and 55 volume will normally cross back beyond zero at nearly the same time.

1500/55 Volume Setup 2 - During a deep 5000-consolidation pullback, price deeply probes beyond the 18-ma and 18-ma turns opposite the trade direction (circle, left). 1500 volume (middle, bottom) moves beyond zero, but holds the -5 area. A good long entry is <u>confirmed</u> when 1500-price moves back through the long term-ma (circle, middle), and when both 1500 and 55 volume move back past the zero line in the direction of the trade (arrows, middle/right).

Created with TradeStation

VOLUME SUMMARY - In trading, price action is always number one, but volume confirmation is a strong number two.

You simply cannot have strong price movement in either direction without volume confirmation, so $E=MC^2$ looks to put this principle to use.

Monitoring up volume vs. down volume will take your trading to a whole new level. (See volume appendix for more details on volume and day trading).

If you have never viewed volume in this way before, I am certain this one area alone can improve your trading.

When we discuss trade management we will introduce the concept of volume divergence. Here we use volume theory to help time our trade exits.

For example, if price is heading higher and higher, but volume momentum is weakening, this is often a great place to exit and/or tighten your trailing stops considerably.

We will discuss this, and more, later.

Volume confirmation is a very important part of the $E=MC^2$ method. While you can successfully trade without it (because nothing is more important than price action), there is no doubt you will make overall better trading decisions when you bring volume analysis into the mix.

Volume analysis will help with trade selectivity, it will always confirm the best trade setups, and it will put you on alert when a trade isn't likely to work out.

<u>5-MINUTE CHART - GAPS/BIG PICTURE</u>

The 5-minute chart plays a very important role to monitor the big picture direction of the overall market, which can improve your trading decisions greatly.

Zoom the 5-minute chart out to include at least yesterdays, and preferably several days' worth of price action.

The set up for the 5-minute chart is @ES.D data (day session only), including an 18-period moving average.

It is important to know if your trade setups are "with or against the big picture."

It is important to know how <u>gap openings</u> from day to day fall into the big picture.

The big picture is determined from observing price swings that develop on the 5-minute chart relative to a "trend line" of the 18-ma tied in with the end of yesterday's price action.

<u>YOU DO NOT NEED TO OVERCOMLPICATE THIS! You do not always have to get 5-minute chart analysis exactly right or wrong. It is just a guide, and often a very clear and easy to interpret guide. If at any moment you can't interpret the 5-minute chart, don't worry, and just go about managing your trades according to Day session Part 1 and Day session Part 2 analysis (to be discussed).</u>

At a glance, the 5-minute chart should tell all you need to know about the big picture. You can easily see if price is swinging up or down, making new highs or new lows, trending higher or lower, or perhaps moving sideways relative to yesterday.

This simple analysis helps determine the potential for many trade setups.

<u>How to view the 5-minute chart</u> - Just like the 5000 chart, look at 5-minute price swings, but also add one more piece to the analysis – a mental trend line of 5-minute price swings relative to the 18 ma.

Zoom the 5-minute chart out and estimate a rough trend line that connects prior pullbacks.

You need this trend line to be violated before a big picture trend change takes place.

This trend line normally slopes about 45 degrees.

When price momentum sets in, the trend line grows much more steep.

A trend line can last for half a day, or can run for days at a time. In general, big picture trend lines do not change on a dime and this is one of their main values.

When you see 5000 and 1500 price gyrating wildly, or you feel like a good trade will run forever, or you feel you are missing out on some forceful price action, etc, always take a step back and see how this price action relates to the big picture 5-minute chart.

At times strong price moves are nothing more than pullbacks to obvious trend line support/resistance areas in the big picture.

You must be aware of limited profit potential beyond such areas. This will allow you to tighten up stops if you are already in a trade, or be very careful about how you manage, or enter new trades in this area.

Also, key trend line pullback areas help determine the structure of the market at otherwise confusing C3 consolidation chop areas where the 5000 18-ma crosses the 89-ma, but the 5000 89-ma is still heading in the trend direction.

When price movement is in line with the 5-minute trend, C3 interpretation defers to the big picture, and C1 continuation and C2 consolidation trades have tremendous potential and are often worth sticking with longer than other less clear big picture supported trades (i.e. consider 5-minute chart price swings to exit, especially if clear momentum develops after the 5000 extreme is penetrated (to be discussed)).

If you take the very first trade after a 5-minute trend change, you should expect the next price swing after a pullback to create a new big picture 5-minute high or low based on simple price swing behavior.

Below is a 5-minute chart with an 18-ma to help visualize a trend line. Big picture trend is determined by viewing a rough trend line, and connecting price swings after 5-minute price pullbacks to the 18-ma/trend line area.

(Note how trend lines are drawn in very liberal fashion with respect to both 18-ma and price swing extremes. Brief 5-minute price probes near the 18-ma will not change big picture trend. Always allow a bit of slack relative to the slope of the 18-ma)

When price penetrates key pivots that develop near the 18-ma (arrows on chart), big picture trend changes. It's really this simple.

As stated, big picture trend changes don't happen "on a dime" (other than gaps), and there is no rush to detect exactly when a trend change takes place.

Therefore, you can stay very relaxed as you analyze big picture structure in real time. This relaxation helps during real time, especially as it relates to putting explosive intra-day price moves into proper context.

In many cases, explosive intra-day price moves are nothing more than pullbacks during a 5-minute trend. This is why explosive price moves will often turn right around and head the other way. The big picture trend doesn't change quickly, and if price has moved a long way to a 5-minute trend line area near the 18-ma, it will often stall right in this area.

In the chart above, I have drawn 4 rough trend lines relative to price pivot points near the 18 ma, and marked with arrows the spots where trend changes take place.

As price moves strongly higher during a trend (see line 1), the trend line grows steeper.

Remember, explosive moves don't last forever, and aggressive steep trend line penetrations can get you in on a new trend nice and early.

The three other trend lines on the chart fall more in line with the normal 45-degree angle of price that takes place during most big picture trends.

A breakout from a shallow trend line (consolidation range) often signals very strong continuation to follow. (See context section on how to handle and identify chop, and breakouts from chop).

Putting the 5-minute chart to use – Let's examine the 5-minute chart above more closely to show how you can integrate the 5-minute big picture chart into the 5000/1500/55 trading plan.

The Gap – At 8:30 CST, the 5-minute chart (day session only - @ES.D) will usually show some type of <u>opening gap up or down</u> from the previous days' close.

This gap is often closed, or "filled-in" at some point during the trading session, but all we want to determine is whether the <u>opening gap starts a new trend, or if the opening gap is a pullback within an existing trend relative to yesterday's price action.</u>

For example, a gap up in a down trend from yesterday will likely move lower to fill the gap at some point, but will also very likely move all the way down to test any price extreme lows that are in place.

A gap up in an uptrend from yesterday might try to fill the gap lower, but don't be surprised if the uptrend eventually kicks in, and new extreme highs for the day are established.

5-minute price analysis allows you to view gaps in a very clear way, which can often provide meaningful information for trade setups that develop early in the trading session.

In our chart example, we see <u>three gaps over three days</u>.

We always take the trades that set up according to Day Session 1 rules, but let's see how big picture/gap analysis helps. The following gap explanations occur left to right on the 5-minute chart below.

<u>Gap 1</u> – <u>An up gap during an uptrend (middle of first trend line)</u>. First signal is a C1 continuation buy. There is no resistance overhead to stop the explosive move up from continuing. Can we predict this type of move will unfold? Of course not, but moves like this happen all the time in the ES.

<u>Gap 2</u> – <u>An up gap that turns a downtrend into an uptrend</u>. The market behaves just as expected in this scenario. A move down to fill the gap occurs first, and look where this move ends and reverses? Right at a pivot area near the 18-ma/trend line area. Price eventually moves up to make new highs for the day in accordance with the new uptrend in place. Again, you can't predict any of this, but I would tighten up stops for any early shorts as price nears the trend line, and I would expect longs that develop near the trend line to have very good potential as a new big picture uptrend unfolds.

<u>Gap 3</u> – <u>Gap up in an uptrend</u>. Just like the previous day, the market first moves down to fill the gap- down to the 5-min 18-ma/trend line area. Choppiness sets in and an attempt at uptrend continuation fails.(Important sign). The subsequent down move that develops moves right through the pivot/trend line area and turns the uptrend into a downtrend. Is it any wonder the market starts an explosive and lengthy move down? When a key pivot/trend line level is penetrated to change trend, you can certainly expect many nice C1 continuation, and C2 consolidation trades.

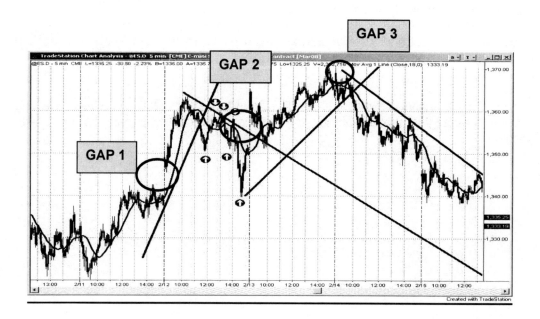

Between gap 1 and 2, 6 price swings that take place <u>after</u> the trend changes from up to down are isolated (first steep trend line is broken). There are 3 swings up and 3 swings down, during this new downtrend (arrows).

Here are some key highlights. All 3 up swings carry price only to the new 5-minute trend line/resistance area. You see this time and time again. Big picture trends don't quickly turn from up to down to up, etc.

Therefore, if you take countertrend long trades, keep your expectations realistic according to the big picture. This doesn't mean countertrend long trades in a big picture down trend aren't very good trades.

In this example, long swings 1 and 3 offer larger gains than short swings 1 and 2, and the only losing trade in the series was short swing 1, a short swing in a big picture down trend.

All types of trades can work, especially if there is enough room to move to key areas on the big picture chart. Short swing 3 was also a big winner (short swing in a down trend), and F=MC2 C1 continuation trades along with a good momentum trailing stop technique, would have allowed you to capture much of this gain.

<u>Big Picture helps with analyzing C3 consolidation chop</u> – 5000-price moves to consolidation chop when the 18-ma crosses below a rising 89-ma (circle, left). Is this the start of a new downtrend? Big picture analysis (right) says no! Big picture trend has just turned up with a break of a steep trend line.

Therefore, the C3 consolidation chop pullback is nothing more than a pullback to a key trend line/support area in the big picture (circle, right) Look to go long in the C3 consolidation chop area for a push to new highs.

Section 5 – Trade Entry

<u>5000/1500/55 CHARTS</u>

<u>The 1500 and 55 charts are used to enter all trades. The 1500-medium timeframe chart is always used for confirmation</u>. The 55-chart is used to establish initial risk, and subsequent 1500 price swings determine risk adjustment parameters as soon as possible after a trade is entered.

The 55-tick chart contains paint bars with a value=8. (both price greater than, and price less than 8), and the way the paint bars <u>group together</u>, combined with the way 55-tick price action unfolds, becomes the key to entering C1 and some C2/C3 trades.

Entering trades with $E=MC^2$ is on one hand very clear, and on the other hand, a bit eclectic with some flexibility thrown into the mix.

<u>We consider a flexible entry approach to be a strength of the $E=MC^2$ method</u> because conceptually we are consistent to look for entries the same way each time, but practically we remain flexible, realizing the market never moves the exact same way each time.

There are two types of orders for entering trades, and you can use both types of orders as you gain experience observing price movement.

You can enter a trade with a <u>market order</u> after a signal is generated , or you can enter a trade with a <u>stop order</u> that falls beyond a signal level 1500/55 pivot point, or 55 flat looking congestion area that forms.

A market order fills you instantly, and you can get either a better or worse fill from current price.

A stop order is a <u>resting order ahead of price action</u>. This entry technique can often control a better fill price, but sometimes you get filled on a price probe that quickly reverses against the trade.

With both techniques, good and bad fills average out over time, so don't worry about this too much. <u>As a general rule, market orders are used to enter after C1 continuation pullbacks, and stop orders are used to enter after C2/C3 consolidation pullbacks.</u>

We use market and/or stop orders over <u>limit orders</u> because we don't want miss a trade by fussing over a tick.

With $E=MC^2$ we are comfortable buying at the ask price, and selling at the bid price and not missing a great trade by trying to save a tick or two at entry.

Paint Bar Groupings – The 55 tick chart moves very fast. Bars form in a matter of seconds. The paint bar indicator (price > avg., price < avg.; input=8) allows us to monitor a microscopic view of the subtle up and down price action taking place.

We set paint bars to draw **UP bars "<u>THICKER</u>" than DOWN bars.**

We are most interested in monitoring:

(1) The <u>alternating</u> up and down paint bar grouping flow that forms during a pullback.
(2) The obvious high/low swing pivot points that form during a pullback.
(3) The 4-paint bars that follow a "signal" paint bar.

An up or down grouping consists of one or many paint bars of the same type in a row. We watch the back and forth alternating formations of up groupings and down groupings.

<u>Alternating 55-Paint Bar Grouping Flow</u> – Notice how 55-price action alternates up and down by paint bar grouping. The arrows in the chart below show the alternating flow of up and down paint bar groupings.
(Note- Single alternating bars do count, but don't worry about these for now. Instead, just get an overall feel for the alternating flow of up and down groupings)

Trade signals – A pullback that develops on the long and medium timeframe charts (5000/1500), sets up a trade in the direction of these longer timeframes.

There are three types of "with trend" pullbacks: (1) C1-Continuation (2) C2-Consolidation normal (3) C3-Consolidation chop.

Each type of pullback requires a unique entry approach.

During a pullback, we look to the short timeframe (55), which clearly will be moving in a mini-trend opposite the direction we are looking to enter.

If we are looking to go long, 55-price will be moving down - making lower lows, and lower highs. If we are looking to go short, 55-price will be moving up – making higher highs, and higher lows.

At first, this may seem a bit confusing, but all you are doing is monitoring the "nature of the pullback" and considering a choice of 55-price options to enter trades depending upon which type of pullback develops.

Furthermore, each type of pullback flows into the next- so you always look for C1 continuation trades first, C2 normal consolidation trades second, and C3 chop consolidation trades third.

As you further examine the flexibility offered by this multi-faceted entry approach you will (1) See how easy it is to put these criteria into practical use (2) Love the flexible nature of how this criteria allows you to react to price action that never acts in the exact same way in all pullback situations.

I welcome you to do your own homework. Perhaps you will be more comfortable waiting for only one of these conditions to form every time, and for every entry (i.e.- only take first C1 after a new 5-minute trend change and/or volume ratio reversal).

Perhaps you will choose to be even more aggressive with subsequent entries during an established 1500-trend (i.e. - two C1's in a row with room to run to support/resistance).

For now, it is best to show this multi-faceted approach to enter trades, and as time goes on you can decide for yourself, what works best for you.

There will never be a single, perfect entry method.

No matter which entry method you chose, there's always an entry that will be too early, or too late. There will always be entries that will stop you out for a loss in otherwise perfect long timeframe set up condition.

The $E=MC^2$ method attempts to strike a balance between risk and reward. To do so, we attempt to enter on the short timeframe relative to the long timeframe.

The short timeframe is always less stable than the long timeframe, yet we want to establish as tight a stop as possible commensurate with being able to capture large gains according to unfolding long timeframe market structure.

Therefore, the best approach is to understand the nature of short timeframe price action relative to long timeframe pullbacks, and take aggressive, yet sensible, trade entries according to the unique unfolding nature of pullback price action relative to the risk and potential reward for a given trade.

BUY ENTRIES

BUY TRADE SIGNAL #1 – CONTINUATION BUY (C1)

(1) When 5000-price pulls back down to a rising 18-ma in an uptrend, move to the 55 chart in the 5000 C1 set up area (2) Wait for a <u>55-UP PAINT BAR</u> to form in the C1 continuation pullback area (5000-paint bar change below 18-ma, 1500-price within the long term moving average area). This is the SIGNAL BAR. If the 4th bar after the signal bar "holds," <u>buy at the market</u>.

A 4-bar hold means the <u>close of the forth bar after the signal bar holds above the signal bar high</u>. Of course, if the actual fourth bar is a big down bar approaching the inside of the signal bar, you would use common sense to wait for another bar, and make sure price is actually holding before buying.

<u>A 4-Bar hold can take different forms</u> – The most common 4-bar hold pattern has price remaining at, or above the signal bar high.

<u>4-bar hold pivot</u> – Sometimes a pivot forms within the 4-bar count, close to the signal bar, as price <u>stalls</u> before moving in the trade direction. In these cases, you can play safe and place your entry one-tick beyond the pivot.

<u>4-bar hold runaway</u> – Sometimes price runs strongly away from the signal bar high before 4-bars complete. If you sense a runaway pattern developing, you can use your judgment and place a market order long on the second or third bar.

In most cases, once you see a 4th bar that holds, and the fourth bar isn't moving strongly downward, you can enter an order to buy at the market.

(Volume – Remember, the typical continuation buy has 1500-volume holding above zero, as 55-volume "brushes the zero-line" either slightly above or below)

Continuation Buy – When 5000-price pulls back to a rising 18-ma in an uptrend (circle, left) we look to the 55-chart for a 4-bar count C1 continuation entry. Up paint bar1 (arrow 1, "not in buy zone") doesn't hold after 4 bars. Up paint bar 2 (arrow 2 "not in buy zone") doesn't hold after 4 bars. Up paint bar 3 (early in circle), which is in the continuation pullback area (5000-price below 18-ma) *does* hold after 4 bars (arrow 3, right) and we enter long with a Market Order (Note- You can set up a one button push market order using macros in Tradestation).

REMEMBER, FOR C1 BUY TRADES 1500-PRICE HOLDS INSIDE, OR RIGHT AT THE 1500-LTMA LINE. C1 MOMENTUM TURNS INTO C2 NORMAL PULLBACK WHEN 1500-PRICE PENETRATES AND HOLDS BELOW THE 1500-89 LT MA.

Created with TradeStation

4-Bar hold alternatives – The most common 4-bar hold pattern has price remaining fairly close to the up or down signal bar high or low.

4-bar hold pivot – Sometimes a pivot forms within the 4-bar count, close to the signal bar, as price **stalls** before moving in the trade direction (circle, top). In these cases, place your entry one-tick beyond the pivot (Horizontal line, First chart below)

4-bar hold runaway – Sometimes price runs strongly away from the signal bar before 4-bars. If you sense a runaway pattern developing, you can use your judgment and place a market order on the second or third bar. (circle, bottom)

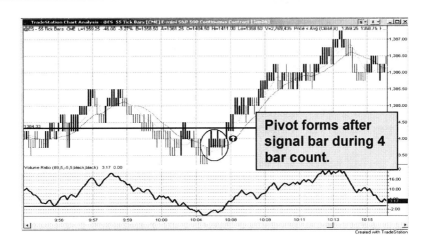

Pivot forms after signal bar during 4 bar count.

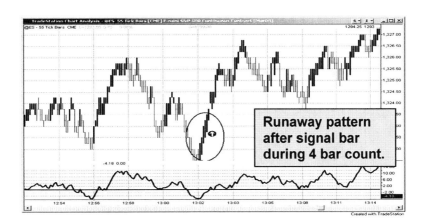

Runaway pattern after signal bar during 4 bar count.

BUY TRADE SIGNAL #2 – CONSOLIDATION BUY (NORMAL- C2)

When 5000-price pulls back to the18-ma in an uptrend, <u>and the 18-ma rolls over and turns down</u>, follow 1500 and 55 price action that moves lower.

1500-price will <u>move below its' 89 LT moving average</u> (as 5000 18-ma turns down) and this signals you to start monitoring for C2 consolidation entries vs. C1 continuation entries.

<u>1500-price moving back above the LT-ma is the key to C2/C3 consolidation buy entries, and it develops in two different ways:</u>

(A) 1500 89 LT-ma is still moving up in trade direction. Enter aggressively on first 1500 1-2-3 price pattern as price moves back above the LT-ma

(B) 1500 89 LT-ma rolls over and turns down (i.e.- 1500-price moves way below the LT-ma), and we look to enter as follows:

Do not enter on the first 1500 1-2-3 that forms way below the LT ma...If two waves in a row (1-2-3-4-5 pattern) form near the LT ma you can enter...If the second wave in a row doesn't form, and price moves back down, <u>start a whole new 1-2-3 count on the next push up, and see if this 1-2-3 is near the LT-ma</u>. In other words, you'll see an extreme high form during the first 1-2-3 pattern up, price will pull back below wave 2, and sometimes shoot right back up through the wave 1 extreme on a single push. This single push is not the entry, but instead wave 1 of the next 1-2-3 count....

So the key is, when the 1500 LT ma is moving down, and price is way below, and you don't get an initial two wave push up, keep starting new 1-2-3 counts over again, looking for 1-2-3 price patterns to eventually form near the 89 LT-ma line.

The main point is that once the 1500 89 LT MA turns against the main trend, relax a bit, and get more conservative with your entry, because this is usually a short-term trend in the opposite direction for a while.

There is one more, less common, consolidation entry we monitor for. The most common way to enter is with a 1-2-3 pattern, but if you see 55-price action flattening out with a long, sideways boxy pattern, showing matching boxy pivot highs, etc., then you can enter a consolidation trade on a breakout of this 55-sideways pattern to the upside.

(Note- A 1-2-3 pattern up is a wave up (1), wave (2) down <u>that holds above wave 1 low</u>, and a wave (3) up that goes higher than wave 1 extreme. Buy one tick above wave 1 extreme)

Consolidation Buy Volume - The main volume consideration with consolidation buy setups is that 1550-volume doesn't move considerably below -5. (In more volatile conditions, normal volume swings can move between +/- 10).

The key is that if the volume move up preceding the pullback reached an upper volume extreme, and the volume pullback is shallow, then the next push up in price likely includes the double strength of anxious buyers and patient sellers. (See volume appendix for more details).

<u>**VERY IMPORTANT**</u>**- TO SEE 1-2-3 PATTERNS CLEARLY (1) NARROW YOUR 1500-BARS AS CLOSE TOGETHER AS POSSIBLE (2) ZOOM 1500-CHART OUT AS MUCH AS POSSIBLE SO YOU CAN VISUALLY SEE A "TRENDLINE" OF THE 1500-PULLBACK.**

<u>**THE LOGIC OF A 1-2-3, OR 1-2-3-4-5 IS THAT PRICE IS BREAKING A TRENDLINE OF THE PULLBACK NEAR THE 1500-LT MA LINE!**</u>

<u>**1500 1-2-3 Buy Pattern with LT ma rising**</u> **– When the 18-ma turns down and a 5000-price C2 consolidation buy setup develops (circle, left), we look to the 1500 (right). When 1500-price drops below the LT ma, but the LT-ma is still rising, buy one tick above wave 1 on a 1-2-3 pattern as price is crossing back above the LT ma. THE KEY HERE IS THAT THIS IS C1 THAT HAS BARELY TURNED INTO A C2 AND YOU CAN LOOK FOR A TIGHT 1-2-3 PATTERN THAT IS BREAKING THE PULLBACK DOWNTREND LINE BACK ABOVE THE STILL RISING 1500-89 LT MA.**

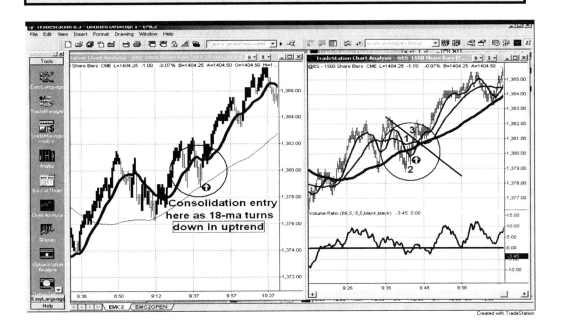

1500 1-2-3-4-5 Buy Pattern with LT ma falling – When the 18-ma turns down and a 5000-price C2 consolidation buy setup develops (circle, left), we look to the 1500 (right). When 1500-price drops below the LT ma, and the LT-ma rolls over and is falling, first look to buy if a two-wave up move develops (i.e.- A 1-2-3 near the 1500 LT ma, immediately followed by another wave higher)

In this instance buy one tick above wave 3 (arrow, right).

THE KEY HERE IS THAT THIS IS A DEEP C2 PULLBACK AND WE WANT TO MAKE SURE THE 1-2-3-4-5 PATTERN IS DEVELOPING BACK THROUGH THE 1500 LT MA, PREFERABLY IN LINE WITH BREAKING A DOWN TREND LINE FORMED BY PRICE AND THE DOWN SLOPING 1500-LT MA. THEREFORE, DO NOT BUY A 1-2-3-4-5 WIGGLE <u>THAT IS BELOW THE 1500-LT MA AND/OR NOT BREAKING A DOWNTREND LINE.</u>

1500 1-2-3 Recount Buy Pattern with LT ma falling – When the 18-ma turns down and a 5000-price C2 consolidation buy setup develops (circle, left), we look to the 1500 (right). When 1500-price drops below the LT ma, and the LT-ma rolls over and is falling, if a 1-2-3-4-5 count doesn't form as described above, keep starting over with new 1-2-3 counts until you can buy one tick above wave 1 near the LT ma (arrow, right). This is the most common type of C2 entry!

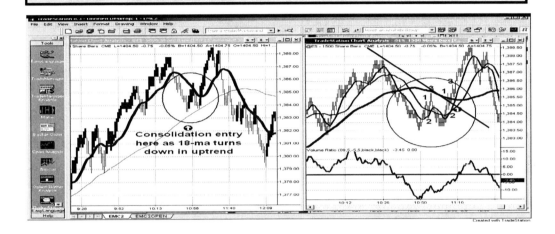

55-Tick Consolidation Buy – Remember, if 1500-price dips below the long term-ma, we generally look for 1-2-3, or 1-2-3-4-5 patterns for consolidation entries.

However, if we see a "perfect flat box" develop on the 55 ahead of a 1500 1-2-3 pattern (rectangle, right) it is ok to buy this upside breakout as a C2 consolidation buy trade.

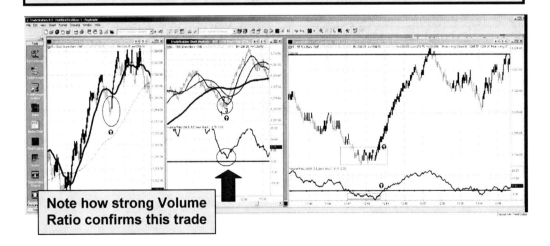

Note how strong Volume Ratio confirms this trade

A word on Buy Logic - We look to buy when 5000-price moves lower towards a rising 18-ma (C1 continuation), or when a falling 18-ma coincides with a rising 89-ma (C2/C3 consolidation).

This causes a series of lower waves in price. (Note - During very strong momentum, there may only be one lower wave down)

We always look to the medium (1500) timeframe chart to see if the pullback is either "shallow (C1) or normal (C2,C3)" according to where the pullback moves in relation to the three moving averages.

As price moves down, the high price for each wave is a "reference area" for where the last seller gets filled as price moves lower during the pullback.

Sellers normally look to sell as high as possible, unless they become very anxious to sell (i.e. during downside momentum). Therefore, as price moves lower and lower during an uptrend pullback; sellers in the market are getting a little anxious but still looking to be filled at higher prices they find to be of value.

Shallow Pullbacks (Continuation-C1) - When price can't move beyond the 1500-long term moving average, and 55-up action "holds" (4-bar count) this represents the point where we can "safely" say that no more short-term seller anxiety is entering the picture (they will now remain patient to sell). This is the point we want to buy during shallow pullbacks.

55-MARKET ACTION CONFIRMS THE DRYING UP OF SELLER ANXIETY, AND WE CAN BUY ASSUMING THE SELLERS ARE NOW WAITING FOR HIGHER PRICES TO SELL.

Normal Pullbacks (Consolidation-C2,C3) – When price declines past the 1500-LTma we want market action to confirm not only when the sellers lose anxiety, but also when the buyers increase their anxiety. As successive selling waves lose momentum and fail to move lower (1-2-3 patterns form up), this is a sign the sellers aren't as "anxious" to sell, but since a larger than normal pullback is taking place it is clear the buyers have been exhibiting patience buying. (Remember, under normal conditions, sellers look to sell high, and buyers look to buy low.)

Therefore, when price eventually breaks above the 1500 89 LT ma with a 1-2-3 penetrating a downtrend line, this indicates that sellers are now willing to sit back and sell at higher prices, and the buyers (who can sense they will no longer get the lower prices they seek), become anxious to buy.

This is the point we can "safely" buy during a deeper pullback as price moves higher from the dual force of anxious buyers, and the inactive force of patient sellers waiting to sell at higher prices.

BUY TRADE SIGNAL #3 – CONSOLIDATION BUY (CHOP)- (C3)

When 5000-price pulls back to the 18-ma in an uptrend, and the 18-ma rolls over and turns down, <u>and the 18-ma crosses below a rising 89-ma</u>, we follow 1500-price action for a C3 consolidation chop trade in the very same manner we follow 1500-price for a normal C2 consolidation trade.

<u>Whenever the 18 ma, crosses the 89-ma this represents an inflection point in the market</u>. Therefore, we always check two things in an effort to remain consistent to either stay with the current uptrend (C3 BUY), or change bias to a downtrend (LOOK FOR C1 SELL). (1) Check the 5-minute big picture chart to see if we are breaking a key pivot low to change to a downtrend. (2) Monitor the 5000 low of the first probe down that caused the 18-ma to cross the 89-ma, and see if this low is penetrated again on a subsequent swing.

If either of these two take place we know the 18-ma crossing the 89-ma is the start of a new down trend (C1 SELL), and not the C3 deep consolidation buy pullback for the uptrend.

We preferably want to see the 5000-89 ma start rolling over down to take new C1 sell trades (and will watch for this rolling over closely), but price action is more important, and if price action is saying the trend has changed after the 18-ma crosses the 89-ma, then it is best to try to aggressively get in on the new trend as early as possible with a C1 Sell, as the 5000 89-ma is "just about to rollover."

If the 5-minute trend is still up, or 5000 price holds just one probe down as the 18-ma crosses the 89 ma, then the overall logic for the consolidation chop trade (C3 BUY) is similar to normal consolidation trade (C2) in that we look for pullback momentum to "flatten out," and we want the medium timeframe to confirm the long timeframe by making sure 1500-price crosses above the 1500 LT-ma line in the direction of the trade.

Because of the deeper nature of the pullback, we simply want to make sure we are still trading with the main trend in accordance with the big picture and price action whenever we see the 18-ma cross the 89-ma.

Also, if the 18-ma crosses the 89-ma and <u>time</u> goes by without a C3 buy setup, and 5000-price is far beyond the 89-ma during the pullback, it is likely the 89-ma will roll over and change direction, and our trade direction bias will change.

(Volume – The main volume consideration with C3 consolidation chop buy setups is that 1500-volume doesn't move considerably below -5, -10, etc. Also, 55-volume should cross back above zero at nearly the same time the buy entry signal is given).

Consolidation Chop Buy – A deep pullback often sets up an inflection point for the market. In an uptrend, the 5000 18-ma crosses a rising 89-ma (circle, left). We look at the 5-minute big picture chart (circle, right) and first probe of 5000 price action (circle, left), to make sure we are still in an uptrend. In this case (and in most cases), C3 consolidation chop buy pullbacks move right to the big picture trend line /support area.

1500-volume is holding nicely above –5 (circle, middle/bottom), and we look for an entry that coincides with 1500-price moving back above the 89 long term moving average with a 1-2-3 pattern in line with a break of down trend pullback line (circle, middle).

In this case, a classic flattening, box area develops on the 55-chart (rectangle), that coincides with our 1500 1-2-3 pattern, and we buy on a breakout from this area (arrow at right of rectangle) for a push to test highs.

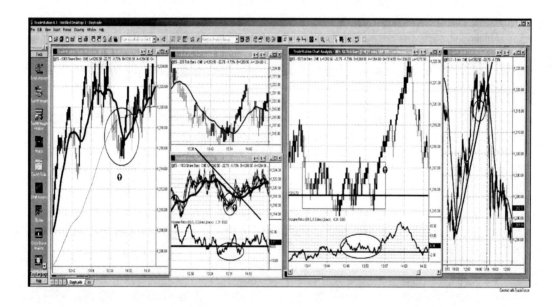

SELL ENTRIES

SELL TRADE SIGNAL #1 – CONTINUATION SELL (C1)

(1) When 5000-price pulls back up to a falling 18-ma in a down trend, move to the 55 chart in the 5000 C1 setup area (2) Wait for a 55-<u>DOWN PAINT BAR</u> to form in the C1 continuation pullback area (5000-paint bar change above 18-ma, 1500-price within the long term moving average area). THIS IS THE SIGNAL BAR. If the 4th bar after the signal bar "holds," <u>sell at the market</u>.

A 4-bar hold means the <u>close of the fourth bar after the signal bar holds below the signal bar low</u>. Of course, if the actual fourth bar is a big up bar approaching the inside of the signal bar, you would use common sense to wait for another bar to make sure price actually holds before selling.

<u>A 4-Bar hold can take different forms</u> – The most common 4-bar hold pattern has price remaining at, or below the signal bar low.

<u>4-bar hold pivot</u> – Sometimes a pivot forms within the 4-bar count, close to the signal bar, as price <u>stalls</u> before resuming in the trade direction. In these cases, place your entry one-tick beyond the pivot.

<u>4-bar hold runaway</u> – Sometimes price runs strongly away from the signal bar low before 4-bars complete. If you sense a runaway pattern developing, you can use your judgment and place a market order on the second or third bar.

In most cases, once you see a 4th bar that holds, and the fourth bar isn't moving strongly upward, you can enter an order to sell at the market.

(Volume- Remember, the typical continuation sell has 1500-volume holding below zero, as 55-volume "brushes the zero-line" either slightly above or below).

Continuation Sell – When 5000-price pulls back to a falling 18-ma in a downtrend trend (circle, left) we look to the 55-chart for a 4-bar count C1 continuation entry (right).

Down paint bar1 (arrow 1 "not in sell zone") doesn't hold after 4 bars. Down paint bar 2 (early in circle), which is in the C1 continuation pullback area (5000-price above 18-ma) does hold after 4 bars (arrow, right) and we enter short with a **Market Order. (Note- You can set up a one button push market order using macros in Tradestation)**

REMEMBER, FOR C1 SELL TRADES 1500-PRICE HOLDS INSIDE, OR AT THE 1500-89 LT MA LINE. C1 MOMENTUM TURNS INTO C2 NORMAL PULLBACK WHEN 1500-PRICE PENETRATES AND HOLDS ABOVE THE 1500-LT MA.

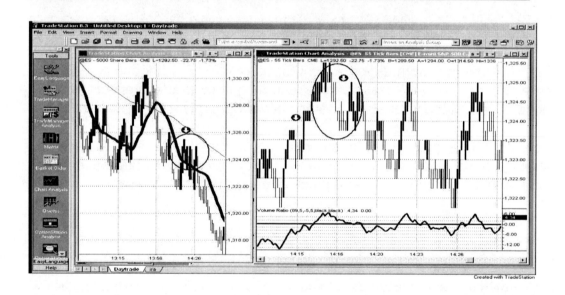

Created with TradeStation

4-Bar hold alternatives – The most common 4-bar hold pattern has price remaining fairly close to the up or down signal bar.

4-bar hold pivot – Sometimes a pivot forms within the 4-bar count, close to the signal bar, as price stalls before moving in the trade direction (circle, top). In these cases, place your entry one-tick beyond the pivot (Horizontal line, First chart below)

4-bar hold runaway – Sometimes price runs strongly away from the signal bar before 4-bars. If you sense a runaway pattern developing, you can use your judgment and place a market order on the second or third bar (circle, bottom)

Pivot forms after signal bar during 4 bar count.

Runaway pattern after signal bar during 4 bar

SELL TRADE SIGNAL #2 – CONSOLIDATION SELL (NORMAL- C2)

When 5000-price pulls back to the18-ma in an down trend, <u>and the 18-ma rolls over and turns up</u>, follow 1500 and 55 price action that moves higher.

1500-price will <u>move above the 89 LT moving average</u> (as 5000 18-ma turns up) and this signals you to start monitoring for C2 consolidation entries vs. C1 continuation entries.

<u>1500-price moving back below the 89 LT-ma is the key to C2 consolidation sell entries, and it develops in two different ways:</u>

(A) 1500 89 LT-ma is still moving down in the trade direction. Enter on a 1500 1-2-3 price pattern as price moves back below the 89 LT-ma

(B) 1500 89 LT-ma rolls over and turns up (i.e.- 1500-price moves way above the LT-ma), and we look to enter as follows:

Do not enter on the first 1500 1-2-3 that forms way above the LT ma...If two waves in a row (1,2,3,4,5 pattern) form near the LT ma you can enter...If the second wave in a row doesn't form, and price moves back up, <u>start a whole new 1-2-3 count on the next push down, and see if this 1-2-3 is near the LT-ma</u>. In other words, you'll see an extreme low form during the first 1-2-3 pattern down, price will pull back above wave 2, and sometimes shoot right back down through the wave 1 extreme on a single push. This single push is not the entry, but instead wave 1 of the next 1-2-3 count....

So the key is, when the 89 LT ma is moving up, and price is way above, and you don't get an initial two wave push down, keep starting new 1-2-3 counts over again, looking for 1-2-3 price patterns to eventually form near the LT-ma

The main point is that once the 1500 LT MA turns up against the main trend, relax a bit, and get more conservative with your sell entry, because this is usually a short-term trend in the opposite direction for a while.

There is one more, less common, consolidation entry we monitor for. The most common way to enter is with a 1500 1-2-3 pattern, but if you see 55-price action flattening out with a long, sideways boxy pattern, showing matching boxy pivot lows, etc., then you can enter a C2 consolidation trade on a breakout of this 55-sideways pattern to the downside.

(<u>Note</u>- A 1-2-3 pattern down is a wave down (1), wave (2) up <u>that holds below wave 1 high</u>, and a wave (3) down that goes lower than wave 1. Sell one tick below wave 1 low)

<u>Consolidation Sell Volume</u> - The main volume consideration with C2 consolidation sell setups is that 1550-volume doesn't move considerably above +5. (In more volatile conditions, normal volume swings can move between +/- 10).

The key is that if the volume move down preceding the pullback reached a lower volume extreme, and the volume pullback is shallow, then the next push down in price likely includes the double strength of anxious sellers and patient buyers. (See volume appendix for more details).

VERY IMPORTANT- TO SEE 1-2-3 PATTERNS CLEARLY (1) NARROW YOUR 1500-BARS AS CLOSE TOGETHER AS POSSIBLE (2) ZOOM 1500-CHART OUT AS MUCH AS POSSIBLE SO YOU CAN VISUALLY SEE A TRENDLINE OF THE 1500-PULLBACK.

THE LOGIC OF A 1-2-3, OR 1-2-3-4-5 IS THAT PRICE IS BREAKING A TRENDLINE OF THE PULLBACK NEAR THE 1500-LT MA LINE!

1500 1-2-3 Sell Pattern with LT ma falling – When the 18-ma turns up and a 5000-price C2 consolidation sell setup develops (circle, left), we look to the 1500 (right). When 1500-price rises above the LT ma, but the LT-ma is still falling, sell one tick below wave 1 on a 1-2-3 pattern as price is crossing back below the LT ma. THE KEY HERE IS THAT THIS IS A C1 THAT HAS BARELY TURNED INTO A C2 AND YOU CAN LOOK FOR A TIGHT 1-2-3 PATTERN THAT IS BREAKING THE PULLBACK UPTREND LINE BACK BELOW THE 1500-LT MA.

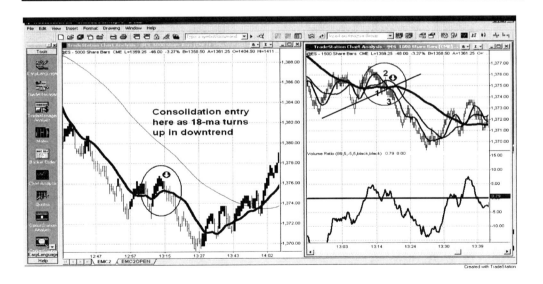

1500 1-2-3-4-5 Sell Pattern with LT ma rising – When the 18-ma turns up and a 5000-price C2 consolidation sell setup develops (circle, left), we look to the 1500 (right). When 1500-price rises above the 89 LT ma, and the LT-ma rolls over and is rising, first look to sell if a two-wave down move develops (i.e.- A 1-2-3 near the 1500-LT ma immediately followed by another wave lower)

In this instance sell one tick below wave 3 (arrow, right).

THE KEY HERE IS THAT THIS IS A DEEP C2 PULLBACK AND WE WANT TO MAKE SURE THE 1-2-3-4-5 PATTERN IS DEVELOPING BACK THROUGH THE 1500 LT MA, PREFERABLY IN LINE WITH BREAKING A UP TREND LINE FORMED BY PRICE AND THE UP SLOPING 1500-LT MA. THEREFORE, DO NOT SELL A 1-2-3-4-5 WIGGLE THAT IS ABOVE THE 1500-LT MA AND/OR NOT BREAKING AN UPTREND PULLBACK LINE.

1500 1-2-3 Recount Sell Pattern with LT ma rising – When the 18-ma turns up and a 5000-price C2 consolidation sell setup develops (circle, left), we look to the 1500 (right). When 1500-price rises above the 89 LT ma, and the LT-ma rolls over and is rising, if a 1-2-3-4-5 count doesn't form as described above, keep starting over with new 1-2-3 counts until you can sell one tick below wave 1 near the LT ma (arrow, right). (Most common C2 sell pattern)

55-Tick Consolidation Sell – Remember, if 1500-price rises above the 89 long term-ma, we generally look for 1-2-3, or 1-2-3-4-5 patterns for consolidation entries.

However, if we see a "perfect flat box" develop on the 55 ahead of a 1500 1-2-3 pattern (rectangle, right) it is ok to sell this downside breakout as a C2 consolidation sell trade.

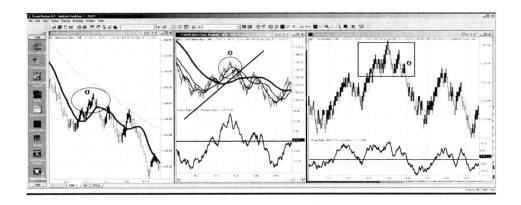

A word on Sell Logic - We look to sell when 5000-price moves higher towards a falling 18-ma (C1 continuation), or when a rising 18-ma coincides with a falling 89-ma (C2/C3 consolidation).

This causes a series of higher waves in price. (Note - During very strong momentum, there may only be one higher wave up)

We always look to the medium (1500) timeframe chart to see if the pullback is either "shallow (C1) or normal (C2,C3)" according to where the pullback moves in relation to the three moving averages.

As price moves up, the low price for each wave is a "reference area" for where the last buyer gets filled as price moves higher during the pullback.

Buyers normally look to buy as low as possible, unless they become very anxious to buy (i.e. during upside momentum). Therefore, as price moves higher and higher during an down trend pullback, buyers in the market are getting a little anxious but still looking to be filled at lower prices they find to be of value.

Shallow Pullbacks (Continuation-C1) - When price can't move beyond the 1500-long term moving average, and 55-up action "holds" (4-bar count) this represents the point where we can "safely" say that no more short-term buyer anxiety is entering the picture. This is the point we want to sell during shallow pullbacks.

55-MARKET ACTION CONFIRMS THE DRYING UP OF BUYER ANXIETY, AND WE CAN SELL ASSUMING THE BUYERS ARE NOW WAITING FOR LOWER PRICES TO BUY!

Normal Pullbacks (Consolidation-C2, C3) – When price rises past the 1500-LTma we want market action to confirm not only when the buyers lose anxiety, but also when the sellers increase their anxiety. As successive buying waves lose momentum and fail to move higher (1-2-3 patterns form down), this is a sign the buyers aren't as "anxious" to buy, but since a larger than normal pullback is taking place it is clear the sellers have been exhibiting patience selling. (Remember, under normal conditions, sellers look to sell high, and buyers look to buy low.)

Therefore, when price eventually breaks below the 1500 89 LT ma with a 1-2-3 penetrating an uptrend line, this indicates that buyers are now willing to sit back and buy at lower prices, and the sellers (who can sense they will no longer get the higher prices they seek), become anxious to sell.

This is the point we can "safely" sell during a deeper pullback as price moves lower from the dual force of anxious sellers, and the inactive force of patient buyers waiting to buy at lower prices.

SELL TRADE SIGNAL #3 – CONSOLIDATION SELL (CHOP)- (C3)

When 5000-price pulls back to the 18-ma in an downtrend, and the 18-ma rolls over and turns up, <u>and the 18-ma crosses above a falling 89-ma</u>, we follow 1500-price action for a C3 consolidation chop trade in the very same manner we follow 1500-price for a normal consolidation trade.

<u>Whenever the 18-ma, crosses the 89-ma this represents an inflection point in the market</u>. Therefore, we always check two things in an effort to remain consistent to either stay with the current down trend (C3 SELL), or change bias to a uptrend (LOOK FOR C1 BUY). (1) Check the 5-minute big picture chart to see if we are breaking a key pivot high to change to a uptrend. (2) Monitor the high of the first 5000 probe up that caused the 18-ma to cross the 89-ma, and see if this high is penetrated again on a subsequent swing.

If either of these two take place we know the 5000 18-ma crossing the 89-ma is the start of a new uptrend (C1 BUY), and not the C3 deep consolidation sell pullback for the down trend.

We preferably want to see the 5000-89 ma start rolling over up to take new C1 buy trades (and will watch for this rolling over closely), but price action is more important, and if price action is saying the trend has changed after the 5000 18-ma crosses the 89-ma, then it is best to try to aggressively get in on the new trend as early as possible with a C1Buy, as the 5000 89-ma is "just about to rollover."

If the 5-minute trend is still down, or 5000 price holds just one probe up as the 18-ma crosses the 89 ma, then the overall logic for the consolidation chop trade (C3 SELL) is similar to normal consolidation trade (C2) in that we look for pullback momentum to "flatten out," and we want the medium timeframe to confirm the long timeframe by making sure 1500-price crosses below the 1500 89 LT-ma line in the direction of the trade.

Because of the deeper nature of the C3 pullback, we simply want to make sure we are still trading with the main trend in accordance with the big picture and price action whenever we see the 5000 18-ma cross the 89-ma.

Also, if the 5000 18-ma crosses the 89-ma and <u>time</u> goes by without a C3 setup, and 5000-price is far beyond the 89-ma during the pullback, it is likely the 89-ma will roll over and change direction, and our trade direction bias will change.

(Volume – The main volume consideration with C3 consolidation chop sell setups is that 1550-volume doesn't move considerably above 5, 10, etc. Also, 55-volume should cross back below zero at nearly the same time the sell entry signal is given).

Consolidation Chop Sell – A deep pullback often sets up an inflection point for the market. In a downtrend, the 5000 18-ma rises and crosses a falling 89-ma (circle, left). We look at the 5-minute big picture chart (clrcle, right), and first probe price action (circle, left) to make sure we are still in a downtrend.

In this case (and in most cases), C3 sell consolidation chop pullbacks move right to the big picture trend line /resistance area. (See 5-minute chart (right) - On this day price gapped strongly higher to create an uptrend. Price worked lower as expected, and did so enough to start a new 5000 18/89 downtrend. Price then rallied higher to turn 5000 18/89 trend up.

The C3 sell trade below was pullback to trend line/resistance during the downtrend phase before price turned back up. 1500-volume moves to +10 area (circle, middle/bottom), and we look for an entry with a 55-box, or 1500-1-2-3 price pattern that moves back below the long term moving average in line with a break of an uptrend pullback line (circle, middle/top).

A classic 1500-1-2-3, and classic 55-flattening, box area develops at the same time, and we sell on a breakout from this area (arrow at right of rectangle) to test lows of day.

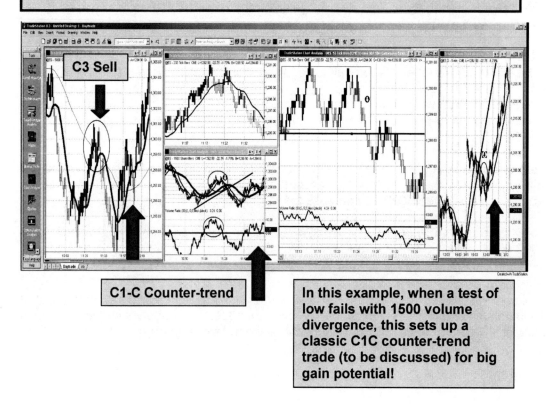

C3 Sell

C1-C Counter-trend

In this example, when a test of low fails with 1500 volume divergence, this sets up a classic C1C counter-trend trade (to be discussed) for big gain potential!

TRADE RE-ENTRY

As previously mentioned, no entry method will ever be perfect. There will simply be times you enter a trade too early in an otherwise perfectly acceptable long timeframe setup.

The best course of action to take if you enter too early is to take a <u>small loss and immediately look to re-enter if conditions for the original trade are still in place</u>.

If you are stopped out of a C1 continuation trade, then watch for another C1 continuation trade to immediately develop.

Sometimes a continuation entry takes two entry attempts in a row.

If you are stopped out of a C1 continuation trade, and a deeper pullback develops (18-ma rolls over), then look for a C2 consolidation trade.

Being stopped out and re-entering during the next setup is the best tradeoff vs. holding onto a pullback trade with a larger than normal loss, and "hoping" the market turns back around in accordance with normal, or chop consolidation behavior.

The best traders always reduce risk as soon, and as much as possible, and always know they can jump right back into a trade.

The $E=MC^2$ trading approach is designed to allow you to get right back into stopped-out trade using the same setup, so you will never truly "miss" a move that first goes against you for a small loss, but eventually turns around in your direction.

Also, as you may have already figured out, the $E=MC^2$ trading approach <u>never gets caught in reversing positions from long to short, or short to long.</u>

If you get stopped out of a C2 consolidation trade, and the market starts a new trend, you wait for the first new C1 continuation, or C2 consolidation trade to setup before entering a trade in the new trend direction. (Under the right conditions a C1-C counter-trend trade can get you in on the new trend early- to be discussed).

RE-ENTRY – (Continuation to Continuation) - **This is an example of a C1 continuation trade that gets stopped out and remains a C1 continuation trade for re-entry.**

The initial 5000-pullback (circle, left) is below a rising 18-ma. 1500-price is above the long term-ma, and 1500-volume is above zero (middle, bottom).

A 55-tick, 4-bar count holds (first circle 1, right) and we buy (arrow 1). This trade gets stopped out below the horizontal line (stops to be discussed later), but the18-ma is still moving up, so we keep our focus on another C1 continuation setup.

55-price forms another 4-bar count that holds (circle 2, right), 1500-volume holds above zero, and we buy again on a re-entry trade (arrow 2, right).

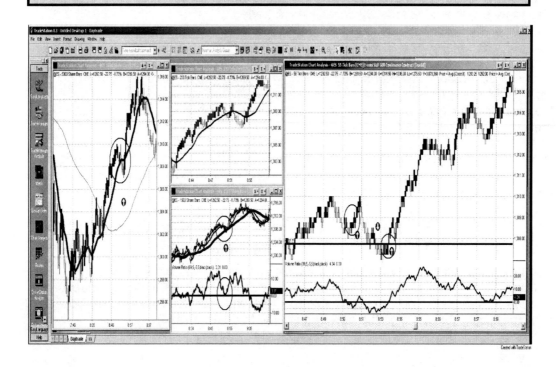

RE-ENTRY (Continuation to Consolidation) – This is an example of a C1 continuation trade that gets stopped out and turns into a C2 consolidation trade.

The initial 5000-pullback (circle, left) is below a rising 18-ma. 1500-price is above the long term-ma, and 1500-volume is above zero.

A 55-tick, 4-bar count holds (circle, right) and we buy. This trade gets stopped out below the horizontal line (stops to be discussed later), <u>the 18-ma turns down</u>, so we immediately begin to focus on a C2 consolidation setup.

55-price forms a nice flat box (rectangle), 1500-volume holds above –5, and the breakout of the box (arrow, right) coincides with 1500-price moving back above the long term-ma with a 1-2-3 pattern - a perfect consolidation buy!

AGGRESSIVE TRADES - The Shallow Pullback – Below is an aggressive, shallow pullback, long trade. We prefer to take most C1 continuation trades when 5000 price pulls back <u>to the 18-ma</u>, but in some cases, the pullback is more shallow, and you can consider these aggressive trades <u>if they occur at the start of a new trend, or after a breakout from a trading range</u>. You only want to take these trades at the start of a move, and not after a move has been in force for some time! If stopped out, you can always wait for a regular C1 continuation trade to set up to re-enter.

<u>Long timeframe</u> – 5000-price has just broken out of a trading range to the upside above a rising 18 and 89-ma (left). These breakout moves can be powerful! 5000 price begins to pull back to18-ma (circle) setting up for a long continuation entry, but price never reaches the 18-ma before turning around, which denotes a very strong market.

<u>Medium timeframe</u> - 1500-price pulls back to the short/medium ma area (circle, middle/bottom), which is a sign of a shallow pullback trade if 55-tick confirms. Volume ratio is holding above zero.

<u>Short timeframe</u> 55-tick down groupings (thin bars) move lower and lose momentum down (circle, right). 55-volume on pullback brushes the zero-line area. Buy on the first 4-bar count that holds after an UP signal bar forms within the pullback (arrow, right). This is an aggressive buy because we normally wait for a 5000-price pullback to the 18-ma before looking to enter. In this case, 55-price action told us this wasn't going to happen. (Note how the next two C1 continuation pullbacks did pull back to the 18-ma if you missed this one). The key, however, is not to miss a big picture, breakout trade!

Later in this book, we will show many more "case study" trade examples like the one highlighted above.

This example gives you a quick taste of how all phases of the $E=MC^2$ method come together (big picture analysis + entry method).

In no time, you will be able to glance at your charts, and know in an instant exactly what is going on in the overall market, and what trade setups to be looking for.

For example, you may sit down at your screen for the first time 2-hours into the trading session. You see 5000-price has been in a downtrend for quite some time, and a C1 continuation and C2 consolidation sell trade have been successful.

Immediately you know additional trades with the trend carry low probability, so you decide not to take any more short trades that setup. Instead, you wait for either consolidation chop to develop, or a new 5000- uptrend to emerge, while keeping an eye out for a counter-trend trade.

If C3 consolidation chop develops as volume ratio holds below zero you will look for another short trade. If an uptrend develops, you are ready to try the first aggressive C1 pullback long trade that sets up.

Furthermore, you note the big picture 5-minute chart has gapped up to signal a big picture up trend, and the recent down trend is nothing more than a move to the big picture trend line/support area on the 5-minute chart.

This further excites you to take the first <u>long trade</u> that sets up after 5000-price makes a trend change higher (18-ma moves above 89-ma that starts to turn up).

This is the type of thought process we put into place at all times using the $E=MC^2$ method.

Where is 5000-price? Is price forming a new uptrend, or new downtrend? Is price continuing, or consolidating? If an existing trend is in place, how many continuation/pullbacks have taken place, as only the first two of each carry the highest probability.

How does 5000 price behavior fall into the big 5-minute picture? Is price action with the 5-minute trend, or pulling back to an obvious trend line support/resistance area on the 5-minute chart?

What type of trade is setting up (1) First trend change pullback on 5000 (2) First, or second continuation pullback (3) First, or second consolidation, etc? How does price action look on the medium 1500 chart? Is the medium timeframe pullback shallow, or normal according to the 3-ma's on the medium chart? Is 1500-volume providing confirmation or not?

Finally, when we are ready to pull the trigger, what type of 55-price action develops? Does 55-price form and take out a flattening pivot area? Does a 4-bar count hold after the first paint bar forms in the trade direction? Does 1500-price confirm with a 1-2-3 pattern crossing the long term moving average?

Also, does 1500 volume ratio confirm a high probability shallow, or normal pullback entry or not. If not, does the overall weight of the evidence still point to a good trade?

All parts of the descriptions above will become second nature to you as you learn the $E=MC^2$ method. In an instant you will always know the big picture, the long, medium and short timeframe relationships, the setups you are looking for, and whether or not the setups are confirmed by volume and/or big picture analysis.

You will learn to become selective with respect to trade setups that offer the best, high probability outcomes.

Always remember, you don't have to take every trade setup that comes along!

We have already discussed how successive C1 continuation setups carry lower and lower probabilities. Setups where 5000-price formation is unclear (choppy 5000 price action) also carry lower probabilities of success because it often means price is moving sideways in the short term rather than directionally. In these conditions price movement is often quite volatile up or down.

You only need to take a few good trades a day to be successful trading!

Wait for the absolute best setups, and don't worry about missing a trade or two.

If you sit back, relax, and watch price action, the great setups will come to you and stand out like a sore thumb when they do! Don't force the action.

As you become more and more experienced with $E=MC^2$, you will develop a sixth sense about what is taking place in the market. Clear momentum will be obvious. Normal pullbacks will be obvious. Chop will be obvious.

You will understand when a pullback trade is almost certain to at least test the most recent swing point, which can offer a virtual no-risk trade with proper trade management (to be explained later).

I hope you are beginning to see how the entire picture comes together as you trade with $E=MC^2$. You will no longer be trading in a vacuum. Price movement will have overall context, and with patience, discipline, and common sense, you can turn trading into a very successful venture.

COUNTER-TREND TRADE (C1-C)

EMC2 is a "go with the trend" trading approach. There are select times, however, when counter-trend trades make sense, and I want to present these opportunities here as an advanced form of trading once you have standard C1, C2 and C3 trades mastered.

The three times to look for counter-trend trades are:

(1) Gap at the open (Fade).
(2) Failure after a key high or low is tested.
(3) Volume ratio reversal after a trend has been in place for some time.

The counter-trend trade (C1-C) is just a C1 trade with the 5000 18-ma against the main 18/89 trend. Enter the same way as a C1. 1500-volume moving beyond zero in the C1-C direction provides key confirmation. The tricky part of a C1-C trade is where to exit.

In some cases, you may be getting in very early before a major trend change, and in other cases price will only work its way back to the main trend pullback area.

Developing intra-day structure and big picture price action leading up to the C1-C entry determines this.

As a rule of thumb, C1-C trades after a long trend run carry expectations to pullback to big picture trend line areas, and you should make sure your entry gives you plenty of room for price to work its way to this pullback area.

C1-C trades to "Fade a Gap," or after a High/Low Failure have the potential to run much further, and you might want to consider holding these trades longer than just the first 5000-price swing extension (exits to be discussed) to see if a new 5000 18/89 trend forms, or a key high/low area is tested.

The classic C1-C trade has 1500-price breaking beyond its LT 89-ma and making its first pullback, with volume first moving past zero, and then holding zero on a pullback.

The E=MC2 trading approach is all about taking advantage of sound market logic.

Therefore, if an opening gap is met with a volume surge in the opposite direction, or a key High/Low Fails, or a trend is in place for a long time followed by a volume reversal, odds are strong that price will move counter to the existing 5000 18/89 trend for awhile.

The astute trader should always look for these unique counter-trend opportunities.

C1-C - After a long trend is in place to resistance (left), you can look for a C1-C counter-trend trade where volume ratio leads the way. In this example, 1500-price rolls over, volume holds below zero on a 1500 pullback to the 89-ma, and a C1-C counter trend trade develops with a price target to the 5000-89 (or 5-min) trend line pullback area (circle 2, left).

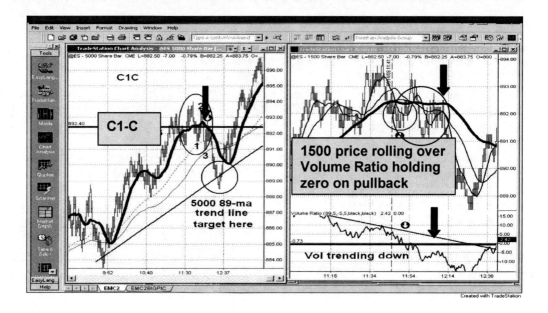

Section 6 – Trade Management

__TRADE EXIT__

Trading is a three part game, and you must perform all three parts well to succeed.

We've discussed the first part in detail- a method to select trades that in the long run provide you with a probability edge. The discussion of multiple timeframe analysis, continuation vs. consolidation pullbacks, counter-trend setups, short timeframe entry relative to large timeframe picture, etc. makes up about 1/3 of the trading game.

The next 1/3 of the trading game is what to do after you are in a trade. This discussion centers first and foremost about managing risk, and second about taking profits. We call this "trade management."

The final 1/3 ingredient necessary to trade successfully is far subtler than the first 2/3. The third piece to the puzzle is you must have the mental strength to carry out your method with proper trade management.

If you took a survey, I would guess a majority of traders place most of their efforts into method, some effort into trade management, and very little effort into the mental discipline necessary to carry it all out.

The breakdown is probably something like 70/20/10.

When it comes to successful trading, all three areas must carry equal weight, and the level of difficulty for each area easily moves from method (easiest) to mental discipline (hardest).

This means we not only need to redistribute our trading priorities, but we also must work exponentially harder to manage risk and execute our method in accordance with the probabilities.

Many traders yearn for all aspects of trading to fall into one nice neat package, including exact places to enter and exit all trades, and exact rules to apply to all trading situations etc.

There are ways to set up such nice neat packages, but the best traders do not act this way.

Market conditions are never exactly the same from trade setup to trade setup, and trade selection often dictates the best way to manage a trade.

Many successful traders trade with a multiple contract set and scale out of winning trades. Other successful traders trade one contract set "all in and all out."

All successful traders know good trading is about "<u>managing risk</u>" above all else, and it is important to reduce this risk as soon as possible.

Many successful traders manage risk by moving stops to "break even plus a tick" after a trade moves "X" ticks in their favor, even if they get stopped out on normal pullbacks within a trend that would otherwise produce gains if they stayed with the trade during first pullback.

Other traders are comfortable sitting through an initial pullback as long as this pullback is within their initial risk range.

Many successful traders never exit winning trades with a set target, but instead only trail their positions by moving ("trailing") their initial stop in the direction of the trade.

Other successful traders do take profits at logical extension points (Fibonacci extension points, Major support/resistance areas etc.), and many traders take quick partial profits, primarily as a means to :reduce risk."

Different trading styles are dictated by a variety of factors.

If you find your entry locations produce 70-percent trades that initially move in your favor, then it is often best to trade with a multiple contract set, take quick profits with either ½ or 2/3 of the contract set, and then move your stop on the remaining contract(s) in the direction of the trade to eliminate risk on the entire position, allowing your remaining contract(s) to run as far as possible with a trailing stop.

If you find your entry locations produce closer to 50-50 results, and many of your losses hit your initial maximum stop, then you cannot afford to scale out of your winners as described above.

With 50-50 results, your total position has to be allowed to run as far as possible according to market conditions to cover the losses you experience due to your trade selection process.

The $E=MC^2$ method, combined with some discretion in terms of trade selection, can easily put you in a position to enter trades that 70% of the time move in your favor, or allow you to reduce risk, before your initial stop is hit.

This gives you wide flexibility with regard to setting up a trading plan.

The best traders always do a few things the same regardless of what trading plan they use.

First, an initial "catastrophic" stop loss point is always entered on every trade. Even though I use the term catastrophic, this initial stop loss is still very small.

$E=MC^2$ uses the short timeframe to keep risk small. Initial stops are set beyond the most recent 55-tick pivot. Most of the time this pivot is about 2-3 ES points.

SMALL INITIAL RISK - Using the shorter timeframe charts, we are able to keep initial risk small relative to our long timeframe aspirations. An initial stop always goes <u>two-ticks</u> beyond the most recent 55-pivot (C1 trades), or 1500 pivot (C2/C3 trades) after the trade is entered.

Next, every successful trader reduces initial risk as soon as possible according to their trading plan and/or trading conditions.

Reducing initial risk can take one of three forms. (1) Scaling out of some of your position early (i.e. 1-point) (2) Moving stops to breakeven plus a tick after "X" ticks (i.e. 7-8 ticks) (3) Moving stops above/below logical 1500 swing points that develop in the trade direction after the trade is entered.

Finally, every good trader uses some approach to let all, or some portion of a winning trade ride, either as far as the market will take it, or at the very least to a logical extension area.

If you let winning trades run as far as the market will take it, then you simply keep trailing your stop behind your position, <u>and only your trailing stop will take you out of a trade.</u>

When you find yourself in a trade where obvious momentum develops, this is a great strategy to implement.

With E=MC^2 we always view winning trades as a function of "price moving past the most recent 5000-pivot extreme."

We enter all trades on pullbacks from a 5000-pivot extreme, and expect all winning trades to move past this extreme in accordance with logical price swing behavior.

Therefore, one of the key E=MC^2 trade management principles is to see what happens to price as 5000-pivot extremes are approached after the trade is entered.

> **WINNING TRADES – A winning trade will always move beyond the most recent 5000-pivot extreme. This is our initial expectation for every trade we enter.**

THREE EVENTS AT PIVOT EXTREMES - A 5000-pivot extreme represents a point where price direction previously halted. The question is– "Was this a temporary halt, or a more permanent halt?"

We can often gauge this answer by watching the reaction of price the next time price approaches this 5000-pivot extreme area.

When price moves to a 5000-pivot extreme one of three outcomes will develop. (1) Price will blow through the pivot area (2) Price will pause at the pivot area before blowing through (3) Price will be rejected at the pivot area.

Two of these outcomes are positive, one negative, for a trade that we are already in as price "tests" the 5000-pivot extreme.

<u>This is why it is so important to already be in a trade before the 5000-pivot extreme is tested</u>. You can benefit from two out of three outcomes, and you have room to manage risk for the one negative outcome!

Most of the time, a big battle takes place between buyer and seller at pivot extremes. There is a lot of anxiety at these price areas, and it is very difficult to gauge what the outcome will be.

Under most circumstances, $E=MC^2$ allows <u>one battle</u> to take place at the pivot extreme before taking action.

As buyers and sellers struggle for control, **we allow one 1500-pullback from the 5000 extreme to develop before moving our initial stop.**

If price blows right through the pivot extreme without a pullback, great!

If price never reaches the pivot extreme, we hope enough time has gone by that we can reduce our initial risk in other ways.

But if price tests the pivot extreme with indecision (moves through by just a few ticks), we allow one pause (buyer/seller battle) to take place in case price is ready to move beyond the extreme after the buy/sell battle is over.

The 1500 medium timeframe allows us to monitor this pause relative to what's happening in the 5000 long timeframe, and therefore allows us to manage our trade in accordance with sticking with the probabilities in the best way possible.

(Note – If you take a very aggressive trade such as the third C1 continuation trade in a row, you shouldn't give price action at the pivot extreme much leeway. Very aggressive trades require you to reduce risk as soon as possible because you know probabilities have been reduced. Therefore, in practical terms, when you take this, or any type of aggressive trade, consider moving your stop to breakeven plus a tick as soon as the pivot extreme is tested. (Also, consider quick exits just past the extreme).

> **TRADE MANAGEMENT AT PRICE EXTREMES** – A C1 continuation sell develops on a 5000-pullback (arrow, left). We watch price action closely as it approaches the pivot extreme (horizontal line, circle, left).
>
> As price hesitates at the pivot extreme (circle, right), we use the 1500-chart to allow one pullback to develop. We then move our initial stop to one tick beyond this pullback extreme to reduce risk, and attempt to ride gains further.

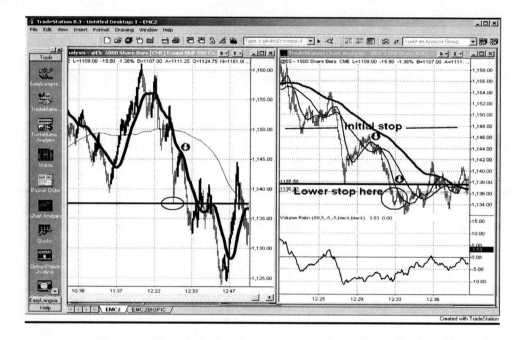

Momentum vs. Extension - The hope for every E=MC^2 trade is that price moves strongly past the 5000-pivot extreme. Price movement beyond the 5000-pivot extreme represents our winning trades, and we must manage these trades appropriately.

Most price movement beyond a pivot extreme forms some sort of "extension" before another pullback begins.

Once in a while, price extension turns into price momentum, and price travels much further than expected before another pullback begins.

MOMENTUM - Strong momentum usually comes out of nowhere. It is impossible to predict ahead of time when it will occur.

There are times you have a sense momentum may be developing (shallow pullbacks, strong +/- volume ratio, price structure moving past key support/resistance areas (either intra-day or daily), overall strength or weakness in the market (i.e. - break past a key support/resistance level with gap in the charts to move to the next big picture target, etc.)

These conditions are always important to be aware of, and set the stage for many momentum moves, but you still never know.

It is easy, however, to spot momentum when it develops before your eyes.

Hopefully you are already in the trade, because when momentum sets in, price action speeds up considerably and price just keeps moving in a straight line up, or down.

I know this sounds very straightforward and obvious, but price momentum is truly this simple, and easy to recognize.

When you are in a trade and strong momentum unfolds, you need to go right to a trailing stop mode!

You may move your stop 4 or 5 times in a matter of minutes in the direction of the trade, trying to lock in as much of the momentum move as possible.

At first, you may trail price action by 1.50 points or so beyond 1500 pullbacks as momentum unfolds. Then, as momentum builds stronger and stronger, you want to bring your trailing stop very close to price action to lock in as much of the profit as possible.

Trailing your stops in this manner is an art form, and we use the 1500 and/or 55 chart.

You will never get it perfect, and if you get stopped out a bit too soon, don't look upon this negatively. If you make 4 points on a trade instead of a possible 6 points, that's fine! The key with momentum is don't relax and be fooled into thinking that the move will last forever. Understand that these types of momentum moves are the moves that truly increase your equity, and you want to try to capture as much of the move as possible without giving much back.

An aggressive trailing stop approach is the best way to do this.

Momentum details – The signs of unfolding momentum are that after a brief battle at the 5000-price extreme, price blows strongly through the extreme and doesn't look back. The medium timeframe 1500-chart will show shallow pullbacks to the short/medium term moving average area (nowhere near the long term average), and 55-tick price swings will be confirmed by volume swings (no divergences) into a logical 5000-price swing extension areas (More on 5000 extension later).

Momentum often coincides with some big picture breakout or reversal area, and/or you could simply be in Trend day type of market day where the Advance/Decline line is either very weak or strong (holding beyond +/-1200) and the Dow Jones Average is also very weak or strong (holding at +/-80, 100, etc.)

If you find yourself in a momentum environment, the general rule of thumb is to try to ride your winners for about <u>twice as long as normal,</u> into 5000 price extension areas. In other words, begin to trail your stops tightly on the 1500-chart into new 1500 price swings that are confirmed by 55 swings in volume in an effort to ride these trades for as long as possible for maximum profit. (vs. exiting sooner on a 55-volume divergence-to be explained later)

<u>Riding winners twice as long as normal is very subjective</u>. In a moment we will discuss "normal equilibrium extension," but as time goes on you will get a sense for normal extension with volume divergence vs. momentum extension with volume confirmation into 5000 extension areas.

When you sense momentum extension is in force, you can try to ride these extensions for longer than normal using an aggressive trailing stop technique.

(Note – The Dow Jones Average is plotted with the symbol $INDU. The Advance/Decline line is calculated in TradeStation by opening a chart and plotting: $ADV- 1minute. Right click on chart, and select Insert Symbol, and add $DECL- 1 minute. Then select Insert/Indicator/Spread-Diff. You then can make the $ADV and $DECL plots very small, and focus on the reading of the "<u>Spread Difference</u>" plot which represents the advance/decline line. Sustained readings of +/-1200 denote trend type days)

MOMENTUM – The chart below highlights momentum. The 5000-chart (left) moves very fast and flies through the 5000-pivot extreme. Steep 5000 18-ma develops. Pullbacks are shallow and barely reach the 18-ma. 1500-chart (middle) shows 3 ma's separate. Pullbacks only reach short/medium-ma area. Volume Ratio is strongly negative. 55-chart (right) creates 55 volume ratio swings that confirm 1500 price action, and 1500 volume pullbacks do not reach the zero line.

Looking at the chart above, momentum is handled by trailing stops beyond high pivots formed as 1500-price swings lower.

The stop is lowered **7-times** before the short trade is finally exited!

Once 1500-swings move strongly past beyond the 5000-pivot extreme and are confirmed by 55-volume swings (no divergence), we know to go into a momentum trailing stop mode using 1500 and/or 55-price swings.

After the strong momentum move ends, odds favor that further momentum will subside.

STANDARD EXTENSION – Although you never know ahead of time exactly when strong momentum will develop, you do know ahead of time that strong momentum develops only about 20 percent of the time.

The other <u>80 percent of the time</u> price just swings back and forth, and we must do our best to learn how to take normal extension profits.

With most trades, we still want to try ride 5000-extension as far as the market will allow, but at the same time we realize that we still have to bank profits when a confluence of conditions unfold, even at the expense of missing further gains that may develop.

If we think about the probability nature of trading, we have to accept that there are many high probability set ups, but most trades only carry a high probability for modest gains.

We will take the big gains when the market hands them to us, but in the end, it is better to bank profits over and over again, rather than wait for every trade to turn into a homerun.

With this in mind we use a triple timeframe concept to help us with exiting winning trades that display "normal" extension.

Triple Timeframe Volume Divergence Exit – Assuming obvious momentum never enters the picture on a trade (if it does, go to active trailing stop mode), here is the best three-pronged approach to take extension profits on most trades.

1. Long timeframe - Allow price to move beyond the latest 5000-swing point with one 1500-pullback.

2. Medium time frame – Allow price to make another 1500-swing in the trade direction.

3. Short timeframe – Look to exit when a new 1500-price swing, creates a 55- "<u>volume swing divergence</u>."

<u>**When we see a 55-volume swing divergence develop on a 1500 price swing in the 5000-extension area (often the second swing), tighten trailing stops to beyond the short-term 55-pivot extremes that form, or simply exit immediately into strength (buys), weakness (sells) at the market.**</u>

A volume divergence swing means 1500-price makes a new high or low in the trade direction, and 55 volume ratio doesn't.

Triple Timeframe Volume Divergence Exit – 5000 pullback area (left, circle) sets up a long C1 continuation trade. Price moves nicely up through the recent 5000-pivot extreme. Medium timeframe (middle) confirms a high probability trade setup as price moves back to 1500-long term ma area, and volume ratio still has a strong overall up bias.

As 1500-price makes swings higher beyond the pivot extreme after one pullback (middle 1 and 2), a volume divergence develops on the 55-chart (right 1 and 2) as seen by a declining trend line (right, bottom). The horizontal line shows the how we now look to trail with 55-pivots, and represents a very nice exit point for the trade.

You can also exit into strength at the market immediately.

Volume Divergence means 1500-price swings higher or lower, but 55-volume doesn't. In most cases, the volume divergence exit approach provides great exit points that prevent you from giving back much of your hard earned gain.

Either exit at the market into strength, or tighten trailing stop to beyond short-term 55 pivots.

55 volume divergence

The triple timeframe approach to extension exit will still allow you to ride big gains if they develop, but in most cases will allow you to bank nice profits when normal market conditions are in place.

The philosophy is you want to try to guide your winning exits according to the long timeframe, 5000-chart.

A good pullback trade on the 5000-chart should always move past the most recent 5000-price pivot extreme during the next move in the trade direction.

If so, try to stay with this move beyond the swing extreme for one minor pullback, and then for as long as possible before another major pullback develops.

In many cases you can "feel" how far a move will extend just by looking at prior price swings.

Price movement often occurs with a "sense of equilibrium." This means successive price swings move proportionally to each other.

Many good traders will exit at specific extension points beyond a price swing extreme.

Actually, this type of exit approach is fine, especially if you sense normal market conditions are in place, or long term price is nearing a key support/resistance area, etc.

PRICE SWING EQUILIBRIUM – Many times price swings move proportionally, and tend to mirror each other. Keep an eye out for these conditions to help guide your extension exits. Remember, the goal is not to catch every single tick of a move, or to hit a homerun with every trade.

Instead, we want to take pieces of high probability price action, with the understanding that the market will provides us with big pieces from time to time.

In the circles below, note the __DOWN__ price swings before and after the arrow. See how both swings tend to mirror each other in normal trading conditions.

Equilibrium price action can often guide you with respect to extension exit areas.

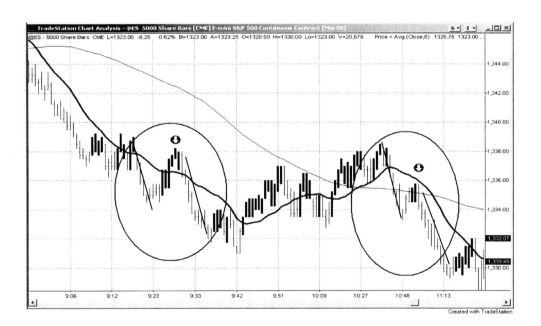

If you can exit at logical swing extension points in normal market conditions, and ride a few trades to bigger gains when obvious momentum develops, you will do very well in your trading. In many cases, 5000-swing extension points coincide with big picture (5-minute) support/resistance trend line areas, or big picture swing extension points.

If you want to let the market tell you when to exit a trade vs. a predefined swing extension level, volume divergence on the short (55) timeframe chart is one of the best ways to do this after a 5000-swing extension takes place.

This means stay with the trade past the 5000-swing extension and for as long as 55-volume confirms continued 1500-price swings in the trade direction.

As soon as 55 volume doesn't confirm a new price swing in the trade direction, <u>look to exit!</u>

These exits will often be in the exact area where another long timeframe pullback begins.

Again, when it comes to probabilities in trading, it is best to not get greedy unless markets conditions scream out for you to do so. Otherwise take your profits, and don't look back.

At the very least, tighten your trailing stops within logical extension areas!

I will repeat, "<u>You only need a few good trades a day to very well in trading</u>."

You can be very selective and wait for only the best trade setups in the best trading environments. If you sense choppy price movement, or many wild up and down price bars, stand aside until you see the charts begin to display more normal directional price action.

This may be a new thought for many of you, especially for those of you that love to "pull the trade trigger" all day long.

If you are successful making many trades, fine, but if not, I highly recommend that you take a step back and try to be much more selective with your trading.

<u>Many great traders take just a few trades a day!</u>

If you are new to trading, it is best to start off being selective with respect to taking only the best setups that develop, and then banking profits (even small ones at first), to see where this leads you.

See if you find yourself over, or under trading? Do you take too many iffy setups? Do you miss too many good trades waiting for the best setups?

Do you take profits too quickly? Do you give too much of your gains back trying to hit the homerun every time?

The best way to apply E=MC^2 method until you gain trading experience is to only look to take the new trades after a trend change with volume confirmation. These are the highest probability price direction trades.

<u>The longer a trend continues, the lower the probability for extensions.</u>

<u>Limit your trade selection to early trend trades at first</u> and try to take only the best setups according to price, volume, current market conditions, and big picture analysis.

Next, look to take gains in two ways. If you sense good momentum, try to trail your stop aggressively and lock in as much of the momentum move as possible. If you don't sense momentum, look to lock in your gains past 5000-swing points (allowing for one minor pullback) in accordance with either common sense swing extension/equilibrium analysis, or volume divergence on the short timeframe, which allows the market to tell you when to exit beyond a swing extreme.

As you gain more trading experience, you can try other exit approaches as well.

For instance, you can try to hold strong momentum trades through a series of 5000 C1 and C2 pullbacks. Or, if you choose to take a second or third pullback trade in a row, you can always reduce initial risk to breakeven plus a tick "the moment price tests the latest swing point." (More on breakeven plus a tick later)

Many times you will only break even on these trades, but you still give yourself the opportunity for nice gains if the market decides to keep running through the swing extreme in the trade direction.

<u>As you can see, exiting trades is by far the most discretionary part of successful trading.</u>

Trade selection is another discretionary part of trading as some trades carry different winning probabilities than other trades (early trend vs. late trend).

As long as you have an overall trade selection process that produces a high degree of trades that initially move in your favor, you will be able to incorporate a trade management approach that will allow you to be successful with your overall trading plan in the long run.

With experience, you can improve your trading as you learn to filter trades within the context of big picture, volume, and market structure, etc.

The E=MC^2 method is designed to produce a high degree of trades that at least initially move in your favor, towards the 5000-price extreme, before the catastrophic initial stop loss point is hit.

As you monitor your progress with trade selection etc, you can set up a trading plan that fits your trading style and personality.

I wish such a plan was the same for everyone, but the reality is we all have to act in ways that we are most comfortable, even in the same overall structural environment.

As I said earlier, no two traders will ever trade E=MC^2 exactly the same.

That's why I cannot sit here and write the same rules for everyone.

The good news is that there are many ways to make this work. Also, there are many common rules that apply to all trading styles.

You as a trader have to do your homework, look to your own personality, and find out what works best for you. This is the reality of trading!

Initial Risk, and Reducing Initial Risk As Soon As Possible - The E=MC^2 method produces two main types of trades (beyond the counter-trend trade) – Continuation trades, and Consolidation trades.

All trades are based on long/medium timeframe pullbacks with entry on the shorter timeframes after a pullback.

Therefore, the initial stop loss is always "two ticks" beyond the last major swing point that forms on the 55 or 1500-chart prior to entry.

If we are stopped out, we watch for re-entry in the same trade direction only. We never reverse a position.

Our initial stop is always considered a catastrophic stop.

You may want to bypass a trade altogether if volatility makes this initial stop too large.

In most cases, your initial stop will be within 2-3 ES points which is a very acceptable even for the smallest trading accounts.

> **INITIAL STOP REVIEW** – The initial stop always starts out two ticks beyond the most recent low or high on the 55 (C1) or 1500 (C2/C3) chart prior to entry. In the chart below we enter C1 long at the arrow, and place our initial stop two ticks below the recent 55-tick low (horizontal line).

Moving initial stop to reduce risk – All successful traders try to reduce initial risk as soon as reasonably possible.

When a trade begins to move in our favor (to the 5000 extreme) we look to move our initial stop to reduce risk.

Our number one priority is to move our stop to "Breakeven plus a tick" and create a free trade!

Breakeven plus a tick - One of the most desirable ways to reduce risk is to move your stop to "break even plus a tick" after the trade moves "X" ticks in your favor.

For the ES, approx 2-points, or 7-8-ticks is a very good starting point to implement such a strategy, but we also want to throw a bit of common sense into the mix according to unfolding market structure.

The benefit of breakeven plus a tick is that you cannot lose on these trades. Your trades literally become "free trades."

The cons of this strategy are that there are times price will retrace and stop you out plus a tick, and then move on to larger gains if you had stayed in, with overall small risk.

In the end, the benefits of breakeven plus a tick outweigh the cons.

You must expect a dose of "breakeven" trades that would otherwise end up as nice winners, but understand that this prevents many small losses as well.

In successful trading, not losing money is more important than making money!

Many great traders trade this way, and accept this tradeoff. I suggest you implement this approach, especially when starting out.

Also, if you sense you are taking an overly aggressive trade, or are making a trade after you've already made some nice profits on the day, I would recommend moving to break even plus a tick as soon as possible.

For instance, if you are taking the second or third C1 continuation trade in a trend, you know you are beginning to push the odds. Therefore, a good tradeoff is to move to "break even plus a tick" as soon as possible, and accept a breakeven outcome for the "chance" to make additional gains.

Again, there are many very good traders who trade this way on every trade. You simply have to accept the tradeoff that you will break even on some trades that will go on to do exactly what you had hoped for moments later.

The positive angle is that you will be preserving capital for trades that would have otherwise gone on to produce a small loss, and this type of trading approach is akin to running a very tight ship.

There is nothing wrong with this! Remember, most winning trades never look back, and there are many of these trades that are right around the corner. DON'T WORRY IF YOU MISS A GREAT TRADE!

<u>Some common sense</u> – Basic breakeven plus a tick philosophy takes place after the ES moves about 2 points in your favor. Here is the way to adjust a pure, predefined, "move your stop to BE after 2-points approach."

You need to use common sense relative to where your entry takes place in relation to the 5000-swing extreme.

Remember, the goal for every trade is to have price move beyond the 5000-pivot extreme, and to take some type of profit beyond this extreme. We want to give each trade ample opportunity to do this, so we allow for one minor pullback after the 5000 extreme is reached.

Sometimes price breaks the pivot extreme, retraces, and doesn't make a nice one-time, minor pullback/continuation we are looking for. (Price is being rejected at the pivot).

If you receive good trade location, and price moves past the pivot extreme, move your stop to breakeven plus a tick immediately. <u>You never want to lose money when you enter with good trade location.</u>

The common sense exception to the BE +1 tick rule is if you enter very close to the pivot extreme (poor trade location), and breakeven plus a tick represents a logical minor pullback area, which means you should wait for a minor pullback to form before moving your initial stop.

Another common sense exception is when you enter a C2/C3 consolidation trade with very good trade location relative to the 5000 pivot extreme. Here, you should move your stop to breakeven plus a tick even before the price extreme is reached as the price extreme area is being tested.

Most of the time you will enter C2/C3 trades far away from the 5000 pivot extreme. With good trade entry location, you never want to lose money once price approaches the 5000-pivot extreme.

BREAK EVEN PLUS A TICK – **A very sound approach to successful trading is to move your initial stop to breakeven plus a tick after "X" ticks have accumulated on a trade, or as price approaches a pivot extreme depending upon the type of trade entered, and/or the trade entry location.**

In the chart below, price moves 2 points above entry and beyond pivot extreme (circle). Move your initial stop to stop to BE +1 tick (horizontal line). You never want to lose money after price moves beyond a pivot extreme, unless you entered very close to the extreme and decide to ride the trade through one minor pullback.

In this example, note good trade entry location relative to distance to the pivot extreme (arrow). With good trade location, you don't want to lose money if price is rejected at the pivot extreme.

We always hope we will get an immediate test of the 5000-pivot extreme, which will set up either a breakeven plus a tick scenario, or a "first pause" pullback level to move the initial stop.

If price doesn't test the 5000-pivot extreme, the next hope is that price vacillates long enough to cause a new pullback pivot to form closer to entry than the original initial risk pivot extreme.

If a new 1500 pullback pivot develops before the 5000 price extreme is reached, we move our initial stop to beyond this level. If you are stopped out you can always re-enter in the direction of the original trade on a renewed price signal.

MOVE INTIAL STOP TO REDUCE RISK – As a general rule use the 1500-medium timeframe as the overall guide to unfolding market structure. After you enter a trade, monitor the price swings that develop on the1500-chart relative to the trend of the 1500 LT moving average in the direction of the trade in order to move the initial stop beyond 1500 pullback points that form before the 5000-price extreme is reached.

In the example below, notice that after a C3 consolidation trade is entered on the 5000-chart (circle, left), 1500-price swings pivots are used (right arrows) to progressively move the initial stop higher until the 5000 price extreme is eventually reached.

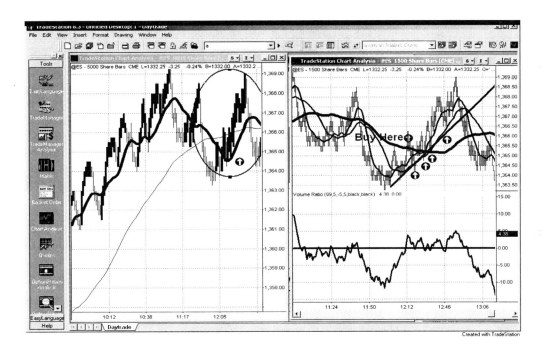

127

TRADE MANAGEMENT OPTIONS

In a moment we will expand upon trade management by discussing trading with multiple contracts, etc, but here is a basic wrap up of how we look to manage trades after entry.

Always set an initial stop loss 2-ticks beyond the most recent 55, or 1500 pivot extreme (For C2/C3 consolidation entries, choose point 2 of a 1-2-3 entry, unless point 2 and the start of wave 1 are very close in which case you will set initial stop 2 ticks below the start of wave 1). Try to let 2.0 - 2.5 points initial risk be your guide

Patiently allow price to move to the 5000-price extreme target area.

As price works its way to 5000-price extreme, prepare to move initial stop beyond pivots formed on 1500 for C2/C3 trades, and in line with 1500-pivots that when penetrated will break the price trend of 1500-price relative to its LT moving average for C1 trades (this takes time to form).

Move initial stop to breakeven plus a tick if entry location is good, and price either moves to, or breaks through 5000-pivot extreme target after 2 points. (Note- You may look to take profits on C2/C3 consolidation trades before the 5000-price extreme is reached if there is significant space between entry and the 5000 extreme, where the 5000 18-ma has rolled back over in the direction of the trade and a new pullback in price will allow for another C1 continuation entry in the direction of the trade. In other words, if 5000-price has already moved a long way back to the 5000-extreme, it will often pause here, before generating continued momentum through the extreme in the trade direction.

If entry location is poor, allow one minor 1500-pullback to form after the 5000-pivot extreme is reached before moving initial stop.

After 5000-pivot extreme is penetrated allow one 1500-pullback to form, then move initial stop (or breakeven plus a tick stop), to 1-tick beyond this new 1500-pullback extreme.

Once price moves favorably past the 5000-pivot extreme in our trade direction, look to exit in one of three ways.

(1) Momentum – If momentum develops, implement an aggressive 1500-trailing stop technique. Try to ride gains 2x longer than normal.

(2) Price Swing Extension Option – Exit trade at logical swing extensions proportional to prior 5000-price swings. At the very least, tighten trailing stops at when logical extension areas are reached.

(3) Volume Divergence – If momentum doesn't enter the picture, exit a trade when a 1500-price swing isn't confirmed by a 55-tick volume swing. You will be selling into strength, or buying into weakness.

ALL IN - AlI OUT VS. ALL-IN SCALE OUT - Most traders start with an "all in, all out" contract approach to trading, and then decide if they want to adopt a scaling out approach using multiple contracts.

An all-in, all-out approach is best for new traders, and can often be the only choice for a small, new account that only provides for trading a single contract at a time.

In other cases, the trader simply requires more time and experience before making sure trade selection and execution produces a high degree of trades that initially move a small direction in their favor in order to effectively scale out.

The big difference to between choosing one approach over the other is TRADE SELECTION ABILITY!

Although $E=MC^2$ provides great trade setups over and over again, with an all in-all out approach you actually have to be more selective with your trade selection, and take only the best setups, even if you miss some good trades along the way.

The "all in-scale out" approach, even though it trades more contracts and seems more "risky," actually allows for being more aggressive and taking more setups, even if the setups aren't picture perfect.

The reason you can take more scale out trades is that most $E=MC^2$ trades move a small distance in the desired trade direction even if they don't go all the way to either reach the 5000-price extreme, or produce big winners.

With an "all in-all out" approach "small distance" trades often turn into small losses, which is fine. This just means you have to make sure you ride winners to make up for these small losses over time.

If you can be more selective and pick only the best setups, you will cut "all in-all out" losses down, and therefore not have as much pressure to ride other trades for big winners in order to come out ahead on balance.

The all in-scale out approach takes a different philosophy, and grabs a quick profit as a way to reduce risk, and also as a way to build up small profits on trades that don't pan out as expected.

Many very successful traders use an "all in-scale out" approach.

This means they have a trade selection process that yields a high probability of trades that at least move a small direction in their favor quickly (up to 70 percent of the time).

With an "all-in, scale out" approach, you just cannot afford to take maximum losses on the full contact set, while you scale out of the good trades, and limit your gains on winners.

As always, you will have to do your homework, see what approach fits your style, makes you most comfortable, and of course works best for you.

The main point I want to emphasize is that if you either start out, or are just more comfortable with an "all in-all out" approach, you will have to sharpen your skills, and be as patient as possible to only take the best setups that unfold in the market.

I realize all setups are unpredictable as to outcome, but there are certain setups that are simply more clear than others, which could be due to market conditions, big picture analysis, ease of discerning market structure at the time, volume confirmation, etc.

SCALING OUT WITH A MULTIPLE CONTRACTS - Many very successful traders trade a multiple contract set and scale out of contracts as price moves in their favor.

As stated, you will only be successful doing this if (1) your entries can provide you with small profits almost immediately after the trade is entered about 70 percent of the time, or (2) you are super quick to get out of trades quick to reduce risk, so as to hardly ever approach your maximum initial maximum loss per trade.

Traders who are successful scaling out of multiple contracts have both perfected their entry selection, location and execution, and are extremely quick not only to enter, but also to exit trades as well.

This style is not for everyone, and takes a lot of practice before you develop a comfort level.

Also, this trading style is greatly enhanced by an order execution platform that can automatically be set ahead of time to scale out of partial contracts and move stops automatically, etc. There are several excellent platforms out there that can do this.

As of this writing, the TRADESTATION order execution platform is behind the curve in this regard, and you have to basically handle each part of the "all in-scale out" strategy manually, meaning if you sell 3 contracts, you have to enter another order for an initial stop for 3 contracts, and yet another order to exit 2 contracts at let's say a 1-point profit.

Then, if your 2-contract "profit" order is filed, you will have to go back and manually cancel/replace your 3-contract stop with a new 1-contract stop, etc.

In other words, you have to be very fast on your feet and have a very fast computer that doesn't experience data delays, etc.

As you can see, this is a more advanced form of trading.

The general approach is to trade a 3-contract set and enter while price is moving in your trade direction with the expectation of immediate trade continuation.

You look to take off 2 contracts very quick, let's say at 1-point (4 ticks), then move the stop on contract 3 to a level where you will still make some money on the trade, should a pullback occur, perhaps at a minus 1 or 2 tick level.

The goal is to ride contract number 3 for big gains should price momentum continue, or make many small gains if there is only a small initial move before a pullback takes place.

The logic is you can always re-enter a trade on a dime after being stopped out as long as you keep your risk very small.

You also must be ready to exit 3 contracts very quickly if your first scale out target isn't immediately reached. The common way to do this is to move your initial stop closer to the trade as soon as possible.

Remember with this strategy, you cannot afford to take full losses on 3 contracts often!

Every once in awhile this can't be avoided, but in the end, to make this strategy work, you really need to make sure you identify entry points that provide immediate gains a majority of the time.

For most traders starting out, it is best to start with an all in -all out approach with a single contract, and be very patient with regard to trade selection.

This not only starts you out in very conservative fashion, but also allows you to gain valuable experience observing price movement over time.

If you can't make money with a single contract using an all in - all out approach it will be hard to make money trading multiple contracts in any form.

Therefore start slow, develop your trading plan, and master your trading skills with a single contract set to start. You have a lifetime to trade. There is no hurry.

As time goes on, and you begin to make money, let your profits pay for adding more contracts.

You will also be gathering valuable trading experience along the way to develop a final trading plan that works best for you- including trade selection criteria, trade management criteria, daily/weekly goals, all in-all out vs. scaling approach, etc.

SPLIT THE DIFFERENCE SCALE OUT APPROACH - Only the most experienced traders should attempt to implement a 3-contract set scale out trading approach, scaling out of 2 contracts quickly (4 ticks), then lowering the initial stop on contract 3 (2 ticks), then trying to let contract 3 run for big gains.

On the other hand, it can be frustrating trying to trade a 1-contract set because most trades provide small profits from the start, and you are always in the position of deciding whether to hold on for bigger gains at the expense of giving back your profits? This often causes "fear" to set in, and you often sell for a small gain when a bigger gain was easily attainable. These small gains end up offsetting a slew of small losses, and in the end, you end up spinning your wheels.

For many, the most comfortable strategy is to trade a 2-contract set, take small profits on contract 1, and try to ride contract 2 for large profits.

With the $E=MC^2$ approach, the best way to do this is exit one contract at, (or just beyond), the 5000-pivot extreme target, and manage the second contract as described earlier in the material.

You will find that when you take a small profit to start, this relaxes you greatly to manage the rest of the position in the correct way.

Although we have provided very clear rules to manage one contract at a time (initial stop, reduce initial stop, immediate re-entry if necessary, breakeven plus a tick, allow for one 1500 pullback after 5000-extreme is penetrated, exit and ride winners according to either momentum, swing equilibrium, or volume divergence), in actual practice it takes a lot of discipline to carry this out because anxiety sets in as much when you have gains, as when you have losses.

Therefore, if you implement a 2-contract strategy that effectively "splits the difference" by taking partial profits at the first logical target area (most recent 5000-swing point), you will likely find this to be the easiest approach to carry out from a psychological perspective.

But, with all scaling strategies, just make sure you aren't taking full losses on your full contract losing trades, while taking only half and half profits on your winning trades.

If you find this happening, go back and analyze your trade selection process. Most likely you are taking too many trades late into the trend, or low probability extension trades into big picture support/resistance areas.

In the end, the actual $E=MC^2$ method is the easiest part of your trading plan. $E=MC^2$ provides a very consistent way to patiently allow price structure to dictate when to enter high probability trades over and over again.

This is a big first step for developing a trading plan that many traders never successfully reach. But this is only the first step. You also must develop an entire trading plan that includes trade selection, and trade management, and there are many different ways to go.

There are more than enough trade management options for you to choose from. No one option is better or worse than the other, but the key is to develop something consistent that fits your style, stick with it, and adjust as necessary according to your trading outcomes.

The good news is this isn't hard to do. Most traders just either never take the time to do this, never understand they need to do this, or try to do this but don't have the discipline to carry it out.

Hopefully enough has been presented for you to realize the importance of developing and executing a consistent overall trading plan.

Step 1 is to consistently organize market structure to identify high probability trade setups over and over again.

Step 2 is to consistently execute a trade management approach according to your own trading style and personality.

Step 3 entails developing the discipline to carry out steps 1 and 2. The only way to do this is to have the confidence that your trading plan is nothing more than a probability exercise that has placed the odds in your favor.

There have been entire books written about the mental difficulties of trading, but it really all comes down <u>to having confidence that without a doubt your method will work in the long run from a probability perspective.</u>

This means you first need to do your homework, look back on many charts, and see that your setups work more times than not.

In <u>TRADESTATION,</u> there is an excellent feature under "Drawing/ Pointer Tracking/Workspace" that allows you to scroll through all charts at the same time.

You can use this feature to back test and see how the long, medium, and short timeframe charts all look at the same time, just like real trading.

With E=MC^2, you cannot view winning and losing trades as right or wrong, but instead as just pieces of a big probability puzzle.

This attitude and understanding will provide you with the confidence and behavior to take good trade setups over and over again, <u>without fear</u>, and will allow you to follow your trading plan religiously.

<u>DAILY GOAL TRADING</u>

E=MC^2 trades are high probability trades. The best trades are poised to provide large gains. We have explained how we keep risk small, and reduce risk for each trade as soon as possible.

If you don't have the time to trade for most of the trading session, why not consider an approach that sets a very modest daily point goal for each day?

Let's say you choose 3 points as your daily target, and keep taking trades as they set up until your daily target is reached. (More on trading goals later).

Sometimes this will be the first trade of the day and you are done. Other times, you might have to take a few small losses first, and recover later on.

While 3 points may not seem like a lot (relative to today's volatility in the market)...let's say out of 20 trading days a month you make your 3 points on 15 days, and lose an average of 3 points on the other 5 days.

This is a net of 30 points a month, or $1500 per contract...If you build up to 5 contracts, this is $7500/month, 10 contracts $15,000/month, etc.

Again, everyone has different trading styles and objectives. Some traders aren't available every moment of the day to trade, and may only wait for very selective set ups when they have the chance to trade. (i.e. First series of new trend trades). Other traders have all day to trade, but like the thought of the freedom a daily point goal strategy provides, should the daily goal be met early in the trading session.

There are other traders who have all day to trade and like to take every setup that comes along to maximize gains on good trading days, and there are still other traders that have all day to trade, but still like to focus on only the best setups that come along.

Again, there is no single, canned trading approach that fits everyone the same.

You have to do your homework, examine your trading personality, and ultimately figure out a way to turn the strengths of the E=MC^2 approach into something that works best for you.

Section 7 – Case Study Examples

CASE STUDY- 1

TRADE SETUP – Examine the following 10 charts and try to determine what type of set ups are taking place, if any? Look at the right edge of all charts together. This simulates real time trading conditions. All answers and explanations are found after Chart 10.

Remember, everything starts by knowing exactly where you are in the moment on the long and medium timeframe. Is a new trend starting? Is price movement experiencing a pullback (continuation, consolidation)?

CHART ARRANGEMENT

Left - Long Timeframe-5000
Right (top) - Medium timeframe –233
Right (bottom) - Medium timeframe-1500

(Note – The purpose of the 233-tick chart is to monitor the relationship between tick and volume charts in the medium timeframe. The 233-tick and 1500-volume charts should move in very close step together. If this relationship ever changes, you may need to explore input value adjustments down the road)

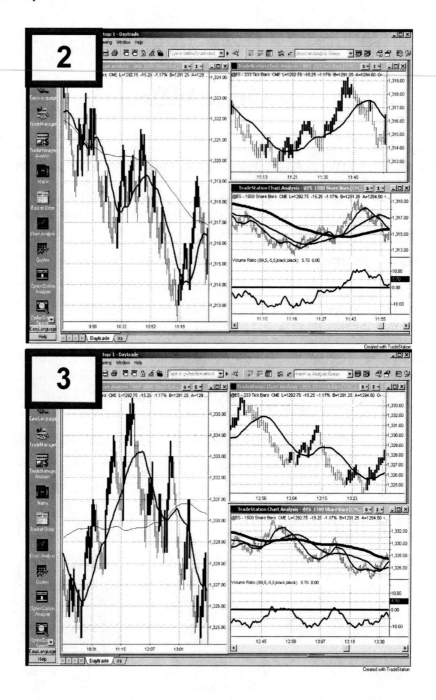

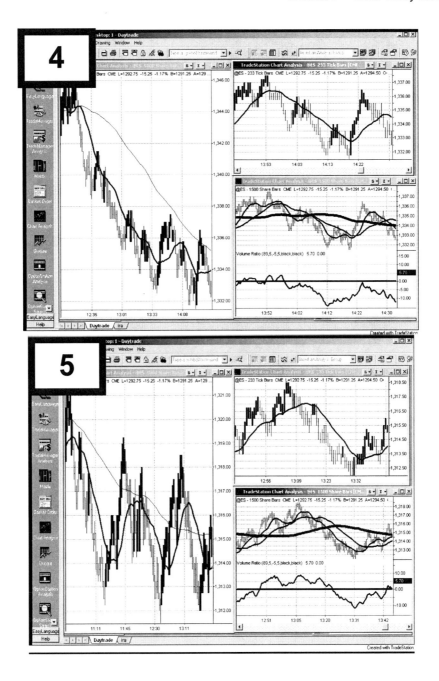

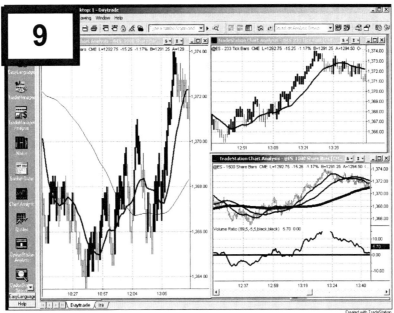

ANSWERS TO CASE STUDY 1 - TRADE SET UP

(1) After a long down trend on the 5000 and many C1 continuation setups, the 18-ma has turned up, and price is rising to a still falling 89-ma. 1500-price has moved above the long-term ma. This is a consolidation sell setup. Volume ratio is still below zero (No C1-C). The 18-ma is still below the 89-ma on the 5000. Be careful. Unless this is a strong down day (big picture), gains on this trade might be limited. You can see how far 5000-price has traveled down already. Momentum really slowed at the bottom, as 1500 volume diverged. A re-test of the low is likely, but it may be nothing more than test. If a C2 consolidation short sets up (1-2-3-1500-break below the 89 long term average), be ready to bring stops to breakeven plus a tick as the low price extreme is tested in case the long down trend is over.

(2) 5000-price is in a choppy downtrend with the 18-ma below a falling 89-ma. There was just a big rally, turning the 18-ma up, and moving 1500-price way above the 89 Lt-ma. This set up a C2 consolidation short, which was likely entered moments ago on a 1-2-3 pivot breakout as 1500-price moved back down through the Lt moving average trend line. Volume ratio did move up close to +10, but this is reasonable if you look at the large price swings taking place on this day. The recent high appears to have stalled right at the big picture trend line/resistance area. The price extreme target for this trade is the low of the day. There is also plenty of room to move stops to breakeven plus a tick if price reaches the low of the day area but can't penetrate through.

(3) 5000-price is clearly in a new downtrend (18-ma below 89-ma) and price shows a classic continuation pullback to the falling 18-ma with a paint bar change for a sell set up. 1500-price moves back to the long-term ma. Volume ratio remains below zero. This is the second continuation trade in a row, near the low of the day, so be careful. During the last move down, price already tested the low of the day. Always remember, the highest probability trades are the <u>first and second pullbacks in a new trend</u>. This down move has been in force for some time (within overall choppy 5000 18/89 structure). This is a trade to bypass, or you would want good C1 trade location (4-bar count develops with space to run to the price extreme) so you can move your initial stop to breakeven plus a tick as the low of the day is tested.

(4) Just one look at the 5000-chart should tell you you're been in a downtrend for a long time already, but let's analyze it further. After a series of strong continuation setups that took price lower, price pulled back for one consolidation trade that nicely moved to new lows. Currently, a second consolidation trade has just been entered. You can see how a nice 55-pivot box formed that coincided with a 1500-break below the long-term moving average (you can tell this by observing the flat 1500-lows that formed near the long term average before the breakout).

Volume pullback never crossed above zero, confirming the trade. Price is now moving once again to test the price extreme (low of the day). Again, I would be very careful, and bring stops to breakeven plus a tick as soon as possible because this is the second consolidation trade trying to take out the lows of the day after a long down move. I hope you are beginning to see how certain trades simply have more potential than other trades dictated by market conditions. The way to make large money on this down move, was to get in on the first continuation set up (left side of the left chart), recognize strong momentum down, and ride a few continuation moves lower before exiting. After such a strong move down, the first consolidation trade provides good trade location for testing the momentum price extreme, but you must maintain realistic expectations for limited follow through. If you look to take modest gains on these trades, it would be very reasonable logic based on market conditions... Remember, most trades don't turn into homeruns, especially back-to-back homeruns!

(5) As always, take a glance at the overall 5000-chart to see what type of price action is unfolding for the day. This chart shows a down bias range day with choppy swings, so don't expect many sustained moves although you never know because at some point price will break out of this pattern. 5000-price has gone from continuation sell, to consolidation (normal) sell, to consolidation (chop) sell, and has made a potential triple bottom. Right now, price is setting up for another consolidation sell, with a 1-2-3-price pullback in place as the 18-ma is starting to turn up below a still falling 89-ma. 1500-price is at the long term moving average, and 1500-volume is back at the zero line.

The exciting potential for this trade is the fact price is narrowing and coiling, which is action that often precedes a strong breakout one way or the other. If a good consolidation sell trade develops, and price breaks below the lows of the day, this can be a big winner. Again, we will not deviate from our trade management, meaning moving initial stop to breakeven plus a tick near the lows, allowing a single minor pullback to develop if the lows are broken before moving our stop even lower, but if price moves strongly through the price extreme low of the day, we know this trade is a major consolidation breakout that can turn into large gains, especially if confirmed by the big picture, volume, price action, etc. Again, we always look at market conditions to put all trades in proper context.

(6) The 18-ma is about to cross below the 89-ma. I hope you can see this a resumption of an overall downtrend rather than a consolidation pullback in a new uptrend that was trying to form at the recent highs. There is no doubt an uptrend briefly formed as the 18 and 89-ma turned up, providing one continuation buy entry that at worst would have provided breakeven plus a tick after the pivot extreme was penetrated. However, look at volume. The entire attempt at an uptrend could barely move volume above zero (a sign the uptrend was suspect), and the current down wave has volume falling sharply below –5. Also the 89-ma is starting to turn down again along with the 18-ma. Therefore, a great C1 continuation sell trade will set up on a price pullback back above the falling 18-ma, which will likely coincide with a 1500-price pullback to the long term moving average area.

(7) This is a classic deep consolidation pullback in an uptrend, where we are looking for the highs of the days to be tested. The buy took place during the latest run up when a 5-wave count developed at about the same time 1500-price moved back above the long term moving average. 1500-volume is crossing zero, and we will monitor if volume can

move strongly past +5, or not. There is plenty of space between entry and the high of the day, so when price approaches this extreme we will move the initial stop to breakeven plus a tick to give ourselves a "free trade" if it develops.

(8) This looks like a big 5000-down trend in force, but price is really just moving sideways as one big leg down moved the 5000 18 past the 89. You should notice the first C2 consolidation sell when the 18-ma tuned up a short while ago. Expectation for this trade was to move to the low of the day, however, price stalled and is now pulling back again. If you look at the 233-chart (top, right), you can see the recent trailing stop pivot which represents where the initial stop was moved very close to entry. You should be stopped out, and looking to either re-enter short on another 1-2-3 setup, or consider a C1-C long if volume holds above zero through this big sideways area. (You can look for both trades).

(9) Classic C1 continuation pullback buy set up, and even more exciting is this is the first pullback after a major sideways breakout. A re-test of the price extreme high is almost assured. Note how 1500-volume exploded past +5 on the first move up. Volume is right at zero during this pullback. Also, 1500-price is right back to the long term moving average. A 55-tick 4-bar count and hold, would present a very good, high probability continuation buy entry.

(NOTE – Set your min/max scale on volume ratio to +/-15 so you can clearly see when volume explodes off the top, or bottom of the chart)

(10) You should be able to look at a chart like this and see that you were just stopped out of a continuation sell trade, and now looking for either an immediate continuation re-entry if it develops on the 55, or a consolidation entry if price pulls back a bit further. 1500-price remains below all 3-ma's. Volume remains below zero. Therefore, the first sell setup that develops looks good. In addition, a new down trend is just starting rather than being over-extended after a long down run. Don't be fooled by 5000-price taking out the recent pivot high, as 5000-price often makes a 1-2-3 pullback before resuming in the major trend direction.

CASE STUDY – 2

ENTRY AND TRADE MANAGEMENT - The following charts highlight a variety of examples pertaining to entries, stops, moving stops, and exits.

Each example shows the 5000-long timeframe setup on the left, and the 55-short timeframe trade management on the right.

The 55-tick short timeframe chart contains:

1. An ellipse showing the swing extreme we expect price to travel to.
2. A rectangle when a pivot overrides a 4-bar count for entry.
3. A solid horizontal line showing the initial stop extreme (2-ticks beyond).
4. Dashed horizontal lines showing where to move initial stop.
5. Entry and exit arrows.

Losing trade – 5000 (left) sets up a long continuation trade. We look to enter after an up bar that continues to hold after 4 bars (arrow 1, right). Initial stop is placed 2-ticks below the most recent pivot low (solid horizontal line). Price works its way to swing extreme (ellipse), but never gets there. If you had good entry location (getting a good fill on bar 5 with a market order after bar 4) price may have moved up enough for you to move initial stop to breakeven plus a tick. If you were trading multiple contracts there was plenty of movement in the trade direction to exit part of your position, and move your stop on the remaining contract(s) to make some money on the trade. If price did not move far enough in your favor to raise stop to breakeven plus a tick, you should have raised your initial stop to below the new pullback low (dashed horizontal line) for a small loss (arrow 2).

Momentum Win – 5000-price sets up for a continuation long trade at the right edge of the screen (left). Enter after an up bar forms and holds after 4-bars (arrow 1, right). Initial stop is placed 2-ticks below pivot low (solid line). When price tests extreme (ellipse) we move initial stop to breakeven plus a tick, and then allow for one pullback.

Price makes one pullback and proceeds higher. Breakeven stop is raised to a tick below the pullback extreme (dash line). Momentum sets in, so we ride the gains with 1500 trailing stops (dashed lines). When a clear volume divergence develops as price makes higher highs, while volume doesn't (2-arrows, bottom right) we either exit into strength (top arrow, right), or tighten our trailing stop considerably (55 pivots).

Buy Win – 5000-price sets up a for a C1 continuation pullback long trade. Note how pullback just touches a rising 18-ma (circle, left). We watch 55 to see if a 4-bar count develops. In this case it does. 4-bars hold above signal bar high, and we but at market (arrow 1, right)

Initial stop is placed 2-ticks below pivot low (solid line). When price tests extreme (ellipse), move stop to breakeven plus a tick, and allow for one pullback. Price makes one pullback and proceeds higher. Breakeven stop is raised to a tick below the pullback pivot (dash line). Price moves higher.

We look for momentum, swing equilibrium, and/or volume divergence to exit. In this case swing equilibrium is very clear (see waves before and after circle on 5000-chart, left). We move to aggressive trailing stop mode.

When price movement levels off, confirmed by volume leveling off (rectangle on volume line), exit via trailing stop with a nice gain in swing equilibrium area (arrow 2, right)

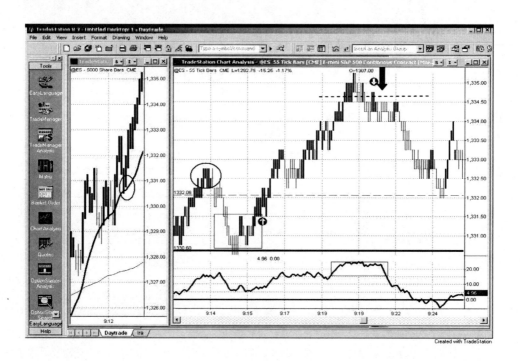

Created with TradeStation

Sell Win – 5000-price sets up a shallow pullback after the 18-ma crosses the 89-ma and trend changes down (left). Note how pullback doesn't reach 18-ma. We watch 55 to see if a shallow pullback entry develops, because this is early in a new trend aggressive trade. In this case it does. A 4-bar count creates a nice pivot low (rectangle, top). Sell below pivot low (arrow 1).

Note – You can also sell at market after 4-bars with price moving up. It's a judgment call. The track record records entry if bar 4 closes beyond the signal bar. Initial stop is placed 2-ticks above pivot high (solid line). When price tests extreme (ellipse), this is a case where we allow for one pullback if you sold below the pivot extreme because BE+1 is too close. Price makes one pullback and proceeds lower. Initial stop is raised to a tick above the pullback extreme (dash line). Price moves lower.

We look for swing equilibrium and/or volume divergence to exit. Often these appear together, but not always. In this case they do. Swing equilibrium is very clear (see 2-waves on 5000 chart). Volume divergence also develops (price makes lower low, while volume doesn't, 2 arrows below). We exit into weakness (arrow 2, right).

(Note – there is nothing wrong with exiting into weakness into 5000-swing equilibrium. This would have been the 55-wave down right before arrow 2)

Small Loss – 5000-price sets up a continuation pullback long trade. Note how pullback doesn't reach 18-ma, and how 5000-price has already moved strongly higher. We only want to take shallow pullbacks like this early in the trend, but let's say you take this trade anyway. A shallow pullback 4-bar count entry develops (right side of rectangle). Buy at market (arrow 1). Initial stop is placed 2-ticks below pivot low (solid line). Price works its way to swing extreme (ellipse), but never gets there. If you were trading multiple contracts there was enough movement in the trade direction to exit part of your position.

There is not enough movement for breakeven plus a tick. Price begins to head lower towards our stop. Time goes by and another pullback pivot low forms above the initial stop. You can raise your initial stop to below new pullback low (dashed horizontal line) for a small loss (arrow 2). Remember, good trades move in your favor almost immediately. If too much time goes by, look to move your initial stop, limit your loss, and wait for the next setup- in this case, either a C1 continuation or C2 consolidation buy.

RE-ENTRY – 5000 (left) first sets up a shallow pullback short trade (ellipse). Note how first pullback doesn't reach 18-ma, with a downtrend that's been in place for some time. (Shallow pullbacks deep into a trend are too risky and should be bypassed, but for the sake of example let's say you took this trade (arrow 1, right) instead of waiting for the better continuation setup beyond the 18-ma) Initial stop is placed 2-ticks above pivot high (solid line). When price tests extreme (ellipse) we allow for one pullback. Price makes one pullback and proceeds lower. Initial stop is raised to a tick above the pullback extreme (dash line). Price stops us out for a small loss (arrow 2). <u>After a loss on a shallow pullback trade, look for the better continuation trade setup.</u> Enter after a down bar forms and holds after 4-bars (arrow 3). Initial stop is placed 2-ticks above pivot high as always.

I didn't want to draw too many lines on this chart but you can see price moves short of the extreme, then pulls back, forming a new pivot high to lower stop. Price then moves lower again to take out extreme, and you would look to exit either with a momentum trail, equilibrium extreme, or volume divergence area. Also, if a new pivot-high forms before either of these three exit conditions develop, trail and lower stop again to protect profits.

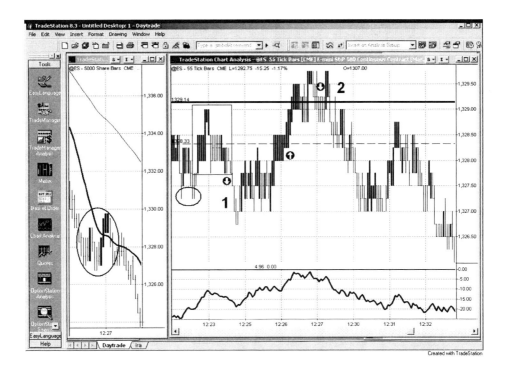

149

Sell Win (Hidden Volume Divergence) – 5000-price sets up a continuation pullback short trade (circle, left). Enter after a down bar forms and holds after 4-bars (arrow 1, pivot break). Initial stop is placed 2-ticks above pivot high (solid line). When price tests extreme (ellipse) we move stop to breakeven plus a tick and allow for one pullback. Price makes one pullback and proceeds lower. Initial stop is raised to a tick above the pullback extreme (dash line). Price moves lower. We look for momentum, swing equilibrium and/or volume divergence to exit. In this case a "hidden" volume divergence develops in a 5000 swing equilibrium area where volume makes lower low, while price doesn't (2-arrows, bottom). We exit into weakness (arrow 2, right).

A hidden divergence is exactly the opposite of a regular divergence. It is often a sign of a price turn to come (heavy volume ratio down can't take price lower). In his case it is especially significant because it occurs near a swing equilibrium level where we are looking to tighten up our stops any way we can!

RE-ENTRY/ DOUBLE LOSS – Here is an example of what can happen if you aggressively take trades near big picture trend line support/resistance levels. In this case, price gapped up, and then strongly trended down to 5-minute trend line support. If you weren't cautious taking additional short trades in this area here is what could result.

5000-price first sets up a shallow pullback short trade (ellipse). Again, avoid shallow pullback trades deep into a trend. If you take this trade, however, you would sell after a 4-bar count holds (arrow 1, trade1).

Initial stop is placed 2-ticks above pivot high (solid line). When price tests extreme (circle, right) allow for one pullback. Price makes one pullback and starts lower. Initial stop is raised to one tick above the pullback extreme (dash line). Price stops us out for a small loss (up arrow 1).

<u>After a loss on a shallow pullback trade, you look for a continuation trade setup where 5000-prices crosses the 18-ma.</u> Enter after a 4-bar count pivot break (arrow trade 2). Initial stop is placed 2-ticks above pivot high as always This trade gets stopped out for a small loss too. You have to know market structure. Taking two aggressive C1 trades (shallow pullback, continuation) at key big picture support/resistance is low probability trading!

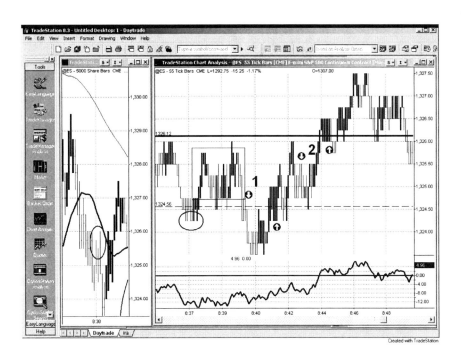

GOOD RE-ENTRIES – 5000-price sets up a continuation pullback short trade, at the <u>beginning of a new trend</u> as 18-ma crosses 89-ma (left). 55-price provides a 4-bar count that holds to enter short (arrow 1) Initial stop is placed 2-ticks above pivot high (solid line). We are stopped out.

<u>C1 Pullback conditions are still in place</u>, so immediately re-enter on next 4-bar count that holds (arrow 2) This trades moves below pivot extreme. Stop is lowered to breakeven plus a tick, and we allow for one pullback. Price makes one pullback and proceeds lower. Initial stop is raised to one tick above the pullback extreme (dash line).

Price stops us out for a small gain (arrow 3). We note price making another C1 pullback in this area. (Circle 2, left). A pivot forms near the next 4-bar count (rectangle) and we re-enter short again at arrow 4 (aggressive trade) for another winning trade.

CONSOLIDATION TRADES – Consolidation trades come in two forms: (1) High potential extension trades with the big picture, or early in a new trend (2) Low potential extension trades against the big picture, or after a trend has been in place for some time.

The low potential trades are still good to take because there is usually "enough room" to test the pivot extreme even if an extension fails, but you must be aware of a potential failure, and apply sound trade management accordingly (breakeven plus a tick, etc.)

<u>Buy Win/Re-entry Win</u> – 5000-price sets up for a consolidation buy entry as the 18-ma turns down in an uptrend (circle 1, left). Buy on a breakout of clear 55-flattening pattern (rectangle). Price approaches swing extreme with "plenty of room," so raise stop to breakeven plus a tick near swing extreme. Price breaks thru extreme, and we allow for one pullback. Raise breakeven stop to below minor pullback after swing extreme is penetrated (horizontal line). We are stopped out for a nice gain. Price is in a C1 continuation pullback area now (circle 2, left). Buy when 4-bar count holds (circle 2, right). Manage trade with initial stop, breakeven plus a tick stop, and extreme pullback pivot stop, and extension exit as always. This trade provides another nice gain.

CASE STUDY – 3

THE BIG PICTURE – Some setups carry higher probabilities for strong follow (extension) than other setups. We can often gauge price extension potential by looking at where setup develops in relation to the big picture.

The 5-minute chart is used to categorize the big picture. There are three types big picture analysis conditions that are meaningful: (1) Gap analysis relative to big picture trend (2) Price moving towards a trend line support/resistance level (Countertrend) (3) Price moving away from a trend line support/resistance level (With Trend).

The following examples describe the relationship between trade setups on the 5000-chart (left), and big picture structure on the 5-minute chart (right).

> **Consolidation trades near resistance** – The 5-minute chart (right, circle) clearly shows price in a big picture down trend. The first 5000-C2 consolidation pullback (circle, left) nears trend line resistance on the 5-minute chart (circle, right). Price moves to test extreme, generating a breakeven plus a tick trade when another pullback rally occurs. Price is currently setting up for another consolidation sell trade (right edge of 5000-chart). We see on the 5-minute chart (right) that this set up eventually produces a trade that moves strongly to new lows. Consolidation trades that set up near big picture trend line areas are high probability trades.

Gap Down in Down trend – The morning provides some of the best trade setups, in part because of <u>gaps</u>. In this example, price gaps down from the previous days' close (circle, far right). This is a gap down in a downtrend.

A gap can continue in the big picture direction, but most often will retrace some of the gap first.

This is a classic example of a retrace back to the trend line resistance area first. Note limited extension for long countertrend trades against big picture (circle 1, left).

Price turns back in direction of big picture (18-ma crosses below 89-ma), and short trades with trend (shallow pullbacks, continuations, consolidations, etc.) carry much greater extension potential (i.e. circle 2, left)

<u>Gap up in an uptrend</u> – As stated, although gaps often retrace first, they can also follow thru in the direction of the big picture. All we can do is "go with the flow" and then **assess** the extension probabilities.

When a price gap continues, moving with big picture direction, there is often no support or resistance to get in the way of the move.

In this example, price gaps up in an uptrend (circle, right), and the continuation pullback buy trade that sets up (circle, left), moves with great momentum higher in the direction of the big picture.

Gap Down in a Downtrend - This is another classic example of gap down in a downtrend, and a retrace back to the trend line support/resistance area first (circle, right).

In this case, however, look at how much room price has to travel back to the trend line area.

The long setups (not shown) provided strong big picture countertrend momentum gains. This is why it always helps to know where setups take place relative to the big picture, and why both trend and countertrend trades can offer great potential.

As you can see on the 5-minute chart (right) price eventually turns back in direction of big picture (right at trend line resistance area), and short trades with the big picture trend (circle, left) carry great extension potential.

Resistance at Trend line area - Looking at the 5-minute chart (right), you can see resistance at the trend line area (i.e. circle, right) occurs many times, including the entire previous day.

Over and over again, you see consolidation trades (circle1, left) and continuation trades (circle 2, left) provide excellent extension past price extremes.

"With trend, big picture" setups always provide the highest probability extension trades, especially if price still hasn't reached a big picture support or resistance area (to be discussed).

CASE STUDY – 4

VOLUME CONFIRMATION - The most powerful way to view overall market action is to place triple timeframe analysis into big picture analysis, and see if volume confirms or not. <u>Multiple timeframes, Big Picture and Volume - that is what the fully integrated $E=MC^2$ approach is all about</u>!

The following charts highlight the way volume analysis can assist you with trading decisions.

Displayed from left to right are the 5000 chart (setup) and the corresponding 1500 and 55 charts, with a vertical line drawn on the 1500 and 55 charts to show volume action at the point of 5000-setup.

<u>Strong Volume Confirmation</u> – During a C1 continuation pullback (circle, left) very strong volume confirmation is in place on both the 1500 and 55. 1500-volume (middle) is strongly above zero and moving past +5.

55-volume (right) doesn't cross the zero line on the pullback.

These are very strong conditions and the subsequent up move unfolds with strong momentum.

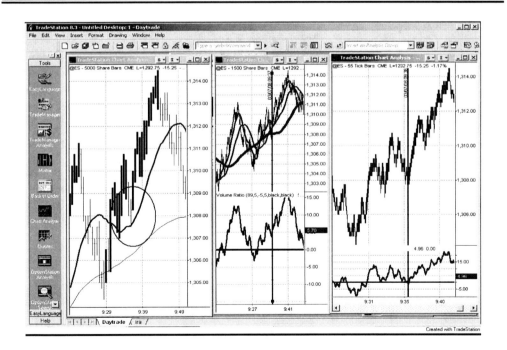

159

<u>Continuation Pullback with Volume Confirmation</u> – During a normal continuation 5000-pullback (circle, left) volume confirms the buy entry. 1500-volume (middle) pulls back to the zero line (remember, it can pull back as far negative 5 area, but it's always best when it stays above zero). 55-volume ratio dips below the zero line (right). A 55-pullback beyond the zero line is very common during normal pullbacks, and often represents the exact pullback extreme area assuming other conditions are aligned.

The up move turns out to be very powerful, and you are alerted to this when 1500-volume (middle) moves strongly past +5. Again, if other conditions are in alignment (big picture analysis, etc.) strong volume confirmation after a trade moves your way is a good sign to ride the trade for further gains. In other words, you should be more comfortable staying with such a trade for a 55-volume divergence swing, even if you are in a price equilibrium extension area.

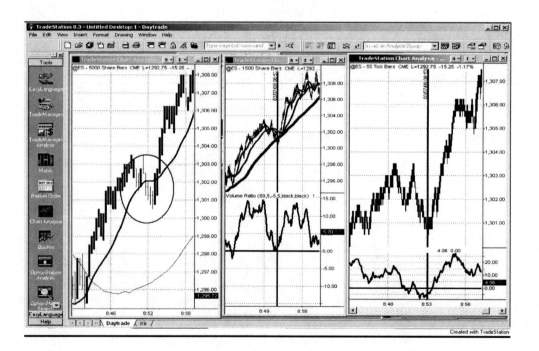

Continuation sell #2 – Let's say you are watching 5000 price at the right edge of the screen in real time (circle, left), and you are wondering if a second continuation trade in a row is worth taking.

A quick check of volume would tell you yes.

1500-volume (middle) is not ready to cross zero as 1500-price is back to the long-term moving average area. 55-volume (right) hasn't yet crossed the zero line, and when it finally does, it's without price confirmation (negative divergence).

Volume is a great way to confirm trade setups!

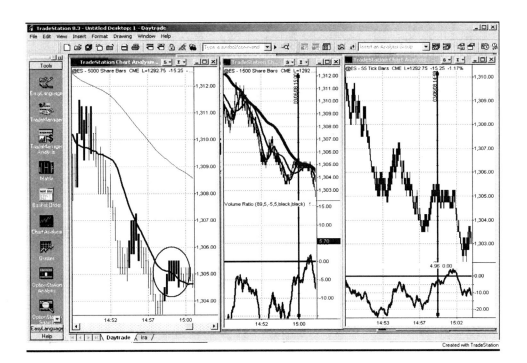

Volume Non-confirmation – The 5000-pullback in a downtrend looks quite strong (circle, left). Notice, however, at the pullback extreme 1500-volume (middle) hasn't crossed zero. Big Picture analysis alerts as well, as the up move is nothing more than a move to the trend line/resistance area in a big picture down trend.

Also, if you look at the 18 and 89-ma on the 5000-chart (left), you will see the 18-ma never crossed the 89-ma, so the consolidation pullback isn't even in C3 chop mode yet. This was an excellent C2 consolidation sell trade as soon as price made a 5-wave move down that coincided with 1500-price moving back below the long term moving average, all confirmed by big picture analysis, and unfolding volume activity.

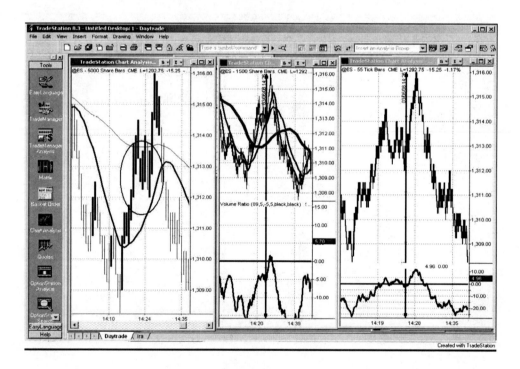

Volume + Momentum – The very best trades develop after the first pullback in a new trend confirmed by a volume ratio surge. I don't want to imply anything is ever guaranteed in trading, but this condition comes closest. Notice how 1500-volume crashes below the low end of the chart during the first push down (middle).

This means whatever price extreme forms during the first move down will almost always be tested again after a pullback. In this case, the 5000-continuation pullback (circle, left) sets up with 1500-volume unable to retrace to beyond minus 10 (middle). 55-volume can't make it back above zero (right), which is a key sign of a strong down trend/momentum movement. The sell trade that develops, with all these conditions in place, goes on to provide big gains.

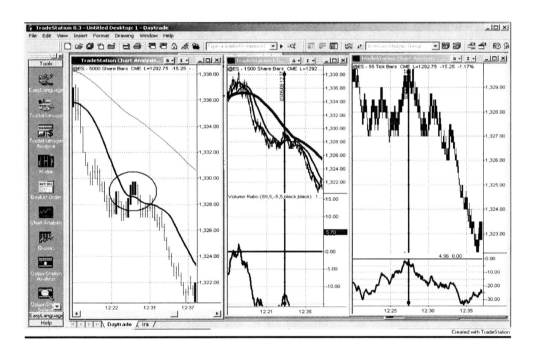

Section 8 - Details

<u>E-MINI BASICS</u>

The E-Mini S&P (ES) is simply a "mini" version of the big S&P futures contract, and trades virtually tick for tick with the S&P market, but 1/5 the size. Therefore, trading 5 E-Mini contracts is equivalent to trading 1 S&P contract.

The E-Mini is traded electronically, whereas the S&P contract is traded through brokers on the floor of the exchange. This leads to quicker fills in the E-Mini market, with less slippage. The only disadvantage to trading the E-Mini, is you must pay five commissions, as opposed to one commission in the S&P, if you plan to trade at higher volumes.

Here is the information on each market:

S&P 500 (SP) Tick size= .10 ($25), Point size =1.00 ($250)
E-MINI (ES) Tick size= .25 ($12.50), Point size=1.00 ($50)

Both futures have four-contract months- March (H), June (M), September (U), and December (Z). The charting symbol consists of the contract, month and year. Thus, if you are trading the December 2008 E-Mini, the symbol would be ESZ08.

<u>You will rollover to the next contract month on the second Thursday of the current expiration month</u>. Thus, you start trading the March contract on the second Thursday of December- the September contract on the second Thursday of June, etc.

Trading $E=MC^2$ offers an opportunity to leverage your trading results over time.

When you reach a point where you trade $E=MC^2$ consistently day in and day out, the sky is the limit when it comes to your trading size. This will be based on your account size, and specific risk/reward tolerances.

The examples in this manual are based on a **minimum contract set**, which means one contract. At current market volatility, it is recommended you start with a $5000 account for a minimum contract set. Each trader must define his/her own comfort level based upon individual risk/reward preferences, as well as trading goals and expectations.

(NOTE – IT IS HIGHLY RECOMMENDED THAT YOU EXIT ALL POSITIONS AHEAD OF THE RELEASE OF KEY ECONOMIC DATA, FEDERAL RESERVE ANNOUNCEMENTS, ETC. ALWAYS KNOW WHEN THESE RELEASES ARE SCHEDULED, BECAUSE MARKET CONDITIONS BECOME WAY TOO VOLATILE TO TRADE IN)

DATA - CHARTING - BROKERAGE SERVICES

Today there are many reliable companies that provide brokerage and charting services at very competitive rates. You can start out examining Tradestation securities (www.tradestation.com), but don't hesitate to go with any other source that you feel offers competitive price and service (Ninjatrader is another very good source).

Price Data and Charting – With Tradestation, the current E-mini data package costs about $40.00 per month. There is also a $100 per month Tradestation fee, <u>but this is waived if you make 10 trades a month</u>, or more. So your fixed cost for data and charting is about $40 per month.

Trading futures has never been easier, and there are many firms out there that would love your business. Once you find a solid company, the most important factors you will need to consider are trading platforms offered, commission costs, and phone back-up service. Today, all firms will send you daily account activity through Email.

The Internet has simplified trading like never before.

In addition to getting your charting services online, you can also execute trades online in just a fraction of a second!

Commissions are a very real cost of doing business. Needless to say, you want to negotiate the lowest commission rate possible. You should never pay over $5.00 a contract, and in most cases you should be able to do better than this.

Most brokerage accounts require a minimum account size of $5,000 to begin trading. Some firms will let you start with a smaller account if you will be day trading (i.e. Balance above $1,000).

One service you must insist on having is a quick, reliable phone back-up desk available in case your Internet platforms/connections temporarily go down. This will happen from time to time, and you want to make sure you have a way to execute orders (exit trades) quickly over the phone if you have to.

Go to **www.futures.tradingcharts.com/brokers.html** to see a very good directory of commodity and futures brokers.

TRADING DIARY

Here is an example of a typical E=MC^2 trading day, and the type of recording keeping effort we recommend that you set up for every trading session.

E=MC^2 trades set up in a logical flow from 8:30 to 3:15 CST. The flow goes back and forth between buy and sell, as price direction changes from up to down. Within each price direction (buy/sell) phase, there is a logical flow between continuation and consolidation trades.

Several continuation trades in a row can represent immediate re-entry after being stopped out, or simply the next trade that sets up after a nice gain.

Deeper pullbacks change continuation setups to consolidation setups, and on and on, until the pullback becomes so deep that direction changes from buy to sell, or sell to buy, as the 18-ma crosses the 89-ma that rolls over in a new trend direction.

Diary Notes – At the top of the diary we list the date, the type of gap opening and the current trend, the distance price is away from trend line support/resistance at the gap opening, and/or the distance price is away from a big picture swing extension at the gap opening.

Trade Type – Monitors the flow of buys and sells, and denotes whether a trade is (C1) - Continuation, (C2) -Consolidation, normal, (C3) -Consolidation, chop. (No C1-C counter-trend trades on this diary)

Entry – Time and price of trade entry according to set ups on the 1500 and 55.

Exit – We list what type of exit takes place on the trade- Initial stop, adjusted stop, breakeven plus a tick, volume divergence, or momentum (or, price swing extension). Again, these exits flow logically according to price behavior.

Results – We keep a running tally of the results for each trade, as well as the cumulative total for these results.

DATE 12-05-08a   **GAP** +0.00 UP IN UPTREND   **DISTANCE TO: T/L** 0.00   **BIG PIC EXT**

TRADE TYPE		ENTRY				EXIT

#	B/S	C1	C2	C3	TIME	ENTRY	PT	Initial Stop	Adj Stop	BE+1	Vol Div	Mom/ Exten.	+/-	Cu
1	Sell			x	843	836.50	x				832.25		4.25	4.2
2				x	857	830.25	x		828.25				2.00	6.2
3		x			906	827.75	x		827.00				.75	7.0
4		x			909	827.25	x				824.75		2.50	9.5
5		x			916	823.50	x			823.25			.25	9.7
6		x			918	824.25	x		821.00				3.25	13.
7			x		929	822.75			824.25				(1.50)	11.
8			x		936	822.25	x		819.50				2.75	14.
9		x			948	820.25		822.00					(1.75)	12.
10				x	1015	825.50	x		825.00				.50	13.
11				x	1024	823.50	x		823.00				.50	13.
12				x	1038	821.75		824.25					(2.50)	11.
13	Buy	x			1047	826.75	x		829.00				2.25	13.
14		x			1059	830.50	x			830.75			.25	13.
15		x			1106	830.25	x		832.50				2.25	15.
16		x			1113	832.25		830.00					(2.25)	13.
17		x			1119	832.00	x			832.25			.25	13.
18		x			1125	832.00	x			832.25			.25	14.
19			x		1205	832.75	x			833.00			.25	14.
20		x			1219	836.00	x			836.25			.25	14.
21		x			1230	835.25	x		836.00				.75	15.
22		x			1237	837.25	x	834.75					(2.50)	12.
23			x		1242	839.00	x				846.00		7.00	19.
24		x			1254	845.25	x		848.00				2.75	22.
25		x			1300	846.00	x			846.25			.25	22.
26			x		1320	843.75	x			844.00			.25	23.
27		x			1329	844.00		842.50					(1.50)	21.

A typical E=MC² trading day – Each trade highlighted below would be listed in a trading diary. See if you can develop a sense for the flow that takes place for the trading session, from buy to sell, sell to buy, and from continuation to consolidation, within each buy and sell phase. You can see that certain trades are stopped out and immediately re-entered (11 and 12), or how continuation trades are stopped out and turn into consolidation trades (7 and 8).

You should be able to gain a sense for the type of winning trades that take place (breakeven plus a tick for 13, volume divergence for 14, momentum for 15). Study this chart, and determine what you think were the highest probability trades according to developing market structure. Note the two C1-C opportunities after lengthy trends(big arrows). If you perform this exercise every day, you will master the E=MC² trading approach.

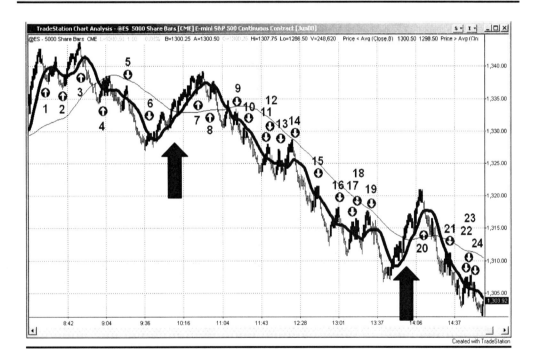

Section 9 – Putting It All Together (Context)

<u>READING THE MARKET</u>

Before you consider trading setups, trading entries, trading exits etc., you must first explore the overall environment in which these setups, entries, and exits develop and exist.

Say you are looking at price action in a complete vacuum. The ES is showing: 988.25 bid / 988.50 ask. Should you buy or sell?

Of course this seems like a ridiculous question without any additional information, or context, but this scenario is not too far out of line from the "out of context" way many traders look to trade.

Would it be helpful to know if the 988.25/988.50 bid-ask spread was right after the market had dropped 10 points to a key big picture support level versus developing soon after an upside breakout where the market had just been consolidating lower for quite some time, and appears to have room to run to the upside?

Yes, this adds "context," but this still may not be completely useful information without knowing how overall developing intra-day structure sets up in a "reading of the market" context.

For instance, if the market had just dropped 10 points to support, you would want to know if the 10 point drop to support may be taking place on the first move of the day, right to a logical pullback area, which means the market may be ready to reverse to new highs on the day.

Or, if the market was breaking out higher from short-term consolidation with further room to run to the upside, a brief stall after the breakout would carry expectations of further upside momentum. In these two examples, intra-day structure (first move of the day), and intra-day price action expectation (momentum after a breakout from intra-day chop) provide further context for your trading decisions.

From a set up pattern standpoint, let's say 988.25 bid/988.50ask has just formed a classic middle of the day buy pattern, with price making new short-term intra-day trend up, then a "pullback" with volume ratio holding zero and confirming.

Perhaps in these conditions you feel the odds of a buy strongly favor the odds of a sell, with such a perfect setup pattern developing, but is this really the case?

What if the in the big picture the market had just broken lower from 5 days of daily overlapping price congestion, and you have a trend day down in effect (to be discussed), in other words, very strong sell continuation conditions based on the big picture.

In this case, does a perfect buy set up pattern either after a 10-point drop, or after a price move higher, really carry strong "overall buy odds" when the more significant big picture odds (Trend day down) point to much lower prices ahead?

In this context, wouldn't it be best to "pass" on dubious buy setups that form against big picture scenarios, and eagerly await the next sell setup instead? Can you see how **TRADING SETUPS AND READING THE MARKET NEED TO GO HAND IN HAND** in order to develop a true edge for your trading decisions.

Lets' say you have a perfect buy setup pattern that develops in line with big picture expectations.

Of course, this is ideal, but does this mean that price will follow thru from this setup for big gains in the same exact manner every single time?

The answer is no, because even with same exact setup, perfectly aligned with big picture, etc. you will never have the "exact same participants" as the last time the setup developed. Therefore, you will never have the same exact outcomes for the same setup.

As a trader, the first thing you must understand is that every trade must first be placed into a bigger picture "read the market" context (i.e.- big picture of developing intra-day structure, small picture of developing price action, etc.), and then once entered, every trade must be observed according to unfolding price action in the present tense.

This is why trade setups, and standard rules, and mechanical trading programs developed from price patterns/indicators alone, without further context, are often meaningless.

The same exact trade setup may develop (1) In-line with big picture structure (2) Counter to big picture structure (3) Unfold with less magnitude than the same previous setup (4) Unfold with greater magnitude than the same previous setup.

As a trader, you must think in this multi-dimensional manner at all times.

This is really no different than when you drive a car, and stepping on the gas pedal takes on a completely different meaning whether you are pulling out of a parking space, stuck in heavy traffic, are in a school zone with children around, or have clear sailing in front of you on an open highway.

In trading, discipline really means having a consistent framework to look to enter and exit trades, but understanding that this "disciplined" framework will have completely different outcome possibilities in different big picture environments, and that each trade with the same setup criteria will never unfold exactly the same way all of the time, nor will the outcomes produced from equal setups match the same outcome results as the time before.

While some feel this multi-dimensional angle adds confusion to the trading mix, the master trader sees this multi-dimensional context as a sign of **flexibility** as he or she works to develop a true trading edge by learning how to read the market and manage trades accordingly.

BRACKETS - CONSOLIDATION - SWING POINTS

You should always know what is happening in the big picture of the market. This will provide context for all E=MC2 mechanical setups and opportunities.

The big picture is determined by observing price action on the daily chart, and then by spreading out the 5-minute chart and seeing how unfolding intra-day structure forms each day relative to what is happening in the daily timeframe.

Daily charts – A glance at the daily charts shows you first how the market is swinging (higher/highs, lower/lows, etc.) and from this action you can see where clear bracket areas (high/low ranges), and swing points form (prior highs and lows that once broken become new support/resistance).

Brackets and Swing points guide us to how price is trying to move from Point A to Point B and also identify big picture support and resistance areas.

A market will tend to move inside a bracket from one bracket extreme to the other extreme, and swing highs and lows inside the bracket tell you which way the market is trying to go at the moment.

Swing points generated within the bracket create support/resistance areas.

If a market breaks out of bracket, price may move into a prior bracket, or to a whole new price area altogether.

If a prior bracket is entered, expect price to run to the opposite edge of this bracket.

If price is moving to a whole new area (gap, space between two brackets etc.) then look for price to find support/resistance at the edge of an old bracket in the distance.

If price is making new all time highs or lows, then there is no telling how far price will travel, and you have to wait for signs that all patient buyers(lows) or sellers (highs) have acted before price will pause and likely retrace and form a new bracket area.

All this information is important in day trading to tie together developing intra-day structure to the predictive aspects of what the daily and 5-minute charts are trying to do.

For instance, if a prior daily swing resistance point is up at 950 (A 950 swing low that was taken out to the downside that will show up as a pivot point on the chart), and an intra-day consolidation breaks out to the upside at 930, you should expect the market to run to 950. Can you see how this 20-pt expectation can help you judge the potential of 5000 18/89 mechanical setups that develop along the way?

Or, if a daily bracket range is identified between 1000-850 (big picture), and the market breaks out of three days of overlapping daily price action to the upside at 950 with trend day conditions, it makes sense to look for a run to the top of the bracket at 1000.

Also, it is very important to know if the market is swinging higher or lower either inside a big picture daily bracket, or outside a big picture daily bracket.

Price swings inside a bracket will likely move to the bracket edges.

Price swings outside a bracket will move to prior bracket edges

Again this just tells you the overall condition of the market and allows you to stay with certain big picture biases until these biases change.

For instance, if you see daily swings making higher/highs and higher/lows inside a 1000-800 bracket, then expect price to work its way to the top of the bracket at 1000 until this condition changes.

Maybe a trend day down will form from the 950 area before 1000 is reached and change this condition in the short run. If so, the top of the trend day (950) sets a new resistance swing point inside the 1000-800 bracket.

The implication here is that if you find yourself in an intra-day trade days later that is moving to the upside (maybe an intra-day consolidation upside breakout at 920), 950 becomes a clear first target and possible resistance point on the way to 1000 based on the daily charts.

So you always need to tie together developing intra-day price structure to what daily charts and 5-minute charts are telling you in terms of bracket /consolidation areas and swing points.

The 5-minute chart (day session only) needs to be spread out to include many days worth of price action. Spreading out the 5-minute chart allows you see "opening gaps" as well as other clear swing points and consolidation areas that make up overall daily price action.

The logic is that price moves from consolidation area to consolidation area on the 5-minute chart and will find support/resistance at pullback to swing points, or at the edges of each consolidation area along the way. Also, when price enters a prior consolidation area, the odds favor price moving all the way to the opposite edge of this consolidation area.

Here are some chart examples that start to tie this big picture thinking together.

DAILY CHART

Here are the key points for daily chart analysis.

1. **A,B,C,D** represent the big picture bracket areas. Price swings back and forth in a bracketed area, and when a bracket area breaks note how the edge of the bracket becomes support/resistance for the next bracket. (Low edge of A = Upper resistance for B, etc.) Also, note how there is space between bracket C and D. If bracket D ever breaks to the upside, there is space to run all the way to the to the low edge of C. Finally, if a bracket is ever re-entered (see false downside probes in brackets B and D) expect price to move to the opposite edge of the bracket. Always know where daily brackets are located!

2. **Point 1** – Note how at the bottom of bracket A, three days of overlapping daily price action develops. This is a very powerful "breakout condition" to monitor in all cases, but since the breakout of 3-days of overlapping daily action is at the bottom of a big picture bracket, note how powerful the subsequent downside move is.

3. **Point 2** – Inside bracket B with price swinging lower (lower highs/lower lows). Since top edge of bracket B held, we expect move to bracket B low. Point 2 is a **Pullback to resistance swing point** inside bracket B

(horizontal line) as price swings to the lower edge of the bracket in the big picture.

4. **Point 3** – Note how bottom of bracket B is resistance for top of bracket C. Intra-day resistance at 1300 area was important to monitor according to the big picture. This could mean not entering C1 long trades that set up in the 1300 area, or exiting long trades that ran up to this area.

5. **Point 4** – Again, note how overlapping daily price action provides a strong big picture breakout condition to monitor. In this case, as before, this breakout occurs at the bottom of a big picture bracket, which makes the breakout very powerful. Use E=MC2 structure to hold for big gains when these exceptional trading conditions develop (Several C1s and at least a C2 swing, etc. See Trend day and Consolidation Breakout section).

6. Bracket D bottom holds after a false probe lower. Therefore, expect price to work towards top of the bracket at 1000. Point 5 provides resistance inside the bracket. Be cautious of new long trades that form at this resistance point, or prior long trades that run up to this resistance until this resistance is taken out. If resistance is taken out, a clear path to top of bracket exists, and this should coincide with very good E=MC2 5000 18/89 long setups.

5-MINUTE CHART

The 5-minute chart is an x-ray view into daily price action. You can see gaps, swing points, and most important, consolidation areas just like daily chart.

Consolidation areas mean so much to big picture analysis as price will flow back and forth between these areas, and break strongly away from these areas into new consolidation areas, etc. The edges of consolidation provide support/resistance as either (1) Price targets from inside a current consolidation area, or (2) Targets to the edge of the consolidation areas in the distance.

Here are the key points for 5-Minute chart analysis:

1. **A, B** represents the two consolidation areas on this 5-minute chart. These are the sideways high/low ranges when the 5-minute chart is spread out. Price moves from one consolidation area to the next, and at times space develops between two consolidation areas.

2. **Point 1** - On this day, intra-day chop develops early in the session at the outer edge of the 880 bracket A. A breakout will be powerful up or down, (Down takes price to 860, Up takes price to daily resistance swing points, etc.) The breakout to the upside moves to an eventual new consolidation high area (915) and the breakout trade to upside could have been held for large gains using the E=MC2 framework.

3. **Point 2** – Gap down creates a "conflict" to stand aside at the open. Overnight price action starts the 5000 18/89 trading trend down, right at pullback to swing support point in uptrend (dashed horizontal line). Mechanical sell trades at the open in this condition are low probability.

4. **Point 3** – Intra-day chop develops for second day in a row after the gap down. We always recognize intra-day chop from an unclear 5000 18/89 relationship. Powerful breakout conditions develop again once the 5000 18/89 trading trend aligns. In this case breakout to upside can be held to obvious resistance point formed at the 915 highs a day earlier. When resistance at this high holds we get a clear 915-880 consolidation area to monitor.

5. **Point 4** - Intra-day chops forms for a third day in a row. You should see how a breakout will take price either to the top or bottom of 915-880 consolidation. Price breaks lower and moves right to 880-consolidation support. This was a 20-point move you could have held onto for big gains because of the chop/breakout condition. After a 20-point move to key support, you should avoid all short mechanical setups for rest of day.

6. **Point 5** - Note how on next day, the breakdown point (900 area) becomes **pullback to swing resistance**. When we saw the trading trend start to the upside on this day, we expected 900 to be a target/pullback to swing resistance point, which would need to be taken out before the top of bracket at 915 could be reached. When 900 failed and the trading trend turned back down, note how next target was back to bottom of consolidation low at 880. This is a perfect example of monitoring price action moving from edge to edge inside a consolidation area and how pullback to swing points inside a consolidation area provide additional support/resistance points to monitor as well.

7. **Point 6** - Bottom of consolidation at 880 continues to hold, and price will not go lower until this area breaks. If 880 area breaks, look for move back to 860 as price re-enters a prior consolidation area and should run to opposite edge. If 880 holds and price starts to move back up to the 915 consolidation top, you can see how the 895 area is the first target/potential resistance point inside the 915-880 consolidation area. This means if the 5000 18/89 trading trend turns up around 885, expect at least 10 points of upside in the big picture to start.

I hope you are beginning to see how to use the daily chart and 5- minute chart together to uncover the big picture condition in the market using the flow of consolidations areas and swing points.

Analyzing the big picture in this way puts 5000 18/89mechanical signals into context and provides you with some very basic common sense rules to add to your trading plan.

1. Use the big picture for target points (Edges of consolidation areas and/or swing points).
2. Avoid mechanical signals that conflict with the big picture. This almost always pertains to uncertain opens (gaps, choppy overnight price action), and new trades after price has worked its way to a big picture support/resistance target area (end of a move from Point A to Point B).
3. Use specific big picture conditions to hold onto winning trades for big gains using the E=MC2 framework. This relates to Trend days and/or consolidation breakouts. Consolidation breakouts develop from overlapping daily price action, or intra-day coiling chop action.

BIG PICTURE - THE "3" UNIVERSAL BASICS

Consolidation Area to Consolidation Area – Inside edges of consolidation are support/resistance targets as price swings back and forth **(AB consolidation)**. When price enters one consolidation area to the next, expect a move to new consolidation area opposite inside edge **(C is target when AB is re-entered).** If there is space between consolidation areas, and a breakout occurs, target outer edge of prior consolidation area in the distance **(D is target when C breaks).**

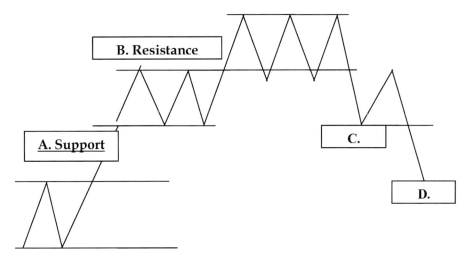

Pullback to Swing Point Support/Resistance – Expect price to target and then find support/resistance at prior pullback to swing points. For instance, If a market is swinging lower, previous low swing points become resistance on pullbacks.

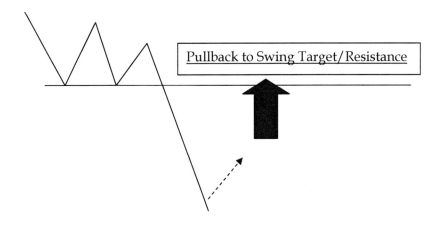

Standard Support/Resistance – Key highs and lows are always support/ resistance to monitor. The most obvious are the consolidation highs and lows in number 1 above. Next are overnight highs and lows to start the trading day. Next are daily highs and lows from previous days. For instance, assume a pullback to swing resistance point is taken out to the upside (below). The next target/resistance above is the obvious next high on the charts. This can be a consolidation area high, or a daily high, etc.

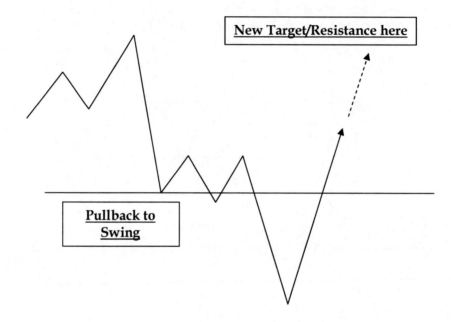

BIG PICTURE AND INTRA-DAY PRICE FLOW

The building blocks to becoming an intuitive trader begins with an understanding of the "very best conditions to trade."

The best conditions to trade combines two things (1) An understanding of big picture support/resistance (2) An understanding of how intra-day structure evolves from opening price action relative to yesterdays price range, and then morphs into today's intra-day structure of its' own.

You need to tie 1 and 2 together to develop expectations for every trade entry setup that develops.

BEST TRADING CONDITION FLOW ANALYSIS

1. Determine Big Picture Support and Resistance areas before the open (View daily and 5-minute charts to identify consolidation, pullback to swing areas, etc.)
2. View the open as an extension of the previous days price action- gap or no gap. (i.e. - 40-50-60 % normal retrace of a move from the end of yesterday can hold direction bias from yesterday early on, etc.)
3. Let today's 5-minute price action morph into a unique current intra-day flow structure.
4. Monitor for today's intra-day structure to "hold, or change."
5. Intra-day flow structure holds if 5-min price continues to swing higher (or lower) with the bias (This is a general starting point- as intra-day structure can change, or be represented in other ways (i.e.- Intra-day chop develops = no bias, Trend day = negates some opposite 5-minute swing changes)
6. Therefore Intraday structure can be classified as either: Range day conditions, Trend day conditions, Intra-day chop conditions.

With these six stages in mind, you can start to look for the best trading opportunities to develop each day relative to a logical sequence . Let's examine the sequential developments that create intra-day structure beginning at 8:30 CST

OPENING GAP - An opening gap at 8:30 CST is viewed in 1 of 2 ways :

(1) Fade Trade (trade opposite the gap) right off the bat back to a logical pullback area which is usually a move to (a) Test overnight highs/lows (b) Test yesterday's close, or a (c) Test logical retrace of yesterdays price action.

(2) Continuation Trade where price first moves in the direction of the opening gap and then pulls back to either (a) Approx 50 percent of the initial move or (b) Pulls back deeper to some logical overall pullback level when yesterdays price action, or today's opening intraday high-low is factored in, etc.

With either a "fade" or "continuation" opening gap trade we watch to see how early 5-minute price action ties in with the end of yesterdays price movement.

For instance, an initial fade trade (gap higher, price moves lower) may retrace 50% of the last leg of yesterday's price action and today's price still be may considered in an overall uptrend with an early move lower. In this case, don't be surprised if the opening price move turns right around and heads back up in the gap direction to make new intra-day highs.

Or, a gap/continuation trade may move to test key big picture support/resistance, overnight highs/lows, etc, so again don't be surprised if a early gap continuation move fails, turns around, and moves back past the opening gap area to form an intra-day structure bias opposite the opening gap continuation direction.

Finally, an early fade or continuation price move may fall in line with key big picture structure (i.e.- daily overlapping breakout with gap trade continuation, or a gap continuation that looks to be breaking out beyond a key bracket level, fails, and then reverses strongly (fades) back into the big picture bracket for the rest of the day.

CURRENT DAY INTRA-DAY STRUCTURE FORMS - At some point after the open, enough time goes by on the 5-minute chart (A first move followed by a retrace attempt, usually within the first hour of trading) and a current intra-day structure forms on its' own (No longer need to consider yesterdays price action after the initial first leg and first retrace attempt completes).

For instance, if opening 5-minute price makes either a large single directional move, or a series of swings in one direction for a period of time, then call this intra-day structure up or down for as long as overall 5-minute trending action holds.

If 5-minute price direction changes later in the trading session, see if a trend day may be in force, in which case the overall intraday structure still holds with the trend day, and not the new 5-minute price direction.

In most cases, however, when a new 5-minute price direction develops, this creates a new directional bias for intra-day structure, or perhaps the onset of intra-day chop.

To conclude, the early 5-minute price flow directly relates to the first move of the day either reaching a key support/resistance area, or pulling back to a logical retrace area relative to yesterday's price action.

Thereafter, look to see if 5-minute price flow develops as either a range day, or trend day in relation to the current intra-day bias.

HOW IT ALL COMES TOGETHER - The 5-minute chart below highlights 8-trading days (June 3,4,5,8,9,10,11,12) and key intra-day structure developments that form relative to the information described above that needs to guide trading each day. During this 8-day period price was moving up and down inside a tight "940-930" 5-minute consolidation area (horizontal lines). So, in this example, we monitor how price tries to breakout from this consolidation area, and/or swings back and forth inside this area which provides logical target/support-resistance points to monitor as intra-day structure unfolds.

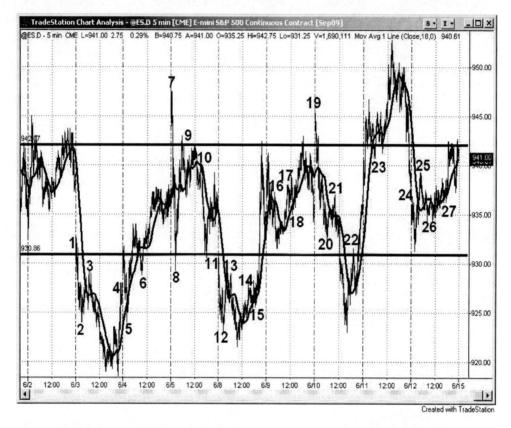

Created with TradeStation

1. Gap down to lower bracket- A continuation trade leads the way vs. a fade the gap trade.
2. Price makes a one direction intra-day move down from the open - Monitor for 50 percent (approx) retrace from open to low point 2 to maintain down bias (Note - In this case, a deeper pullback to point 1 could still maintain a down bias relative to the overall pullback which includes yesterday's price action)
3. Price retraces 50 percent from 1 to 2 and sets up a nice 5-minute pullback sell with expectations for a swing move to new intra-day 5-minute lows.
4. Intra-day bias remains down all day until strong rally at point 4 after a low failure changes the bias up at end the day. This retrace of more than 50-

60 percent of days range (plus new swing high after a failure at intra-day lows) sets up nice long opportunities on a pullback.

5. Next day opens higher to bracket resistance and first moves down to point 5. By looking at previous day price action we know this is an excellent 5-minute pullback buy opportunity after the open moves lower, for an expected move to test the opening intra-day high.

6. Price swings to a higher high on the day after a pullback at point 5, intra-day bias confirmed up (now inside bracket with expectations to bracket high), and a 5-minute pullback develops at point 6 for a classic buy for a move to new 5-minute swing highs. (Note - The 5-minute pullback near the end of the day offers another long opportunity but this is late in the day so the time factor for sustained follow-through is limited).

7. Big gap up way past bracket high resistance. A fade the gap trade develops, and we want to monitor price action as it nears the bracket edge (horizontal line) for signs of acceptance or rejection of the potential breakout higher (Rejection occurs -price back into bracket)

8. Major one directional down move develops back into bracket to point 8, which is also bracket support low. Expect a support bounce here and monitor for 50-60 percent retrace of days range (point 7 to 8) to see if intra-day down bias holds or not.

9. Price bounces to bracket resistance high at point 9, which is approx 50 percent of days range. Very wide opening range with a snap back to the middle of range makes intra-day trading difficult from this point forward, but intra-day bias remains down from the open.

10. With patience, 5-minute chart rolls over to the downside (in line with holding intra-day down bias) sets up a nice short opportunity on a pullback to point 10. Target is a new 5-minute swing low that has clear sailing to bottom of bracket (bracket again holds at 11).

11. Next day gap opens lower below bracket support, and sets up a nice short continuation opening trade to point 12, which is near support from the last breakout attempt lower.(Near points 2 and 5)

12. We monitor pullback that develops from point 12 to see if intra-day down bias will hold? Down bias will hold either with a 50 percent retrace from opening gap, OR a deeper pullback closer to the open which would align with normal retrace pullback to swing from yesterday in line with bracket low resistance.

13. Price pulls back deep to bracket low (point 13)- a normal pullback when yesterdays price action is considered, and sets up a nice short trade area for a test of lows of day.

14. After lows of the day are tested, price makes a large enough retrace of days range at point 14 to change intra-day bias from down to up, (or perhaps intra-day chop if price moves back to the lows).

15. Excellent long trade setup at 15 on first 5-minute pullback after a developing intra-day trend change. Price moves back past intra-day highs, back into bracket, and as expected, all the way back to bracket high.

16. Next day, price opens slightly higher, and first moves up to test high of bracket resistance after which it comes back down to take out opening lows which sets a intra-day down bias inside the bracket. Pullback to point 16 is an excellent short area to test bracket lows.

17. Price then makes a major push higher, retracing well over 50-60 percent of the days' range turning intra-day bias back up.

18. 5-minute price pullback at 18 represents an excellent long area as the first pullback after an intra-day trend change to swing higher to test bracket highs.

19. Next day a big gap up above bracket high resistance. A fade the gap set up develops to signal possible rejection of bracket high. Price moves back into bracket and as expected moves all the way to bracket low at point 20.

20. Trend day down conditions also develop so we monitor for a pullback from point 20 low to sell, and know intra-day down bias will hold on all pullbacks up to 50 percent of opening (19- 20) move.

21. Excellent sell area on pullback to point 21, which is pullback to swing resistance of current days price action. On a strong trend day, expect lows of day to be taken out (also aligns with target to bracket lows as well), and in this case bracket low is taken out for big gains.

22. Pullback to point 22 has all the making of another nice short trade - Trend day down, pullback on 5-minute chart, pullback to bracket low/swing resistance, but when this set up fails, price moves back into bracket (key development!), and an explosive end of the day rally takes price all the way back to upper bracket! (Note- On trend days, expect intraday highs/lows to be taken out at least once after a first deep pullback. Thereafter, price action dictates the likelihood of intraday high/lows to be taken out a second, or third time)

23. Open next day near top of bracket and a pullback on 5-minute chart to bracket high. This time bracket high holds which sets up a nice long trade area to see if price will finally breakout out and hold above bracket or not.

24. A breakout attempt above bracket early in the day clearly fails when price collapses well over 50-60 percent of the days' range, moves back into the bracket, taking out intra-day lows at the close.

25. Next day market opens and moves to first test bracket lows. Pullback to point 25 creates a "pullback sell area with conflict" because (a) big picture support (bottom of bracket) has already been reached during opening move of the day (b) new intraday high develops (is bias now up?) (c) normal pullback in line with yesterday price action (is bias still down?).

You can take such big picture short trades but need to be very cautious, knowing a big picture conflict is in place for a sustained extension.

26. Price fails several times to make big picture swings lows.
27. After several big-picture swing low failures, 5-minute price makes a new swing high, and this provides an excellent pullback long trade at point 27 for a move to test the bracket high area.

When you think BIG PICTURE/DEVELOPING INTRA-DAY STRUCTURE FIRST, you are focused on "reading the market" and trade set ups become an extension of big picture/intra-day structure expectations.

This is how trading intuition enters the picture (1) You wait for good big picture developments before trading (2) You consider holding onto winning trades according to big picture price swings and/or targets if price action develops in line with big picture price swing expectations.

You will soon discover how it is better to trade less rather than to trade more during the trading session- especially as it relates to trying to hold trades for big gains when big picture structure dictates to do so.

If you can adopt a "Big picture/Intra-day structure first, Trade signal second" mindset as you "learn to trade," you will be well on your way to reaping the rewards of allowing intuition and trading context to guide your trading efforts.

DEVELOP AND MAINTAIN A RUNNING VIEW OF THE MARKET

As a trader, it is very important to strive to be in sync with the big picture flow of the market at all times. As you work to develop the skill of "reading the market" you begin to anticipate market developments, and begin to gain intuition regarding price action that either confirms big picture developments, or not.

You should spend 90 percent of your "trading time" focused on analyzing big picture/ intra-day structure developments and expectations, and then intensely watch unfolding intra-day price action to see if these expectations are being confirmed or not.

Trading setups should only enter your mind after you settle on what is developing in the big picture.

Once you define a developing big picture scenario, see if trading setups fall in line with big picture expectations or not.

Start from observing how overnight price action/opening gap at 8:30 CST relates to 5-minute price action from yesterday, and then follow how 5-minute price action forms a unique intra-day structure on its own as the trading session moves on.

Always note if unfolding 5-minute structure is moving back and forth inside an existing consolidation area, or breaking out of a range, or pulling back to a logical support/resistance area.

Monitor overall price swing action on the 5-minute chart, and determine logical targets by spreading out the 5-minute chart to include several days worth of data.

Entries and exits need to have a big picture context.

For example, look at point 21 on the 5-minute chart above. If you enter a short trade in this 5-minute pullback area, expect new 5-minute swing lows past point 20 to develop, in conjunction with a likely price move that will test the low of the bracket area.

Furthermore, if you look at down leg (19 to 20), an equilibrium swing from 21 to lows near 12, 15 is no surprise when the bracket low doesn't hold.

In other words, when price action aligns with the big picture, consider holding trades to logical big picture targets/extensions and monitor price action as these areas are reached. In this particular scenario, you shouldn't be "scared" and exit after a 2-point gain, when a bigger picture price swing gain is likely.

BIG PICTURE DIARY - A very good way to stay in touch with the continuous and never-ending unfolding big picture price flow is to setup and maintain a diary of "price action" that you update each day.

Here are the four areas to update each day (and a sample of what to write). Of course you can add or include anything else that may be helpful to you.

YESTERDAYS WRAP UP - As expected we tested lower 970 bracket support. Market, tried to break thru lower, couldn't, and then worked its way back to top of ever continuing and tightening range near 980.

TODAY'S OPENING GAP/1500-PRICE VOLUME ANALYSIS - Mechanical trend starts down near lower end of 980-970 range. A bigger overnight breakdown than yesterday, so we will watch to see if price/volume action early points to a sign of a deeper daily range pullback to 960 area to start.

BRACKETS/PULLBACK TO SWING ANALYSIS - Range trading if price stays inside 980-970 range. If so, a powerful breakout is developing as we are at 5-days of overlapping daily price action. Daily pullback to swing lower to around 960- 955 area support maintains big picture bias up

DAILY CHART (BIG PICTURE) ANALYSIS - Bounce off big picture 950-870 bracket low at 870 started move back to 950. As long as this recent breakout above 950 area holds, we will start a new daily bracket higher and watch for signs of a reversal to set up a new daily bracket high. It is possible this big picture breakout above 950 could be rejected, but as of now big picture bias clearly up with target to the 1050-1000 area on daily charts.

With these 4 areas updated before the start of each trading session, you know exactly what is taking place in the market, and since you do this every day, you also know how these developments relate to various scenarios that have unfolded in prior days.
In other words, you are not trading in a vacuum!

In this example, you know price action is tightening inside a 10-point range (980-970) that will likely provide a powerful breakout soon.

You know this range has developed above a major daily bracket high (950) and the breakout is holding, which likely means a continuation higher is setting up until proven otherwise.

You also know the gap lower for today's session is right to daily low support from yesterday, so you should be wary of continuation for any sell trades that develop near the open early.

This doesn't mean you won't take sell setup early, but it does mean that you should be ready to exit quickly if you don't sense immediate follow though, compared to other sell trade scenarios (i.e.-new intra-day 5-minute direction changes, etc.) that you likely will give more room to develop.

In this example, you should also be very excited to aggressively take long setups that develop early if an initial move lower fails. You know there is a wide overnight high and low range in place, so any long trades that develop early will likely carry all the way up to test the overnight high to start.

Do you see how pure mechanics and set up patterns by themselves can never capture the entire mental map you can create before trading even begins each day?

You are prepared to go short with caution. You are prepared to aggressively go long.

You have expectations according to the overall big picture that connects several days, and week's worth of price behavior, and will see how unfolding price action supports or rejects these expectations.

Although this may seem like a lot to digest, especially if you are a new trader, I contend that developing this comprehensive thought process each day actually makes trading more logical, and creates more certainty, than if you try to keep things rigid and inflexible.

However, like anything else you wish to master, this comprehensive thought process takes time and experience to blend together, and on top of this, you must realize that you will never get it correct 100 percent of the time.

TREND DAYS AND CONSOLIDATION BREAKOUTS

As mentioned, the E=MC2 method is much more than just mechanical buy and sell signals.

Instead it is an entire framework designed to take advantage of big picture conditions in the market.

Like any method that goes with the trend, E=MC2 does best when the market is trending from Point A to Point B intra-day.

Intra-day moves from point A to point B develop in several different ways.

You can have powerful end-to-end trend days. You can have trends that develop as breakouts from consolidation areas. You can have trends that develop after a market has reversed from obvious support or resistance area.

The first two types of trends (end-to-end trends days, breakouts from consolidation) are the most powerful and long lasting.

They also provide some of the best trading opportunities you will ever find!

Therefore, when you see either of these two conditions develop, why not be flexible and use the E=MC2 framework in an entirely different way.

Instead of exiting gains into the first 5000-swing of a move that is destined to be very powerful, why not hold onto the trade through a series of C1 and eventual C2/C3 price swings?

In some cases these trades can be held all day.

In other cases they can be held to obvious support/resistance targets in the big picture, or at least until a C2/C3 swing shows an obvious 1500 volume divergence etc.

In all cases the goal is to take advantage of a big picture opportunity by using the E=MC2 framework for passive and large gains.

E=MC2 - A Flexible Framework to exploit Price Trends - The E=MC2 approach is a consistent framework to enter and exit trades and is especially effective when it aligns with the big picture.

This means you don't want to see the mechanical E=MC2 signals fighting a key big picture support or resistance area, or an uncertain open.

For instance, a C1 momentum buy trade after the market has already made a long run to a major big picture resistance is low probability compared to a C1 trade that starts a new trend away from support/resistance, or is in the middle of a trend moving from Support point A to Resistance point B.

Also, you don't want to trade mechanical E=MC2 signals that are based on a conflicting 5000 18/89 trend set ups at the open that is based on overnight price action. (i.e. a C1 sell at the open when the market gaps down to a key big picture support area).

So there are times to avoid certain "mechanical signals" based on common sense big picture analysis.

Always remember, E=MC2 is designed to take advantage of various big picture trending scenarios where price is moving from Point A to Point B in the bigger picture.

If price has already moved from Point A to Point B, or possesses uncertain trending characteristics at the open etc, then E=MC2 set ups at these times carry lower probability than otherwise even if there is a "mechanical set up" on the charts.

The goal of E=MC2 is not to take every signal mechanical signal that sets up, but instead to be very patient and wait for the best big picture conditions to either take all the signals during that time, or use the E=MC2 framework as a whole to take advantage of trades that can be held for even bigger gains than the mechanical part of the method suggests.

I hope this point is very clear, and this means you always need to be thinking big picture first, mechanical set ups second!

There are many great mechanical E=MC2 trade set ups each day and each week- more than enough to meet weekly and monthly trading goals.

You don't have to catch every single move that takes place in the market.

Your goal is only to take the best of the best when big picture and mechanical set ups align in an effort to always keep the probabilities squarely tilted in your favor.

For instance, the 5000 18/89 open is always a random time to trade because it is based on overnight price action and nothing has really settled in on the day, however, there are times when opening trades are fine to take because overnight has price action has formed a solid looking trend that is poised to test either the overnight high or low, a key support/resistance area, and/or aligns with other big picture conditions (fade trades) that are in place from prior day price action as trading begins at 8:30.

You will gain a feel for the open with experience, but at the open always look at the overnight trend in place to be sure it looks clean, and then always know where an opening trade aligns relative to "testing" the overnight highs/lows, as well as where it sets up relative to any key big picture support/resistance point from past days.

If overnight price action (i.e. overnight highs) took price to a key pullback to swing point in a down trend, and a sell signal sets up first, this is a much better trade to take than a sell that sets up right after the market has gapped down to a major big picture support area.

If anything is unclear, stand aside at the open!

There are many times you shouldn't even begin trading until about 9:15 CST (45 minutes into the trading session). By then you'll have a much clearer picture of what the market is trying to do intra-day, how it has reacted to the overnight highs and lows, as well as any other key support /resistance points areas that may be relevant, etc.

You can also see if a trend day is forming or not (To be discussed shortly).

You can see if a strong volume ratio bias has formed, or not.

Again trading this method is all about probabilities. The consistent mechanical set ups are just one part of the probability picture, but not the only part, because the positive expectations for these signals are always directly tied to what the big picture of the market is trying to do.

Once the day has settled in a bit, unfolding market conditions and intra-day structure becomes much more clear than at the open.

I really want to emphasize that you don't have to take every single mechanical setup with this approach!

If you can remain patient and wait for clear signals that align with clear big picture conditions, you will trade much less (preferable) and do very well trading E=MC2.

You don't have to be in the market at all times.

Stand aside if anything is unclear or in conflict, even if you miss a price move.

In the end, the odds of your overall success are always best when you are patient enough only to trade when price is logically moving from point A to point B when considering the bigger picture. This occurs during (1) One-direction trend days, (2) Breakouts from consolidation areas, and (3) Before price has reached a big picture support/resistance area (consolidation high/low, or pullback to swing point).

PASSIVE GAINS – Having watched the E=MC2 mechanical framework and inter-related big picture price structure, day after day, for a long time, there are two scenarios where using the E=MC2 framework as a whole can greatly benefit your trading.

Just as there are times to bypass certain mechanical E=MC2 signals, there are times where there is a better approach than just trading E=MC2 purely mechanically.

When you see a **TREND DAY**, or a **CONSOLIDATION BREAKOUT**, there is no reason you can't bypass E=MC2 exits and hold trades longer for larger, passive gains in line with the big picture!

The best trades time and time again have always been these types of trades, and you should always be on the lookout for these two conditions so you can take advantage of them when they develop.

I believe it is always better to trade less rather than trade more.

My best trading days have almost always had very few trades. My worst trading days have almost always had too many trades.

This is why I prefer to be very selective to take only the best E=MC2 setups that align with the big picture. If I see an uncertain open I stand aside. If the market has made a long run to key support/resistance I stand aside with C1 trades. If I see chop developing (via an uncertain 5000 18/89 relationship to be discussed), I stand aside.

Another way to cut down on trades and maximize performance is play for big gains when conditions are right to do so.

If a trend day, or consolidation breakout develops, doesn't it make sense that the market is likely to run and make several new highs or lows on the day (trend day), or move to a new support/resistance areas where patient buyers and sellers are now located.

Why not enter E=MC2 trades early in these scenarios and then hold according to the E=MC2 framework of price trends that likely will exhibit C1 and then C2/C3 price behavior for a period of time.

You can't be afraid to ride winners with E=MC2!

Standard E=MC2 exits always try to hold on for big gains with 1500 price swings that move past the 5000 extreme, but if a big picture trend day or consolidation breakout presents itself, the most aggressive way to play this move is to actually go into a passive "hold" mode.

TREND DAY – A trend day, has three characteristics: (1) The Advance Decline line moves to an extreme early and stays there the whole day (+/-1200 area). (2) The Dow Jones average moves to an extreme and stays there all day (+/- 80-100 and holds). (3) The 5-minute chart shows clear one directional price action intra-day and all day. (This usually takes the form of trend direction/consolidation/trend direction/consolidation, etc.)

(Note – The Dow Jones Average is plotted with the symbol $INDU. The Advance/Decline line is calculated in TradeStation by opening a chart and plotting: $ADV- 1minute. Right click on chart, and select Insert Symbol, and add $DECL- 1 minute. Then select Insert/Indicator/Spread-Diff. You then can make the $ADV and $DECL plots very small, and focus on the reading of the "Spread Difference" plot which represents the advance/decline line. Sustained readings of +/-1200 denote trend type days.

While these 3 characteristics of a trend day are always the same, price action on a trend day is not always the same.

There can be both choppy/slow moving trend days, or much more smooth and cleaner price movement trend days.

Mechanically, E=MC2 will obviously do better in the less choppy type of trend day, and very choppy trend days can be frustrating with E=MC2 with many breakeven trades etc.

In both cases, you should end up with nice gains trading E=MC2 on trend days, but the very best way to trade a trend day is to simply hold on, sometimes all the way to the close, or at the very least to a key support/resistance area, or after E=MC2 has made some type of C2/C3 swing to a new intra-day high/low extension.

If you have never held onto a trade for a long time intra-day, this will take some getting used to psychologically.

Trend days by nature often move slowly and do their best to shake out the "weak hands" along the way as the trend just continues and continues and continues.

I have seen so many of these days over and over again that I just know you have to have faith to hold on thru the variety of price swings (key on the 5-minute charts for structure), and I hope you will learn to do the same.

<u>The very best trend day entry</u> – First, if you see a trend day in force (AD line, Dow, One direction price movement on 5-minute chart), you ***shouldn't*** take a mechanical 5000 18/89 setup that develops against the trend.

In fact, if the 5000 18/89 should ever briefly look like it is making a change against the trend, this is often the very best time to enter with the main trend of the day and hold!

This will often be at the top/bottom of a consolidation/pullback area (5-minute Trend line Pullback area with a false probe, etc.), and if you enter in this area and the market moves back with the main trend as expected, <u>you need to hold on for at least new highs or lows on the day!</u>

Here is a chart that highlights a trend day: (1) One directional price action on 5-minute chart (left) (2) AD Line that is strong/weak and holds all day (center) (3) Excellent 5000 18/89 entries during deeper pullbacks (right).

One of the best ways to enter during a trend day after a big picture pullback to support/resistance (arrows above), is to look for an aggressive C1-C type entry where volume crosses zero and holds on a pullback. Often you will get a brief 1500-pullback to the 89-ma at this time and you can enter aggressively here to get back in on the main trend of the day in an attempt to ride to new highs or lows on the day.

Trend days present a great opportunity for you to grow your account passively by holding onto positions (sometimes all the way to the close), and I hope with experience you will learn to recognize and take advantage of trend day trade opportunities when they develop.

Each trading session develops in a unique way. As the trading session unfolds, the first question always must be "Do we have a trend day, or a more normal range day in place?"

Remember, a trend day doesn't mean a single trend will remain in force all day, although it often does, and a range day doesn't mean the entire day will move back and forth between a high and low point all day long although this can happen too.

Trend days can eventually fail to move higher or lower, and reverse to a trading range.

Range days can be tight (intraday chop) and be setting up for a powerful breakout.

The main point is that there are two main overall ways to view each trading session when it comes to viewing the 5-minute/18-ma flow.

There is a very simple way to define classic trend days vs. range days.

CLASSIC TREND DAY - 3 characteristics (1) Very strong or very weak advance/decline line that starts and holds all day, (2) Strong or weak Dow that starts and holds all day, (3) Confirmation of trending 5-minute price structure that holds all day. Strong/weak advance/decline readings move and hold +/- 1200. Strong/weak Dow readings move and hold +/- 80.

Trending 5-minute price action means overall price action holds approx 50% pullbacks for the unfolding session range, and/or holds above/below any major sideways consolidation that may form in the trending direction.

RANGE DAY - Any day where advance/decline line doesn't start and hold above /below +/- 1200.

Important note - As mentioned, a range day does NOT mean price moves equally up and down inside a high and low range. All a range day means is that you look to follow the 5-minute price flow with the 18-ma. This can form as a mostly one-directional flow, two-directional flow, or some combination flow etc.

Trading a trend day - A trend day is viewed differently from a range day in terms of intra-day structure. With a trend day, you should look to trade only "with the trend" as long as 5-minute price action maintains an overall trend bias by not retracing more than 40-50 percent of the day's range, or breaks an obvious consolidation range that forms opposite the trend, usually after a trend swing extension failure of some kind.

In other words, you can have a new intraday bias from 5-minute price action and the 18-ma (5-minute price above 18-ma on a trend day down), but this is often the best time to look to get back with the main trend of the day, especially if this is the first deep pullback during the session where intra-day lows with the trend are very likely to be taken out.

You always need to know if you have a normal range day vs. trend day in place to guide your view of developing 5 minute/18-ma structure as it relates to trading decisions during the trading session. (Note- There are Non-classic trending-type days too which we will discuss)

DAY SESSION - PART 1

Before you know if you have a trend day or range day, you must first observe three developments to guide trading early in the trading session (1) Overnight Price action (2) Opening Gap and subsequent first price move of the day (3) Retrace of first price move of day en route to an intra-day bias.

Overnight Price action - The ES market trades in a day session between 8:30-15:15 CST, and also in an overnight session as well.

Although we don't look to trade all night long, overnight price action leading up to the 8:30 CST open often provides very valuable trading information (i.e. - overnight highs and lows for initial trade targets) and can also provide good trade opportunities when "pre-open" price action aligns with other big picture/short term developments.

Although we usually don't look to start trading until after 8:30 CST (to determine how to trade a gap open etc.) there are times to enter trades before the actual opening bell if overnight price structure and a short term price action confirms clear trending structure in place with a perfect price + volume pullback setup (Take small gains before 8:30!).

Opening Gap and first move of day - When the day session begins at 8:30 CST there is usually an opening gap from yesterday's close which is clearly seen as "space" on the 5-minute chart at 8:30 CST. (5-minute day session data only) There can be excellent continuation "with the gap" trades, or reversal "fade the gap" trades at the open.

Big picture analysis and price/volume action will guide the way to trade opportunities during the first hour of trading, and whichever way price first moves creates an initial price leg for the day.

This first price leg will often reach logical targets which include (1) Pullback to 5-minute 18-ma area (2) Pullback to normal 40-50-60 percent retrace of a price move continuing from yesterday (3) Follow thru move to test overnight highs or lows, and/or other big picture targets (4) Continuation move after a breakout from a consolidation area with unlimited direction potential.

Again, reading the big picture is the key to determining where an initial opening price move is likely to go.

Retrace of opening move - At some point after an opening move, price will pause, consolidate, and likely retrace. The type of retracement often sets the tone for the initial directional trading bias for the day.

If the first retrace holds approximately 50 percent of the initial price move, then expect a move to a new high/lows in the initial price move direction (and if a move to a new swing high or low fails, be on the lookout for a key reversal or perhaps chop conditions forming early on).

If the retrace of the initial price move carries beyond 50 percent of the initial price move, then look for one of two developments (1) A complete reversal past the gap open to set the initial directional bias for the day opposite the initial price move, or (2) A reversal move past the gap open that still may be just be a normal pullback from yesterdays price action which can create a bit of a conflict as to what the initial bias of the day truly is? (i.e. - gap down, a reversal move up that creates a 5-minute swing high (UP BIAS?) that is still an obvious normal retrace of a down move from yesterday (DOWN BIAS?)

There can be various trade setups that develop within the 3-phase "Gap, First Move, First Retrace," first hour, intra-day structure cycle.

The first move/first retrace can either be a (1) Big Picture counter-trend move if it develops way above the 5-minute trend line (2) Support/resistance bounce if it develops at the 5-minute pullback trend line area, or to a logical pullback area that includes yesterday's price action etc.

Day Session 1 Summary - (1) You can start with a good overnight trade entry setup before the open with a clear pre-open price + volume pullback that "continues" into the opening bell at 8:30 CST (2) Or, you can have either a Continuation or Fade the Gap trade right after the open at 8:30 CST (3) Then, you can look for a reversal trade from the initial price move either as a counter-trend move way beyond the 5-minute trend line, or as a pullback/bounce move from either the 5-minute trend line pullback area, 50 percent pullback area of the first move, or a normal pullback that includes yesterday's price action for an expected move back in the direction of the gap open.

Each of the Day Session 1 trade opportunities will become clear to you as you watch the 1500 price/volume chart early on, and integrate setups with big picture expectations that include yesterdays price action.

Here are several 5-minute charts showing examples of Day Session 1, 3-phase unfolding nature of price action (Gap Fade or Gap Continuation, First Move, First Reversal), highlighting some of the keys points mentioned above. As you review these examples, keep in mind that the first part of the trading session sets the tone for the bias to start the trading day.

(1) Gap down Continues **lower (2)** First move **ends at 2 (3)** Counter-retrace a bit past 50 percent of first move to 3, but right to 5-minute 18-ma pullback area **(4)** Expect move to new lows when price turns down. (Note- Look left on chart to find pullback to swing resistance at 3, and bracket support in area 4. This is also a range day vs. trend day, so even though intra-day structure is down with new lows at 4, trade with 5-minute/18-ma flow, and therefore a 5-minute turn up developing at right edge of screen can be powerful based on big picture/bracket support.

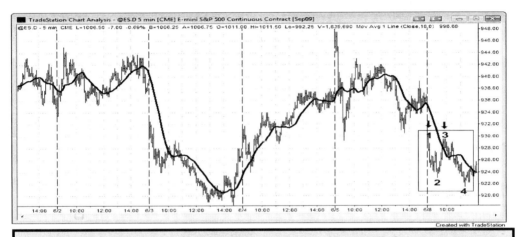

(1) Gap up Fade **moves lower (2)** First move **ends at 2 (3)** Counter-retrace from below 5-minute 18-ma that moves back above 18-ma to 3 and turns 5-minute bias up **(4)** Intraday bias remains up until price dips below 18-ma just prior to 4. 4 is safest place to short once 5-minute flow turns down. (Note -Look left on the chart to see how this day was dominated by strong resistance near bracket high in 1,3 area. Gap up breakout (1) failed, as did rally effort all day after counter-retrace (down arrow at 3). Big Picture alerts for much lower prices after open/failure back into bracket.

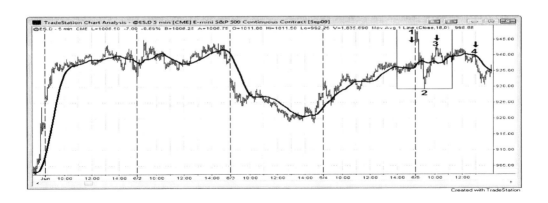

(1) <u>Gap down fade</u> moves up (2) <u>First move</u> ends at 2 (test of yesterday's high = resistance) (3) <u>Counter-retrace</u> at 2 to 50 percent retrace of initial move which holds at 3 but cannot follow through to new highs past resistance (highs of yesterday) even as initial 5-minute bias remains up (4) Price dips below 18-ma between 3 and 4 = look for shorts. (5) Following 5-minute/18-ma flow on range day sets up buy at 5 and up action for rest of day.

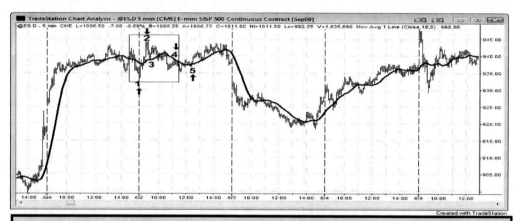

(1) Gap down <u>Continues</u> lower (2) <u>First move</u> ends at 2 (3) <u>Counter-retrace</u> moves past open to 3 and sets intraday bias "up with conflict" because 3 is <u>Up</u> with the 5-minute flow/move past intraday highs, but <u>Down</u> considering a normal retrace when looking at yesterdays price action. (4) Going with 5-minute/18-ma flow on range day sets up sell at 4 after a move below 18-ma (5) Going with 5-minute/ 18-ma flow on range day sets up buy at 5 after a move above 18-ma.

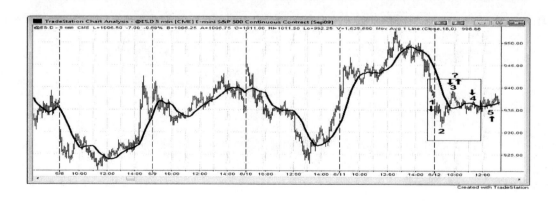

The first part of the trading session starting at 8:30 CST develops in 3-phases and includes a (1) Gap open, (2) First move of the day, (3) Retrace attempt of first move of day, all in the context of the big picture.

Some of the best trades of the day develop near the open because there is usually strong directional movement one way or the other, and when you learn to read the market in this 3-phase, multi-dimensional fashion, price moves near the open contain logical context.

Some trading approaches advocate "avoiding the open" because there is a lot of confusion with regard to overnight price action, gaps, etc. before intra-day structure settles into place, etc.

However, in many more cases than not, trading setups near the open, and in line with understanding the 3-phase nature of opening price movement, provides some of the best trades you will find.

KEY POINT - Look for trades during Day Session Part 1 based upon Gap-First Move-First Retrace development first, and 5000 18/89 structure development second!

The best way to do this is to key on trade set ups that contain volume ratio confirmation (above or below zero) to lead the way for the first trades of the day.

Then place these trade setups in the context of the 5000 18/89 trend in place as it relates to overnight price action.

For instance, if at 8:34, a 5000 pullback to the 18-ma with volume holding above zero sets up a "buy" in a 5000 C2 sell condition, consider this a C1-C fade the down gap buy, and this buy is especially meaningful if overnight price action has reached key support.

Or, if price gaps up in an 5-minute uptrend, and pulls back lower without a fade the gap sell setup in a C2 buy condition, then look for a normal C2 buy as long as volume holds above zero in line with the current 5000 18/89 buy condition that is in place at the open, and expect a test of overnight highs, etc.

DAY SESSION PART 2

When Gap-First move-First retrace price actions completes, you have an up or down bias to the start trading session. An initial up, down (or chop) bias can remain in place all session long, or it can change as intra-day structure unfolds.

Here are some unique Day Session 2 bias developments to monitor for:

Non-Classic Trend Day - A non-classic trend day develops when price action forms a clear one directional bias <u>without</u> confirmation from a strong or weak Dow, or Advance/Decline line.

The two most common forms of non-classic trend day price action are (1) Days that Gap strongly in one direction, and then trade in the opposite direction for the rest of the trading session (Often after an early big picture support/resistance test/failure that reverses) (2) Breakout of early consolidation area to form a main trend for rest of the day.

The implication for a non-classic trend day is that you can look to enter the first deep pullback on the non-classic trend day for an expected test of the highs/lows of the day.

Such entries set up when 5-minute price makes a deep pullback because the range of the non-classic trend day is wide. The key is to take the first deep pullback in line with the non-classic trend day, and not to be fooled by the deep 5-minute pullback.

> **The chart below shows a Classic trend day left (Strong confirmed trend day conditions from the start) and a Non-classic trend day right (powerful breakout from consolidation early), back to back. In both cases, the first deep pullback (sell arrows) were opportunities to enter with the main trend (down) for a test of intra-day lows (target) even though 5-minute price was making a deep pullback.**

Intra-day Trend Change - Intra-day trend changes take two main forms and often both happen at the same time (1) 5-minute price makes a new swing high or low (2) Volume ratio leads the change in trend with a new extreme.

Most significant, however, is when either of these two intra-day trend change events occur after a big picture support-resistance area has been tested. This can happen after a long trend has in place, after a test of the overnight high or low early in the trading session, or after a intra-day chop breakout fails and price moves the other way.

> **After a trend moves to key big picture support/resistance (lows on the chart below), look for a new volume ratio extreme to confirm a mechanical intra-day trend change, usually with a new 5-minute swing as well.**
>
> **In this example, price reaches big picture support, moves back above pullback to swing resistance, and volume ratio explodes off the upper end of the chart- a perfect confluence of events to confirm an intra-day trend change higher.**

Consolidation Breakouts - Consolidation breakouts take two distinct forms, and provide similar opportunities as trend days to hold trades for longer, bigger picture passive gains.

Big Picture Consolidation vs. Intra-day Consolidation – When you spread the 5-minute chart out to include many days of price action, you will see periods of time where overall price action moves sideways inside a distinct high/low consolidation range.

In these instances, note how the daily price chart may be overlapping for days at a time (2, 3, 4 days, etc).

This is big picture consolidation (often tough and limited intra-day trading), and an eventual breakout from consolidation is usually quite powerful to at least the next key support/resistance area, or pullback to swing point on the 5-minute, or daily chart etc.

When a breakout from big picture consolidation develops, there is no reason you can't hold trades passively for big gains to logical big picture targets.

If price moves into a prior consolidation area, expect price to move all the way to the opposite consolidation extreme.

If there is dead space on the charts after the breakout, expect price to move to the edge of a prior consolidation area in the distance- often a pullback to swing point on the higher timeframe chart. This could be "filling a gap," etc. Note the powerful downside breakout that occurs after 5-days of overlapping price action in the chart below after a big picture consolidation area breaks to the downside.

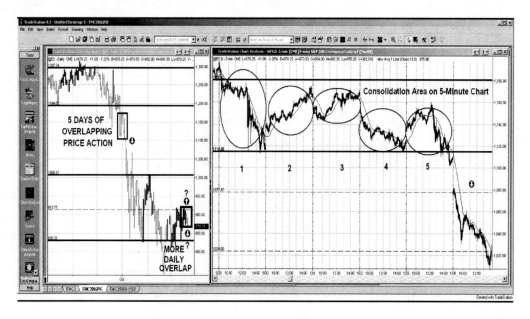

<u>Intra-day consolidation</u> - If you see chop develop intra-day (indicated by an uncertain 5000 18/89 flow - see chop section), you will see intra-day price action coiling between a distinct intra-day high and low price range that forms in the chop area with tightening volume extremes.

First, you should stop trading until the 5000 18/89 re-aligns. (This alignment can and often does take place <u>before</u> the actual high/low range breakout). Also remember, the longer intra-day chop (or a bigger consolidation area) continues, the more powerful the breakout will be, and again, there is no reason you can't hold trades for passive gains to big picture targets when this happens.

At the very least expect such a breakout to contain initial momentum (C1 setups), and then expect the first deep pullback to make a run to the highs or lows (C2/C3 extreme before pullback) established by the momentum swing.

Note below how intra-day chop within a consolidation area (3 examples), breaks and moves strongly to edge of larger consolidation support/resistance targets. Also, note the one pullback to swing resistance point (dashed horizontal line, point 4), that develops on the 5-minute chart as well.

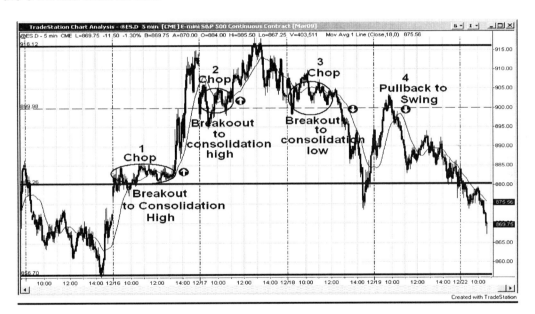

__INTRA-DAY CHOP__

Most trading approaches look to take advantage of directional price movement that results from an imbalance between buyer and seller. Even "counter-trend" moves exhibit an imbalance between buyer and seller to some degree.

There are times, however, where buyers and sellers move into a state of equilibrium.

Neither buyer nor seller has firm control, and as a result, price begins to drift sideways until activity dries up, and eventually price moves to a new area to seek out the buyers, or sellers who want to act.

The key to intra-day (or daily) sideways price movement, or "chop," is that buyer and seller activity is drying up in a narrow range and, is preparing to move to a new area!

Many traders try to play chop by shifting to a strategy of buying low and selling high in the chop range, but this is actually dangerous because price action is winding down in preparation for a breakout of this range.

Since, we can't recognize chop until after we are already in it, and since price is preparing to move to a new area sometime soon, it doesn't make much sense to try to play fading the high and low of the range once you recognize you are in chop, because the odds favor that time is running out in this area (perhaps a brief range trade or two for small gains to the chop edges are fine with a clear pullback entry).

Any small rewards of trading in chop are usually not worth the time and energy, and instead it pays to stand aside until a potential directional move develops out of chop.

Recognizing Chop – While obvious wide intra-day price action back and forth can represent "choppy price action," we define intraday chop as a 5-minute high-low price range that holds as the 5-minute chart begins to move sideways.

This can result in several 5-minute 18/ma flows that do not follow through as expected

If you look back to the 3 examples of intra-day chop in the previous chart, you can see how this 5-minute high-low range can take several forms.

In chop circle 1, 5-minute price first makes a leg higher, retraces to the 18-ma, and then fails to move to new highs for a period of time. Of course, the intraday bias with the 18-ma appeared to be up as chop was forming, but when new highs on the day couldn't be established (or new lows), you knew you were in chop, and this meant a likely powerful breakout was coming later on.

In chop circle 2, a gap down is followed by a retrace to the 18-ma trend line resistance area, and when a new low attempt fails, and then a new high attempt fails on a 5-minute move above the 18-ma, you know you are in chop.

In chop circle 3, price starts lower, and then moves all the way up above the 18-ma (intra-day bias up), but fails to make new highs on the day. Then price moves below the 18-ma (intraday bias down), and you can clearly see chop develop between the initial high and low of the trading session.

In this case, chop was wide enough where the intra-day down bias kept you on the right side of the eventual chop breakout which you expected to be powerful.

WHICH WAY WILL CHOP BREAK - Once intra-day chop becomes clear, we need to become patient with our trading until a trading trend re-establishes itself. We look to the 5000-chart with a 18 and 89 moving averages to get a hint when chop may be ending, and a trading trend may be re-emerging.

We use the 5000 chart in two main ways (1) To clarity of the 5000 18/89 moving average trend to distinguish good trending conditions vs. choppy trading conditions. (2) To consider entering a trend day positions on deep pullbacks to the 5000 89-ma area.

When we see chop develop between a sideways high-low range, this will almost always coincide with an uncertain 5000 18/89 relationship where the 18-ma moves back and forth thru a relatively flat 89-ma.

An intra-day chop breakout will almost always be on the verge of developing when the 5000 18/89-moving averages begin to realign with each other after chop has been in force for a period of time. This means the 5000 18-ma and 89-ma will start to move together in the same direction.

What to do in chop? – As soon as you recognize chop, the thing to do is trade cautiously (especially if you see a tight 5-minute high-low range in place) until the 5000 18 and 89-ma's begin to clearly move together in the same direction again.

This means that early in chop, recognize that pullback/volume trade setups may only take winning trades to the edge of chop, or short-term support/resistance.

Then as chop time expands, a chance for a breakout from a particular pullback trade is more likely.

NOTE - You don't necessarily have to wait for a breakout of the high-low range to trade. In many cases, a breakout of chop will go hand in hand with an early 5000 18/89-ma realignment, and the odds favor a trade setup that develops inside chop will powerfully breakout of chop, which can provide big gains if you continue to hold after the breakout.

Also, the longer chop is in force, the more powerful the breakout from chop usually is.

Sometimes you see the 5000 18/89 ma's flatten for half the trading day. On a wider scale, sometimes the 5-minute chart remains in a trading range for days at a time.

From a big picture standpoint, when a breakout of either of these two consolidation conditions takes place (Big Picture Daily consolidation , Intraday 5000 18/89 chop realignment), it will usually be extremely powerful and last for quite some time, so you should experience excellent gains if you hold onto trades in the breakout direction.

Again, breakouts from intra-day chop/daily consolidation areas represent some of the very best trading conditions and opportunities you will find!

CHOP EXAMPLE – **Price starts session in a strong intra-day downtrend (5000 chart, left, Fade the Gap 5-minute chart, right). Later the 5000 89-ma flattens as chop forms (Rectangles). Note how 5000 18-ma moves back and forth thru flat 89-ma. Note how the 5-minute bias, changes direction twice in the rectangle area. THIS DEFINES CHOP!**

Get defensive trading between the high and low price that forms chop until the 5000 18/89 moving averages realign and start to move in the same direction again after chop has been in force for awhile (circle next to rectangle = 500018/89 realignment). Breakouts from chop can trigger explosive moves (circles on both charts).

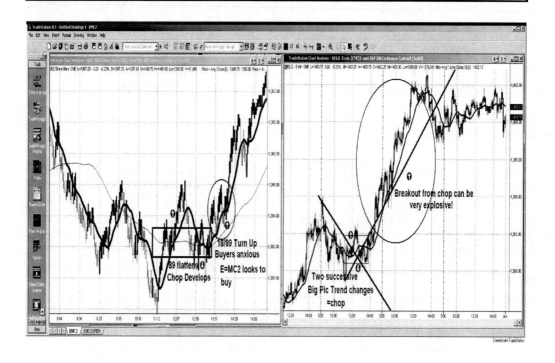

Choppy price conditions develop in all timeframes. A breakout from chop usually means a strong directional move will follow for the particular timeframe in question. It is important to learn to identify chop in your dominant trading timeframe early on so you can know when to "get defensive" until better trading conditions develop.

With patience and experience you will learn to view 5000 18/89 intra-day chop as nothing more than a temporary "lull in the action" that will soon be followed by excellent trading conditions and opportunities.

Summary – The trend day/consolidation breakout "hold for big picture gain opportunity" is just a part of the entire E=MC2 framework.

We know from 5000 18/89 structure that a good trend will likely have several C1 setups, and then at least one if not several C2/C3 pushes to new highs or new lows before the intra-day trend subsides (With an end-to-end trend day the intra-day trend never subsides).

Therefore, when you see these two big picture conditions develop, why not use E=MC2 structure to take advantage by holding for bigger gains!

THERE ARE NO BETTER GAINS IN TRADING THAN HOLDING ON DURING TREND DAYS, AND CONSOLIDATION BREAKOUTS!

Point A to Point B trend conditions don't present themselves all the time, but when they do, they are very powerful, and the flexible trader knows to consider taking advantage of them by holding onto small timeframe entries for big timeframe gains as described.

Expect price to work its way to logical big picture support/resistance target areas.

Expect E=MC2 structure to show several C1 and C2/C3 swings in the trend/breakout direction.

E=MC2 trading is all about big picture first, and mechanical set ups second.

The trend day, and consolidation breakout scenarios present some of the best trading conditions and opportunities you will ever find, and the very best way to take advantage of these conditions is to use the E=MC2 framework to hold onto trades for big picture passive gains.

DAY TRADING AND VOLUME

The E=MC2 approach ties together Price Structure in Multiple Timeframes, Volume, and Big picture analysis all in an effort to uncover trade setups that have a high probability for success.

If you have never considered "**Volume**" in day trading, this information will provide something new for you to consider. It certainly can be applied in many different ways.

We know that price vacillates all over the place, up and down, in the day timeframe. For those of you who have studied Market Profile the following will make a lot of sense. Assume price action up and down, is nothing more than price moving up and down to fill "big patient orders" in the market.

In other words, forget about trends, support, resistance, or anything else other than the fact that **whichever patient participant (buyer or seller) wins the tug of war battle, price is going to go there**. Conversely, if there are no patient orders in a certain price area, price will move to other areas to seek out where the patient orders are.

From this perspective, you can see how lower prices are often not "sellers pushing price lower," but rather price moving lower to find the big orders of patient buyers in control. Higher prices do not have to represent "buying pressure," but instead can be the only course price can travel, after "all" buyers have patiently bought lower, and now the only participant looking to act are patient sellers up above. Price must go higher in response to this imbalance.

Remember in any normal market, buyers prefer to buy low, and sellers prefer to sell high.

When you view price as nothing more than a vacillating entity looking to fill whichever patient participant is currently in control, volume analysis can be the shining light with regard to price movement, showing where the big orders are, when the big orders are drying up, and where price is likely to go next, either to seek out new participants, or continue on its path to satisfy the big orders of existing participants.

For trading purposes, we can keep it very simple.

We start by watching for a "volume extreme" to develop, and then we watch to see what happens next.

When you set a good measure for volume extreme (i.e.- Up and Down volume against price via the Volume Ratio Study), you will be able to see where volume on balance reaches an extreme, or finds an area where a level of big patient orders are in control of the market.

Therefore when a volume extreme is reached (Volume Ratio = +/- 10), either the patient sellers (high extreme) or patient buyers (low extreme) are in control, and price will do one of three things:

1. Immediately move to an opposite extreme to fill opposite big orders (i.e.- all big buy orders are filled low, price goes up to fill big sell orders high),

2. Hang around this area and continue to fill remaining big orders with help from the anxiety of opposite participant big orders that aren't being filled (i.e.- there are more big buy orders to fill at low prices, price rises but never reaches the point where the big sell orders are waiting, so sellers cave in and sell lower, while buyers remain patient and buy lower – a double push in price so to speak), or

3. Hang around in big order area, even though there are less and less big orders to fill (i.e. - Most big buy orders are filled low, and price moves back down to this area with fewer big buy orders remaining).

In case one, the swing in volume extremes means you are in a range with a single set of big orders above and below. This represents balance. Eventually all big orders will dry up in this range, price and volume extremes will contract, and price will have to move far out of this area to find new patient order participants.

In case two, a volume extreme is the beginning to discovering many big orders. This condition is accompanied by opposite participants who are impatient to wait for price to come back to fill their big orders. Therefore, a volume extreme in one direction is followed by a non-extreme in the other direction, and price moves back in the original extreme direction to fill more big orders, but in this case this push in price consists of both buyer and seller –one patient, the other anxious, or impatient.

In case three, a volume extreme discovers a decent amount of big orders, and price continues to hang around in the area to fill these orders without a push from opposite participant anxiety. (Opposite side patiently waits for price to eventually come back to them for now). Therefore, as price continues to fill all big orders of one participant in an area, volume slowly dries up signifying all big, patient orders in this area are filled (Volume/price divergence on chart), and price must either move back in the opposite direction to fill the orders of the patient participants waiting on the other side, or if not, price will move significantly further in the current trend direction because new patient orders are now way beyond this area after drying up.

This means a drying up of orders/volume in one area, can signal either a change of trend, or a forceful continuation of trend.

When you place this understanding in the context of not predicting how this will all unfold, but instead reacting to how it unfolds according to market structure, it can result in very powerful trading opportunities.

Here are a few examples:

1. If you see one volume extreme move to another volume extreme, know activity is starting to dry up in this area, and price is getting ready to move to a new area altogether. <u>The trading implication is to stop taking new trades until you can recognize which patient big picture participant will win the tug of war battle waiting for price to come to it (See 5000 18/89 realignment in "Chop Section").</u>

2. Strong volume extremes, followed by a lack of opposite volume extremes, means a ***continuation*** of current price direction is likely (big orders on both sides contributing to the continuation as one side is anxious, the other side patient). <u>The trading implication is to look to enter new trades on price pullbacks that aren't experiencing opposite volume extremes.</u>

3. Strong volume extremes followed by price continuation "unaccompanied" by new volume extremes, means the patient orders are drying up in this area, and the other side is patiently waiting for price to come back to it. <u>The trading implication means to either exit existing positions, aggressively enter counter-trend trades if other appropriate big picture conditions are in place, or if a counter-trend move doesn't develop, know price will move significantly further in the current trend direction.</u>

With E=MC2 we keep it very simple and broad. When Volume Ratio makes an extreme of +/- 10 that participant is in control until an opposite volume extreme is reached.

Therefore if +10 is reached, the patient sellers are in control, and price is expected move higher until either −10 is reached, or new price highs are met by lower volume extremes (i.e. Volume divergences)

Again, a volume divergence doesn't always mean a price reversal is imminent.

Instead a volume divergence can mean a pause, and strong continuation.

That's why we always wait for either a good counter-trend setup to develop, or the 5000 18/89 trading trend to change direction before entering trades in a new direction.

Also, when a volume extreme moves from one extreme to the other this can signal a new participant in control (New Trend), **OR** it may signal balance is entering the market at the present time (Chop, or a Consolidation Pause during a trend day)

Therefore, If you start watching what happens to price <u>after volume extremes and volume divergences are generated</u>, this will open up a whole new way for you to classify price behavior in the context of what is unfolding in the market according to prices' main role- filling big orders in the market according to the balance or imbalance of big orders that exist, or according to whichever market participant (buyer or seller) is displaying the most patience, or anxiety at the given moment.

You do not have to predict what will happen. If two volume extremes are reached back to back and a new trend doesn't unfold, realize you are entering a balance period and price will move strongly away from this area in time.

Or, if a volume divergence unfolds and price doesn't reverse, expect continuation.

The main use for Volume with E=MC2 is to maintain a trend bias that confirms taking good C1, C2, C3 setups with the trend. (i.e. If a -10 is reached, continue to look to the short side until either an opposite + 10 is reached, or price has moved to expected big picture support target areas).

Volume 1 - The trading range - Price will eventually move to a new area after patient buyers and sellers in this area dry up.

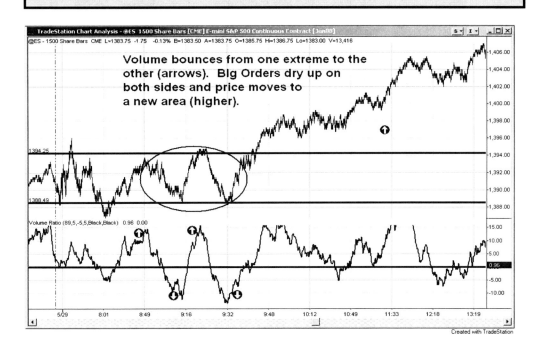

Volume 2 – Continuation - Volume extreme lower followed by lack of opposite volume extreme higher. Original price push continues and includes both participants - one side anxious, one side patient.

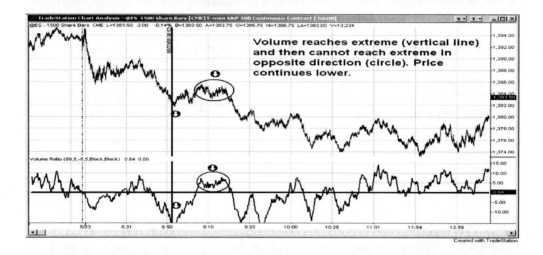

Volume reaches extreme (vertical line) and then cannot reach extreme in opposite direction (circle). Price continues lower.

Volume 3 – Divergence – Volume extreme followed a price probe back to area with no volume extreme. No more patient participants here for now, so price either changes direction to seek out patient participants on the other side, or continues much further in current trend direction.

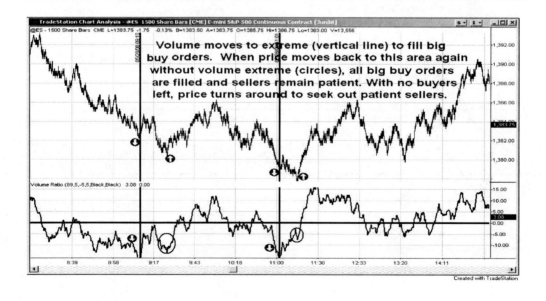

Volume moves to extreme (vertical line) to fill big buy orders. When price moves back to this area again without volume extreme (circles), all big buy orders are filled and sellers remain patient. With no buyers left, price turns around to seek out patient sellers.

PRICE TREND AGAINST A MOVING AVERAGE

We plot moving averages on the charts for several reasons. One important reason is to visually see how "price trends relative to the slope of the moving average."

Price action in trading is everything, not moving average lines.

Moving averages are <u>NOT</u> magical lines that price needs to "bounce off of, remain above/below" or anything like that. Moving averages simply provide a visual trend guide.

Therefore, start to view price action in terms of price trending relative to the slope of the moving average line. This means price may probe the moving average line on pullbacks, etc, but as long as you can detect an overall price trend in place (about 45 degrees), this is what is most important.

PRICE TRENDING WITH A MOVING AVERAGE LINE REPRESENTS ONE OF THE ARTFUL ASPECTS OF ATTEMPTING TO "READ THE MARKET."

For example, in the 1500-volume share bar chart below, note the visual trend lines we draw relative to the way 1500-price action trends with the LT 89-moving average line.

You need to perform the same visual trend line determination for the 5000 chart (relative to 89-ma) and the 5-minute chart (relative to the 18-ma).

This means it will very important to compress your charts an appropriate amount so you can look back and see a large range of price/moving average data together at the same time.

<u>1500 CHART-VOLUME RATIO HOLDING ZERO AREA ON A PULLBACK</u> - While price action is everything in trading, the fuel behind most sustainable price moves is volume.

The Volume Ratio indicator provides an excellent way to measure the ratio of up to down volume contained in a price move.

Sometimes an extreme Volume Ratio reading (+/- 10) represents the onset of strong price action to follow. Sometimes an extreme Volume Ratio reading represents the high and or low price area for the dominant cycle wave in force.

Our concern for trading purposes is a "Volume Ratio that holds the zero area during a price pullback within an established trend."

Using the same 1500-volume share bar chart as before, note the (1) Pullbacks to the 89-ma trend line area where (2) Volume ratio holds the zero area (vertical lines). These conditions represent our best trade entry areas for pullback trades.

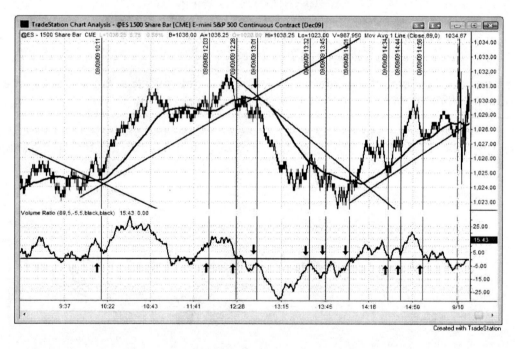

Here are a variety of trade examples that highlight 1500 trend + Volume ratio pullback confirmation to put odds in your favor relative to trade selection.

In these examples, we examine the 1500-chart and the big picture 5-minute chart at the same time.

OPENING GAP CONTINUATION SELLS USING PULLBACK ENTRY AT OPEN BASED VOLUME RATIO CONFIRMATION

OPENING GAP FADE - LONG TRADES OFF KEY SUPPORT WITH VOLUME RATIO CONFIRMATION (ARROWS 1 AND 2)

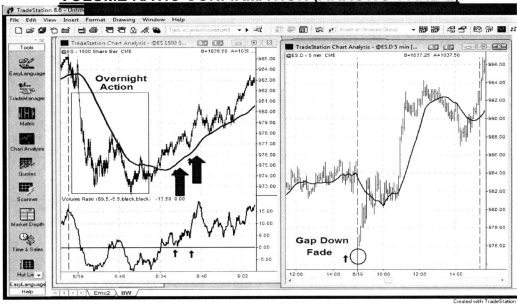

PRE OPEN CONTINUATION (ARROW 1 LEFT) AND GAP FADE (ARROW 2 LEFT) BASED ON VOLUME CONFIRMATION

FIRST MOVE REVERSAL AT BIG PICTURE PULLBACK RESISTANCE - C1-C ENTRY

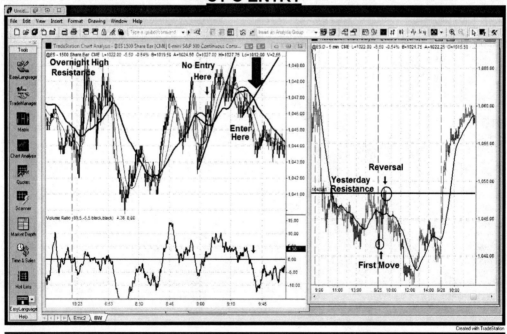

FIRST MOVE REVERSAL AT BIG PICTURE RESISTANCE) - C1-C COUNTERTREND ENTRY

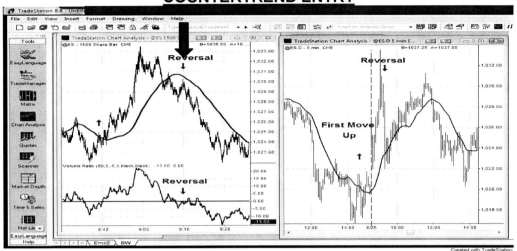

1500 "MOMENTUM" PULLBACK ENTRY (SHALLOW 5-MINUTE PULLBACK)

FIRST 1500 PULLBACK ENTRY WITH 'NEW' 5-MINUTE TREND
(VOLUME RATIO LEADS WAY AFTER FAILURE AT HIGHS)

1500 MA PULLBACK + 5-MINUTE 18-MA PULLBACK
AT SAME TIME

DEEP PULLBACK (TREND DAY) EXAMPLES

5000 PULLBACK 89-MA - 5- MINUTE PULLBACK TO 18- MA
(OPPOSITE VOLUME EXTREME = BEST TREND DAY ENTRY AREA)

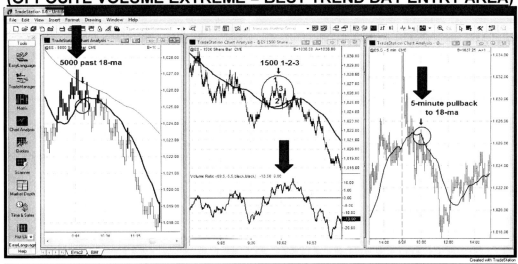

5000 PULLBACK TO 89-MA, DEEP 5-MINUTE PULLBACK
(OPPOSITE VOLUME EXTREME = BEST TREND DAY ENTRY AREA)

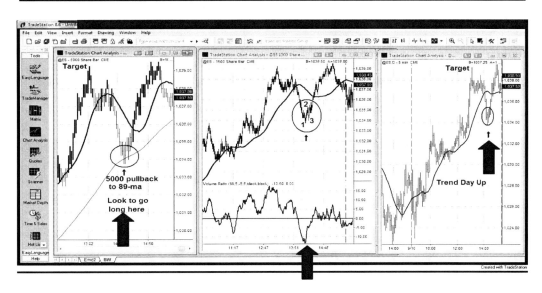

DAY TRADING AND GAMBLING

I had a fellow trader ask about this topic, and thought it was important enough to share my thoughts.

At its core, day trading is very similar to any other form of gambling in the sense that you are making bets (the trade), and you can win or lose.

Also, psychologically day trading can become addictive, and psychologically you can do a lot of damage to your account, and to your family, and to everything else if you are not very, very careful.

So that's the negative aspect of day trading that everyone can rightly point to.

The positive aspect of day trading is that if you can actually embrace day trading as a form of gambling, you can take control over it, and turn it around in your favor (with certain knowledge and mental strength), although this is a tough task for many who try.

From a pure gambling perspective, the big difference between day trading betting, and say football betting, is that in **day trading betting you can take your bet off the table if you are not winning the game!**

In other words, say you bet $100 on a football game, and your team goes down 2 touchdowns in the first quarter. How nice would it be to say, "I don't like my bet anymore, can I please have $90 back."

In another game, your team may be up 3 touchdowns, so you keep that bet on the table. Or what about a game, where its tied with 4 minutes to go, and it's a 50-50 outcome, and you are allowed to pull your bet off the table and walk away breakeven instead of possibly losing $100. Do you think you could devise a betting strategy to win football betting with these rules?

You can bet the favorites for every football game, watch the games, and change your bet as the game unfolds with the option to win the full amount if you win, and pull most of your money off the table according the developing score of each game.

Actually it's even better than this. In day trading, you can win more than your original bet when you are right. Can you imagine betting $100 on a football game, and if it's a blowout in your favor, you win $500!

So, with such rule possibilities in day trading, the odds can move greatly in your favor, but only if you have the discipline make the best bets to start and then pull your money away at the right time from bad bets, and learn to take advantage and maximize your good bets. That's why day trading, if done correctly, is a much better form of gambling than anything else.

(1) The arena offers many good bets, meaning plenty of winning games (trades) to bet on (2) You have control to take back most of your bet if you're wrong (3) You can win more than you put up, when your right.

So, if you can actually embrace the notion that day trading is gambling, and that you're gambling in an arena where you can structure the rules in your favor to win, you'd be better off with that mentality than denying that day trading is gambling- instead thinking you are making trades based on some superior knowledge you have about what is going to happen next in the market.

In fact, it is when you think you have control over the market, and can predict outcomes, etc, that all the damaging aspects of gambling enters the day trading arena, because you get stubborn, and feel you are "right" with all your decisions, and in the end, this prevents you from making the good flexible "rule" judgments that allows you to put the odds in your favor to win- **the rules that allow you to control the nature of your bets during the flow of the game!**

Therefore, if you have a sound plan in place to select only good bets, understand how and when to take advantage of very flexible betting rules, and then have the discipline to understand that this is what it takes to win, and stick with it, then day trading gambling offers much better odds, and more opportunities for success than any other form of gambling.

With that said, because you are going to be tempted to go in other directions (Stubbornness, "I'm right" mentality, Inability to stick with proper odds, taking high risk vs. low risk chances, etc.) or things that can make you very successful in other ventures in life, but not in trading, at the very least you need to respect the damage day trading can cause, and start out by betting with money you can afford to lose, in case you can't implement the proper gambling mindset to succeed.

Or, if you feel you understand how to put the day trading odds in your favor to win, and want to give it a shot, then at least start very small, and do everything in your power to set up your complete gambling plan ahead of time, stick with it, and still start with a small amount to risk until you are sure you can make it work.

In the ES, E-mini market, for example, if you start with $5000, and go very slow to start, and really have all your bases covered with regard to the gambling plan you will implement, you should be able to easily risk no more than $2000 to find out if you have what it takes to be successful.

And if not, like good day trading itself, you can decide to walk away from the arena, and pull the rest of your bet without too much damage.

So, you don't have to throw your life away in order to find out if this can work for you, but if you aren't careful, and really don't take the time to understand the <u>probability</u>

<u>nature of the day trading game</u>, you could end up throwing your life away, because day trading, like any form of gambling, does present serious risks.

Everyone should read Mark Douglas –"Trading in the Zone" for an excellent explanation about probability in trading among other things.

The good news with day trading gambling risks is that you can structure the rules to put the odds in your favor to win. Other forms of gambling are fixed, and just don't allow you to do this.

That said, it is the very flexibility to set your own rules that often gets the day trader in trouble, which is shame, because the day trading arena does offer tremendous opportunity from an odds standpoint if you can take the time to learn how to play the game the right way.

The E=MC2 framework and approach recognizes that day trading is nothing more than a probability game, and as a result, offers one very good way to play the day trading gambling game the right way.

CONFIDENCE TO TRADE E=MC2 FOR A LIVING

A lot of ground has been covered in this material. Consider what is behind a basic C1 buy trade.

The 5000 18-ma is heading up. 1500-price action likely shows a higher/high and is trending with its 89-ma. Volume Ratio is positive. The intra-day trading trend may be up or down, and each scenario provides different expectations for the trade. Finally, the intra-day trend is part of a bigger picture in play that also may provide additional expectations for the trade.

Furthermore, bridging together all these individual parts that make up a particular trade is the "easy" part of trading! This difficult part of trading is threefold-fold: (1) Having the fearlessness to take the trade (2) Managing the exit of trade according to a combination of what happens immediately after the trade is entered in conjunction with monitoring big picture conditions that may allow you to hold for bigger gains when good trades develop in good big picture environments. (3) Understanding how all the wins and losses in the trading game come together in the end to make money.

Fearlessness to take trades – You will only be able to successfully trade this method (or any other method) when you can learn to accept small losses and you can learn to feel comfortable placing every trade into a much bigger probability picture of what you are trying to accomplish.

We intuitively know we <u>must take small losses</u> to trade successfully.

As stated earlier in this book, most of us have taken large losses before, and have seen how difficult it is to recover from large losses. If you take a large loss and continue to stick with your trading plan, it takes a long, long time to catch up.

The best way to learn to accept small losses and maintain steadfast confidence in your trading plan is to set up a complete trading plan ahead of time with <u>realistic goals and expectations</u>.

You need to develop a trading plan that severely curtails high-win expectations, and this is very exciting to do because this sets the stage for a much more realistic trading blueprint.

Eliminate catching the best trade of each day - Assume you will miss the best trade every day, even though the odds are slim you will miss the very best trade for all 20 days during the month.

1-pt/day average – Lower your trading goals and try to make 3-points a day but accept a 1-point per day average. This becomes a very realistic and very reasonable goal to achieve.

Remember, many traders look at ES volatility and think they can make 10- points a day, every day. You must work with "realistic" expectations, which includes time to catch up if the first trades of the day lose.
Also keep in mind, there are many different ways to reach a 1-point per day average.

First, if you have time to trade all day, and try to take the best setups, the odds strongly favor you can take a 10-points worth of volatility, and end up with a 1-point/day net outcome.

Remember, you will have losing trading days.

If you adopt a 3-pt/day trading plan, you can end up winning 3 points on 15 days of the month, and losing 3-pts/day on 5 days of the month.

If you follow the rules of E=MC2, and stick with E=MC2 through thick and thin, this is a conservative and realistic winning/losing plan.

Even if you lose money on some days with E=MC2, if you are appropriately selective you should still come close to averaging 30 pts per month with 6 trades per day:

15(3) – 5(3)= 30 x 50 = $1500. Commissions = 120 X 5 = $600 (6 trades a day average), or a net of $900, or $9000 for 10 contract trading.

Keep in mind, the best part about this trading plan, is that it is conservative and realistic to start!

On many days, the notion of making 3-points a day and stopping is very limiting.

Let's say you have a great breakout of a consolidation condition, or a trend day.

We have discussed over and over again how you can, and should try to hold for substantial gains in very favorable big picture environments.

<u>Why stop at 3-points when you can make 15-points when conditions scream out for you to do so</u>?

Also, on the winning side, if the market is clearly moving from Point A to Point B in the big picture, there is no reason you shouldn't continue to take most of the mechanical trades that set up during this run, from one set up to the next. This also can lead to very nice gains beyond 3-points.

Then there are the losing realities of trading E=MC2. Some days you get off to a great start, and other days you get off to a poor start.

While each trade outcome is almost always directly tied to how close your trading aligns with big picture conditions, the fact is sometimes you start out behind, or make trading mistakes, and need to try to catch up during the day.

So the realities of trading are that you sometimes are in excellent big picture conditions that provide for large gains (Trend days, Breakouts of consolidation, etc.)

Sometimes you start out nicely ahead on the day (Fearlessly taking trades that align with big picture conditions as price moves from Point A to Point B in the big picture). Sometimes you start out behind on the day, and are in a position of trying to catch up for the day in some fashion (Taking trades not in line with big picture conditions, taking trades before you recognize chop settling in, taking trades at an uncertain open, or just taking trades with choppy price action in otherwise good trading conditions).

You must expect your returns to be more scattered than a neat 3-points per day average over the course of any given week!

Therefore, you need to be more focused on weekly, and monthly goals, rather than daily goals when it comes to trading.

You especially need to place your focus on where you end up at the end of the month.

With a large variety of trading options and outcomes available each day, you need to start with a realistic trading goal of trying to make approximately 20-30 points a month, knowing that if volatility is very high for a given month much greater returns are possible, and if volatility is low there may be some months where lower outcomes result.

DAY- TO- DAY DECISIONS – On the way to 30-points a month there will be a variety of daily outcomes and trading decisions to make.

One of the most difficult things to teach in trading is to describe how much to trade each day, and when to continue trading, and when to stop trading relative to the open ended environment you are in, and the trading goals you have in place.

The best I can do is share with you what I find works best. Much of this you will simply have to experience on your own to truly understand.

I have found the best way to meet weekly and monthly goals is to stop trading at some point when you are ahead on the day, continue trading when you are behind on the day in an effort to get to some small win or small loss on the day, and continue trading aggressively when ahead on the day when big picture conditions scream out for you to do so.

Also, always look for trend days and consolidation breakout conditions (daily, intra-day) to stay aggressive and hold for big gains.

I know these conditions by themselves offer the best opportunities of the month and I try to stay very aggressive trading on these days in one form or another.

Finally, there are just bad trading days. You do everything to avoid these days (avoiding trades in conflict with the big picture, avoid trades in chop, avoiding trades after a trend has run a long way and is losing momentum, avoiding trades without a solid volume ratio bias etc.) but it's simply impossible to avoid poor trading days altogether, and sometimes you can do everything right and price action just isn't in sync with the trading timeframes you are looking to exploit with E=MC2.

Again, you have so many options when trading day to day as a variety of trade conditions and setups present themselves over and over again.

Trading outcomes are random and widely dispersed in terms of size and scope.

Therefore, it is best to control your trading based upon the big picture condition of the market, and the actual trading results that develop throughout the trading session.

You have to develop a feel for this over time, but I can tell you there is definitely a **time to stop trading on days when you have gains**, or at least protect as much of these gains as possible, and take very limited risk going forward. There is also a time to stay aggressive, and this always relates to big picture conditions (trend days, breakouts, price clearly moving from Point A to Point B).

Finally, you just have to accept that not every day can, or will be profitable. Do your best to keep losses minimal on these days, wipe the slate clean, and come back strong the next day.

As long as you can keep losses relatively small, there will always be great trading conditions right around the corner, and in the end trading is a marathon much more than a sprint, so where you end up at the end of the month is much more important than where you end up at the end of each trading day.

MAKING A LIVING WITH E=MC2

Here is a theoretical, aggressive, one year plan to make a living trading E=MC2 using conservative estimates.

At 30-points a month avg. starting with a $5000 account, assuming that once you develop trading consistency, you will need $3000 in your account for every contract you trade (10 contracts = $30,000), here is a way to build up your account for a 12-month period if you can develop consistency.

ONE YEAR E=MC2 TRADING PLAN

	# Contracts	$/Month	$Balance
Month 1	Learn Method	0	5000
Month 2	Break even Trading	0	5000
Month 3	1	900	5900
Month 4	1	900	6800
Month 5	2	1800	8600
Month 6	3	2700	11300
Month 7	3	2700	14000
Month 8	4	3600	17600
Month 9	5	4500	22100
Month 10	5	4500	26600
Month 11	5	4500	31100
Month 12	10	9000	40100

If you adopt such a plan, you can see how realistic estimates of performance (30-points a month average) can result in earning $9000 per month in one years' time trading 10 contracts at a time.

At the very least, I hope this information sets you on the path to understanding realistic goals and expectations when trading, and shows you the importance of setting up a very specific trading plan ahead of time, before you ever begin to trade for real.

Only with such a plan will you have the <u>confidence to trade with the consistency required</u> to succeed at game that is all about probabilities in the long run.

You will do very well trading E=MC2 if you start out with realistic trading goals, and adjust these trading goals over time as necessary.

Many traders never take the time to establish realistic trading goals, and then see how their trading plan fits within these goals (assuming they have a solid trading plan to begin with).

Without trading goals, and a trading plan, traders develop a distorted view of trading reality, which often leads them to a host of distorted trading decisions.

If you can start out with a realistic view that successful trading is all about numbers, probabilities, and consistent execution over time, then you will start out with an excellent chance to succeed if you can develop the confidence to apply the rules of your trading plan over and over again.

E=MC² TRACK RECORD

Here are results for the E=MC2 track record for one year (approximately 5000 trades), including a detailed breakdown for one month- designed to highlight <u>the positive expectancy for this approach</u>.

This is a running diary of all setups that develop in order, where each trade exits according to whichever exit trigger develops first. Then, once a trade is exited you look to enter the very next trade that develops next. <u>There are no C1-C counter-trend trades listed in this track record.</u>

Once you understand the continuous trade flow, the key becomes selecting the very best trades according to developing market structure, trading goals etc. For example:

<u>Choppy price action</u> - look to take C1 pullbacks that develop with volume ratio confirmation with an expected move to the upper or lower end of the range in place (Consider early exits). Then, if range conditions tighten and coil, look to be very aggressive on the first breakout, or when the 5000 18/89 starts to re-align in the breakout direction. Consider holding breakout trades for an initial momentum move, and then for at least one C2/C3 pullback with a push to test momentum extreme.

<u>Directional Price Action</u> - (Trend days, Smooth up/down price action) When price action flows smoothly, E=MC2 is very easy to trade. Take the first, and perhaps second C1 in a row. Always look to take a deeper C2/C3 pullback trades for a test of the recent high or low in place. (Especially stay aggressive as long as Volume ratio confirms pullbacks).

Then, look for intra-day trend changes. (New 5-minute price swings and Volume ratio reversal confirmation is often key). Be aggressive on first trades after a trend change.

<u>Trend days</u> - The best trades with E=MC2 are deep C3 pullbacks on trend days that appear to be changing intra-day trend. Look to enter aggressively on the pullback (even before 1-2-3 pattern back in trend direction) and look to hold trades for at least new high or lows on the day, or even to big picture support/resistance if clearly indentified.

Also, always look for <u>countertrend trades</u> (not listed on this trade flow) which are always best after opening gaps, high/low failures, or long intra-day trend runs that change trend with volume ratio reversal confirmation.

<u>Volatility</u> - Finally, as the attached trading diary shows, E=MC2 (like most trading methods) always works best when volatility increases, so stay very aggressive when intra-day price ranges expand.

The exciting part of E=MC2 is that it <u>does well in all conditions</u> when you start with modest trading goals and expectations. You can do very well with this approach from a return on investment standpoint if you average just 1-ES point a day! With appropriate integration of Big Picture, Intraday Structure, Mechanical Trade Flow, and Volume Confirmation, this goal should be very easy for you to achieve.

Month/Year	Days	Points
01/09	20	+115.75
02/09	19	+56.75
03/09	17	+100.25
04/09	21	+227.50
05/09	20	+125.50
06/09	22	+94.25
07/09	21	+94.25
08/08	21	+74.50
09/08	21	+492.25
10/08	23	+829.00
11/08	16	+360.75
12/08	18	+215.75

TRADING DIARY FOR DECEMBER 2008

DATE	12-01-08a	GAP	+0.00 UP IN UPTREND	DISTANCE TO: T/L	0.00	BIG PIC EXT

	TRADE TYPE		ENTRY		EXIT	

#	B/S	C1	C2	C3		TIME	ENTRY		PT	Initial Stop	Adj Stop	BE+1	Vol Div	Mom/ Exten.		+/-	Cu
1	Sell	x				831	868.00		x				863.50			4.50	4.5
2		x				839	863.25		x		861.00					2.25	6.7
3		x				842	859.75		x			859.50				.25	7.0
4		x				846	859.50		x			859.25				.25	7.2
5		x				850	857.25		x			857.00				.25	7.5
6		x				856	855.00			856.50						(1.50)	6.0
7		x				858	855.25		x			855.00				.25	6.2
8		x				900	853.75		x	856.00						(2.25)	4.0
9			x			906	851.75			854.50						(2.75)	1.2
10			x			920	852.75			854.50						(1.75)	(.50
11			x			925	852.75		x			852.50				.25	(.2
12		x				929	851.50		x		850.50					1.00	.75
13		x				934	850.75			852.25						(1.50)	(.7
14		x				937	851.25		x		852.00					(.75)	(1.5
15			x			948	851.25		x				847.25			4.00	2.5
16			x			1026	846.75		x			846.50				.25	2.7
17			x			1100	847.00		x			846.75				.25	3.0
18			x			1120	845.25		x				843.00			2.25	5.2
19		x				1136	842.50		x			842.25				.25	5.5
20		x				1145	841.50			843.25						(1.75)	3.7
21		x				1148	842.50		x		841.50					1.00	4.7
22		x				1159	840.25			842.00						(1.75)	3.0
23			x			1242	843.50			846.00						(2.50)	.50
24			x			1245	842.75		x			842.50				.25	.75
25		x				1254	841.00		x			840.75				.25	1.0
26			x			1302	841.75		x			841.50				.25	1.2
27			x			1315	841.50		x		840.00					1.50	2.7

DATE 12-01-08B **GAP** -00.00 DOWN IN DOWNTREND **DISTANCE TO:** T/L +0.00 **BIG**

| | | | TRADE TYPE | | | | ENTRY | | | | | EXIT | | |

#	B/S	C1	C2	C3	TIME	ENTRY	PT	Initial Stop	Adj Stop	BE+1	Vol Div	Mom/ Exten.	+/-	Cumn
28	Sell			x	1336	842.00			844.25				(2.25)	.50
29		x			1412	841.00	x			840.75			.25	.75
30		x			1417	840.00	x					834.50	5.50	6.25
31		x			1429	834.75	x			834.50			.25	6.50
32		x			1432	833.75	x		833.25				.50	7.00
33		x			1436	831.75	x					822.75	9.00	16.00
34		x			1448	825.25	x			825.00			.25	16.25
35			x		1451	823.25	x		820.25				3.00	19.25
36		x			1455	820.25	x					815.75	4.50	23.75
37														

DATE 12-02-08a **GAP** +0.00 UP IN UPTREND **DISTANCE TO:** T/L 0.00 **BIG PIC EXT**

| | | | TRADE TYPE | | | | ENTRY | | | | | EXIT | | |

#	B/S	C1	C2	C3	TIME	ENTRY	PT	Initial Stop	Adj Stop	BE+1	Vol Div	Mom/ Exten.	+/-	Cu
1	Buy			x	851	823.00	x			823.25			.25	.25
2	Sell	x			856	820.50	x		820.25				.25	.50
3	Buy	x			917	834.00	x			834.25			.25	.75
4		x			919	834.25	x	832.25					(2.00)	(1.
5		x			921	834.25	x			834.50			.25	(1.
6			x		924	835.75	x		836.00				.25	(.7
7			x		930	836.00	x			836.25			.25	(.5
8		x			934	837.00	x			837.25			.25	(.2
9		x			939	838.75	x			839.00			.25	0
10		x			945	838.25	x			838.50			.25	.25
11				x	1024	837.25			834.75				(2.50)	(2.
12		x			1033	83875			837.25				(1.50)	(3.
13			x		1046	838.50	x		841.00				2.50	(1.
14		x			1059	842.75	x	841.00					(1.75)	(3.
15		x			1105	843.00	x		841.75				(1.25)	(4.
16		x			1114	842.50	x		846.00				3.50	(.7
17		x			1135	846.75			844.75				(2.00)	(2.
18	Sell	x			1244	837.00	x		834.75				2.25	(.5
19		x			1256	833.50	x		833.75				(.25)	(.7
20		x			1259	832.75	x				826.00		6.75	6.0
21		x			1311	823.75			826.75				(3.00)	3.0
22			x		1317	826.00	x			825.75			.25	3.2
23		x			1320	823.50	x			823.25			.25	3.5
24		x			1322	822.00	x		820.50				1.50	5.0
25		x			1329	821.00	x	822.50					(1.50)	3.5
26		x			1330	821.75	x	823.00					(1.25)	2.2
27	Buy	x			1402	830.25			828.00				(2.25)	0

DATE 12-02-08B **GAP** -00.00 DOWN IN DOWNTREND **DISTANCE TO:** T/L +0.00 BIG

TRADE TYPE — ENTRY — EXIT

#	B/S	C1	C2	C3	TIME	ENTRY	PT	Initial Stop	Adj Stop	BE+1	Vol Div	Mom/ Exten.	+/-	Cum
28	Buy		x		1417	829.25	x					839.50	10.25	10.25
29		x			1428	841.25	x		843.25				2.00	12.25
30		x			1433	842.00	x		845.75				3.75	16.00
31		x			1438	845.25	x	843.25					(2.00)	14.00
32			x		1442	843.75		840.50					(3.25)	10.75
33				x	1454	842.00				842.25			.25	11.00
34														

DATE 12-03-08a **GAP** +0.00 UP IN UPTREND **DISTANCE TO:** T/L 0.00 BIG PIC EXT

TRADE TYPE — ENTRY — EXIT

#	B/S	C1	C2	C3	TIME	ENTRY	PT	Initial Stop	Adj Stop	BE+1	Vol Div	Mom/ Exten.	+/-	Cum
1	Sell	x			830	829.00	x			828.75			.25	.25
2		x			835	830.00		831.75					(1.75)	(1.50)
3			x		851	832.25	x			832.00			.25	(1.25)
4		x			859	830.50	x		829.00				1.50	.25
5	Buy	x			920	836.00	x			836.25			.25	.50
6			x		926	839.00	x					845.75	6.75	7.25
7		x			939	845.00	x			845.25			.25	7.50
8		x			943	844.50	x					856.25	11.75	19.25
9		x			1002	856.25	x	854.75					(1.50)	17.75
10			x		1011	857.00	x		860.00				3.00	20.75
11		x			1021	861.50			860.25				(1.25)	19.50
12			x		1053	859.00	x		862.50				3.50	23.00
13		x			1102	861.75	x	860.00					(1.75)	21.25
14	Sell		x		1142	854.25		856.50					(2.25)	19.00
15			x		1151	854.00		856.75					(2.75)	16.25
16			x		1201	854.50	x			854.25			.25	16.50
17		x			1219	853.25	x					837.25	16.00	32.50
18		x			1251	837.00	x		836.50				.50	33.00
19		x			1256	836.75		838.25					(1.50)	31.50
20			x		1307	834.25			836.25				(2.00)	29.50
21	Buy	x			1329	850.75	x		854.00				3.25	32.75
22		x			1333	855.25	x			855.50			.25	33.00
23			x		1341	855.25	x			855.50			.25	33.25
24		x			1349	857.75	x		859.00				1.25	34.50
25		x			1355	857.50		856.00					(1.50)	33.00
26				x	1408	858.75		855.50					(3.25)	29.75
27			x		1416	856.75		852.75					(4.00)	25.75

DATE 12-03-08B **GAP** -00.00 DOWN IN DOWNTREND **DISTANCE TO: T/L** +0.00 **BIG**

		TRADE TYPE				ENTRY					EXIT			
#	B/S	C1	C2	C3	TIME	ENTRY	PT	Initial Stop	Adj Stop	BE+1	Vol Div	Mom/ Exten.	+/-	Cu
28	Buy			x	1420	856.25	x			856.50			.25	26.
29	Sell	x			1424	854.00	x		853.50				.50	26.
30		x			1426	852.50		855.50					(3.00)	23.
31			x		1430	852.00		855.00					(3.00)	20.
32	Buy	x			1437	858.75	x			859.00			.25	20.
33		x			1438	860.00	x		866.25				6.25	27.
34			x		1447	865.25	x			865.50			.25	27.
35			x		1451	866.50	x				870.00		3.50	30.
36		x			1456	870.50	x		871.50				1.00	31.
37														
38														
39														

DATE 12-04-08a **GAP** +0.00 UP IN UPTREND **DISTANCE TO: T/L** 0.00 **BIG PIC EXT**

		TRADE TYPE				ENTRY					EXIT			
#	B/S	C1	C2	C3	TIME	ENTRY	PT	Initial Stop	Adj Stop	BE+1	Vol Div	Mom/ Exten.	+/-	Cu
1	Buy	x			856	868.25	x			868.50			.25	.25
2		x			902	869.25	x		870.00				.75	1.0
3		x			905	870.25		868.00					(2.25)	(1.
4				x	921	865.75	x		866.75				1.00	(.2
5		x			928	866.25	x	864.25					(2.00)	(2.
6		x			946	870.25		867.75					(2.50)	(4.
7			x		951	869.50	x		873.50				4.00	(.7
8		x			1002	873.50	x	871.25					(2.25)	(3.
9			x		1024	874.00	x		872.50				(1.50)	(4.
10	Sell	x			1049	865.25		867.00					(1.75)	(6.
11			x		1101	865.50	x			865.25			.25	(6.
12		x			1129	862.00	x			861.75			.25	(5.
13			x		1202	860.75		863.25					(2.50)	(8.
14			x		1212	859.25	x			859.00			.25	(8.
15		x			1226	858.25	x			858.00			.25	(7.
16			x		1244	859.25		862.00					(2.75)	(10
17	Buy	x			1309	866.75	x	865.00					(1.75)	(11
18		x			1332	865.75	x		867.75				2.00	(9.
19	Sell	x			1411	848.00		850.00					(2.00)	(11
20		x			1411	849.50	x				842.00		7.50	(4.
21		x			1418	842.25	x		842.00				.25	(4.
22		x			1420	841.50	x		841.25				.25	(3.
23		x			1422	839.25	x		839.00				.25	(3.
24			x		1425	839.75		842.25					(2.50)	(7.
25			x		1426	840.25	x		840.00				.25	(6.
26		x			1429	838.25	x		838.00				.25	(6.
27		x			1431	837.50		839.75					(2.25)	(8.

DATE 12-05-08a   **GAP** +0.00 UP IN UPTREND   **DISTANCE TO: T/L** 0.00   **BIG PIC EXT**

| | | TRADE TYPE | | | | ENTRY | | | | | | | EXIT | | |

#	B/S	C1	C2	C3	TIME	ENTRY	PT	Initial Stop	Adj Stop	BE+1	Vol Div	Mom/ Exten.	+/-	Cu
1	Sell			x	843	836.50	x				832.25		4.25	4.2
2				x	857	830.25	x		828.25				2.00	6.2
3		x			906	827.75	x		827.00				.75	7.0
4		x			909	827.25	x				824.75		2.50	9.5
5		x			916	823.50	x			823.25			.25	9.7
6		x			918	824.25	x		821.00				3.25	13.
7			x		929	822.75			824.25				(1.50)	11.
8			x		936	822.25	x		819.50				2.75	14.
9		x			948	820.25		822.00					(1.75)	12.
10				x	1015	825.50	x		825.00				.50	13.
11				x	1024	823.50	x		823.00				.50	13.
12				x	1038	821.75		824.25					(2.50)	11.
13	Buy	x			1047	826.75	x		829.00				2.25	13.
14		x			1059	830.50	x			830.75			.25	13.
15		x			1106	830.25	x		832.50				2.25	15.
16		x			1113	832.25		830.00					(2.25)	13.
17		x			1119	832.00	x			832.25			.25	13.
18		x			1125	832.00	x			832.25			.25	14.
19			x		1205	832.75	x			833.00			.25	14.
20		x			1219	836.00	x			836.25			.25	14.
21		x			1230	835.25	x		836.00				.75	15.
22		x			1237	837.25	x	834.75					(2.50)	12.
23			x		1242	839.00	x				846.00		7.00	19.
24		x			1254	845.25	x		848.00				2.75	22.
25		x			1300	846.00	x			846.25			.25	22.
26			x		1320	843.75	x			844.00			.25	23.
27		x			1329	844.00		842.50					(1.50)	21.

DATE 12-05-08B   **GAP** -00.00 DOWN IN DOWNTREND   **DISTANCE TO: T/L** +0.00   **BIG**

| | | TRADE TYPE | | | | ENTRY | | | | | | | EXIT | | |

#	B/S	C1	C2	C3	TIME	ENTRY	PT	Initial Stop	Adj Stop	BE+1	Vol Div	Mom/ Exten.	+/-	Cumr
														21.50
28	Buy		x		1333	844.50	x		847.25				2.75	24.25
29		x			1338	848.00	x					865.75	17.75	42.00
30		x			1351	863.75	x			864.00			.25	42.25
31			x		1400	867.25	x	864.50					(2.75)	39.50
32			x		1412	864.00	x		868.50				4.50	44.00
33		x			1420	866.75		864.25					(2.50)	41.50
34			x		1424	866.75	x			867.00			.25	41.75
35		x			1435	869.75	x		874.25				4.50	45.25
36		x			1439	874.25	x			874.50			.25	45.50
37		x			1442	874.75	x	873.00					(1.75)	43.75
38			x		1444	874.50	x			874.75			.25	44.00
39		x			1446	877.00	x		875.50				(1.50)	42.50
40			x		1450	875.75		872.75					(3.00)	39.50
41														

DATE 12-08-08a   **GAP** +0.00 UP IN UPTREND   **DISTANCE TO:** T/L 0.00   **BIG PIC EXT**

| | | | TRADE TYPE | | | ENTRY | | | | | | | | EXIT | | |

#	B/S	C1	C2	C3	TIME	ENTRY	PT	Initial Stop	Adj Stop	BE+1	Vol Div	Mom/ Exten.	+/-	Cu
1	Buy		x		840	902.25	x		905.00				2.75	2.7
2		x			846	905.00			903.25				(1.75)	1.0
3		x			847	904.50	x			904.75			.25	1.2
4				x	906	900.00	x		900.75				.75	2.0
5				x	915	900.50		898.00					(2.50)	(.5
6		x			931	904.00	x			904.25			.25	(.2
7		x			936	905.00	x				910.00		5.00	4.7
8		x			950	909.50	x	908.25					(1.25)	3.5
9		x			955	909.75		907.75					(2.00)	1.5
10			x		1031	907.50			907.50				0	1.5
11	Sell	x			1102	900.75	x			897.25			3.50	5.0
12			x		1151	900.75	x		899.75				1.00	6.0
13			x		1207	901.00		903.50					(2.50)	3.5
14			x		1215	901.00	x		900.00				1.00	4.5
15			x		1229	899.00	x		895.25				3.75	8.2
16			x		1246	897.00	x		898.25				(1.25)	7.0
17			x		1256	894.50	x	897.75					(3.25)	3.7
18	Buy	x			1329	907.25	x	904.75					(2.50)	1.2
19		x			1334	904.75	x			911.75			7.00	8.2
20		x			1352	911.25	x		913.50				2.25	11.
21		x			1402	913.75	x			914.00			.25	11.
22		x			1409	915.25	x			915.50			.25	11.
23		x			1416	915.50	x			915.75			.25	11.
24		x			1420	917.50		914.75					(2.75)	9.0
25			x		1431	917.25			917.50				.25	9.2
26	Sell	x			1451	906.75		909.50					(2.25)	7.0
27														

DATE 12-09-08a **GAP** +0.00 UP IN UPTREND **DISTANCE TO: T/L** 0.00 **BIG PIC EXT**

	TRADE TYPE					ENTRY						EXIT		
#	B/S	C1	C2	C3	TIME	ENTRY	PT	Initial Stop	Adj Stop	BE+1	Vol Div	Mom/ Exten.	+/-	Cu
1	Sell	x			838	897.50		899.25					(1.75)	(1.
2			x		854	897.00		899.00					(2.00)	(3.
3		x			900	898.25		901.00					(2.75)	(6.
4	Buy	x			920	909.75	x		908.00				(1.75)	(8.
5		x			940	911.25	x			911.50			.25	(8.
6		x			945	913.50	x		914.00				.50	(7.
7		x			948	914.25		912.25					(2.00)	(9.
8		x			950	914.00		911.75					(2.25)	(11
9			x		956	913.25	x			913.50			.25	(11
10	Sell	x			1033	905.25	x			905.00			.25	(11
11			x		1117	906.25				906.00			.25	(11
12		x			1120	906.00	x		905.25				.75	(10
13		x			1131	906.00	x		907.25				(1.25)	(11
14				x	1155	907.25	x		902.75				4.50	(7.
15		x			1209	905.50	x				900.00		5.50	(1.
16		x			1232	898.50	x				896.25		2.25	.75
17		x			1241	897.75		899.00					(1.25)	(.5
18		x			1242	897.75	x		898.50				(.75)	(1.
19			x		1254	898.50	x			898.25			.25	(1.
20			x		1302	896.00	x		893.00				3.00	2.0
21		x			1315	891.25		893.00					(1.75)	(.2
22			x		1321	891.50	x				887.25		4.25	4.0
23		x			1337	887.25	x	889.00					(1.75)	2.2
24			x		1344	887.25		889.25					(2.00)	.25
25				x	1411	895.25	x			895.00			.25	.50
26				x	1425	891.50	x				886.75		4.75	5.2
27		x			1434	888.50	x			888.25			.25	5.5

243

DATE 12-10-08a   **GAP** +0.00 UP IN UPTREND   **DISTANCE TO:** T/L 0.00   **BIG PIC EXT**

| TRADE TYPE | | | | ENTRY | | | | | | | | EXIT | | |

#	B/S	C1	C2	C3	TIME	ENTRY	PT	Initial Stop	Adj Stop	BE+1	Vol Div	Mom/ Exten.	+/-	Cu
1	Buy			x	902	895.50	x		902.50				7.00	7.0
2		x			926	901.75	x		900.25				(1.50)	5.5
3				x	1003	896.75	x			897.00			.25	5.7
4				x	1012	897.00	x		900.50				3.50	9.2
5		x			1029	900.50	x			900.75			.25	9.5
6		x			1036	901.50		899.75					(1.75)	7.7
7			x		1042	901.25	x				904.00		2.75	10.
8		x			1100	904.25		902.25					(2.00)	8.5
9		x			1102	903.75	x			904.00			.25	8.7
10		x			1110	905.50	x		906.75				1.25	10.
11				x	1151	900.25		897.50					(2.75)	7.2
12	Sell		x		1233	898.50	x		895.00				3.50	10.
13		x			1248	894.75	x				888.25		6.50	17.
14		x			1300	887.75	x	890.25					(2.50)	14.
15		x			1325	886.75	x	888.75					(2.00)	12.
16				x	1349	888.75	x	892.00					(3.25)	9.5
17				x	1358	890.50	x		892.25				(1.75)	7.7
18	Buy	x			1413	894.00	x		895.75				1.75	9.5
19		x			1422	895.50		893.25					(2.25)	7.2
20		x			1423	894.75	x			895.00			.25	7.5
21		x			1426	894.75	x		895.25				.50	8.0
22			x		1441	896.00	x		898.50				2.50	10.
23														
24														
25														
26														
27														

DATE 12-11-08a **GAP** +0.00 UP IN UPTREND **DISTANCE TO: T/L** 0.00 **BIG PIC EXT**

TRADE TYPE — ENTRY — EXIT

#	B/S	C1	C2	C3	TIME	ENTRY	PT	Initial Stop	Adj Stop	BE+1	Vol Div	Mom/ Exten.	+/-	Cum
1	Sell	x			832	888.00	x			887.75			.25	.25
2		x			841	890.50	x			890.25			.25	.50
3			x		908	892.25		895.50					(3.25)	(2.75)
4	Buy	x			928	901.00		898.75					(2.25)	(5.00)
5		x			931	900.50	x			900.75			.25	(4.75)
6			x		1042	898.00	x			898.25			.25	(4.50)
7		x			1115	901.25	x	900.00					(1.25)	(5.75)
8			x		1147	900.25	x			900.50			.25	(5.50)
9	Sell	x			1334	892.25		894.00					(1.75)	(7.25)
10		x			1337	892.25	x					879.25	13.00	5.75
11		x			1405	877.00	x		875.50				1.50	7.25
12		x			1410	875.25	x		875.00				.25	7.50
13		x			1415	873.75	x			873.50			.25	7.75
14		x			1421	872.00	x		873.75				(1.75)	6.00
15			x		1458	872.50			873.50				(1.00)	5.00
16														

DATE 12-12-08a **GAP** +0.00 UP IN UPTREND **DISTANCE TO: T/L** 0.00 **BIG PIC EXT**

TRADE TYPE — ENTRY — EXIT

#	B/S	C1	C2	C3	TIME	ENTRY	PT	Initial Stop	Adj Stop	BE+1	Vol Div	Mom/ Exten.	+/-	Cu
1	Sell			x	842	854.25		856.75					(2.50)	(2.
2				x	847	854.00		856.50					(2.50)	(5.
3	Buy	x			853	858.25	x			858.50			.25	(4.
4		x			855	859.50	x		862.00				2.50	(2.
5		x			901	863.00	x		864.75				1.75	(.5
6		x			908	864.25		862.25					(2.00)	(2.
7				x	941	860.25	x			860.50			.25	(2.
8				x	950	863.25	x		866.50				3.25	1.0
9		x			1003	868.25	x		870.00				1.75	2.7
10				x	1100	864.00	x		864.75				.75	3.5
11				x	1123	867.75	x		872.00				4.25	7.7
12		x			1149	872.50	x					877.75	5.25	13.
13		x			1205	877.50		876.00					(1.50)	11.
14	Sell	x			1256	865.50		867.25					(1.75)	9.7
15		x			1259	866.00		868.00					(2.00)	7.7
16		x			1330	865.50	x		863.25				2.25	10.
17		x			1336	864.75	x	866.50					(1.75)	8.2
18	Buy	x			1358	874.50	x		879.25				4.75	13.
19			x		1409	877.25		874.50					(2.75)	10.
20			x		1438	874.75	x			875.00			.25	10.
21		x			1440	876.50	x			876.75			.25	10.
22		x			1445	876.25		874.00					(2.25)	8.5
23				x	1450	874.50			873.75				(.75)	7.7
24				x	1457	873.75	x					885.00	11.25	19.
25														

DATE 12-15-08a **GAP** +0.00 UP IN UPTREND **DISTANCE TO: T/L** 0.00 **BIG PIC EXT**

TRADE TYPE | ENTRY | EXIT

#	B/S	C1	C2	C3	TIME	ENTRY	PT	Initial Stop	Adj Stop	BE+1	Vol Div	Mom/ Exten.	+/-	Cumr
1	Sell	x			906	872.00	x		871.50				.50	.50
2		x			913	870.50	x		869.75				.75	1.25
3			x		947	869.00	x		867.00				2.00	3.25
4		x			1008	866.00	x	867.50					(1.50)	1.75
5			x		1258	865.75		868.50					(2.75)	(1.00)
6			x		1313	867.25	x			867.00			.25	(.75)
7		x			1336	866.50	x		865.25				1.25	.50
8			x		1353	864.00	x		863.50				.50	1.00
9		x			1406	862.25	x		858.25				4.00	5.00
10		x			1426	858.75			859.75				(1.00)	4.00
11	Buy	x			1440	868.25	x		872.00				3.75	7.75
12		x			1443	870.50	x			870.75			.25	8.00
13		x			1445	871.25	x			871.50			.25	8.25
14		x			1448	870.00				870.25			.25	8.50
15														

DATE 12-16-08a **GAP** +0.00 UP IN UPTREND **DISTANCE TO: T/L** 0.00 **BIG PIC EXT**

TRADE TYPE | ENTRY | EXIT

#	B/S	C1	C2	C3	TIME	ENTRY	PT	Initial Stop	Adj Stop	BE+1	Vol Div	Mom/ Exten.	+/-	Cu
1	Buy		x		834	879.50	x		880.75				1.25	1.2
2		x			845	882.25	x			882.50			.25	1.5
3			x		851	880.75	x		880.25				(.50)	1.0
4			x		904	882.00	x		883.75				1.75	2.7
5			x		925	882.25	x		880.25				(2.00)	.75
6			x		952	880.75	x			881.00			.25	1.0
7			x		1021	881.50	x				884.25		2.75	3.7
8		x			1053	884.25	x	883.00					(1.25)	2.5
9			x		1229	884.00		882.00					(2.00)	.50
10			x		1305	883.25	x			883.50			.25	.75
11		x			1317	884.50	x		887.25				2.75	3.5
12		x			1324	891.00		888.25					(2.75)	.75
13			x		1326	889.25	x			889.50			.25	1.0
14			x		1329	890.00	x			890.25			.25	1.2
15		x			1335	896.50	x			896.75			.25	1.5
16				x	1351	891.00	x		892.50				1.50	3.0
17		x			1356	895.25	x		896.25				1.00	4.0
18		x			1358	895.25	x			895.50			.25	4.2
19			x		1408	896.75	x					907.75		11.00	15.
20		x			1420	908.75	x		910.00				1.25	16.
21		x			1423	910.00		908.75					(1.25)	15.
22		x			1424	910.25	x		909.00				(1.25)	14.
23			x		1430	910.75			908.50				(2.25)	11.
24			x		1442	911.00	x		911.00				0	11.
25				x	1454	909.25	x					913.25		4.00	15.
26														
27														

DATE 12-17-08a **GAP** +0.00 UP IN UPTREND **DISTANCE TO:** T/L 0.00 **BIG PIC EXT**

TRADE TYPE — ENTRY — EXIT

#	B/S	C1	C2	C3	TIME	ENTRY	PT	Initial Stop	Adj Stop	BE+1	Vol Div	Mom/ Exten.	+/-	Cum
1	Sell		x		830	900.00	x		899.75				.25	.25
2				x	904	901.50	x					896.75	4.75	5.00
3		x			918	895.75		898.00					(2.25)	2.75
4		x			920	897.25		898.50					(1.25)	1.50
5			x		938	897.50		900.75					(3.25)	(1.75)
6	Buy	x			958	904.25	x		905.50				1.25	(.50)
7		x			1004	904.75		903.25					(1.50)	(2.00)
8			x		1014	904.75		902.25					(2.50)	(4.50)
9				x	1041	902.50	x		904.00				1.50	(3.00)
10		x			1103	904.00	x					908.25	4.25	1.25
11		x			1125	909.00	x		906.75				(2.25)	(1.00)
12			x		1148	907.25	x		910.25				3.00	2.00
13			x		1213	911.00		908.50					(2.50)	(.50)
14			x		1222	911.25	x		912.50				1.25	.75
15		x			1230	912.00	x		914.50				2.50	3.25
16		x			1252	915.00	x	913.50					(1.50)	1.75
17			x		1305	915.50	x			915.75			.25	2.00
18	Sell	x			1342	906.50	x			906.25			.25	2.25
19			x		1355	907.00		909.00					(2.00)	.25
20			x		1423	910.25	x		907.00				3.25	3.50
21		x			1437	905.50	x			905.25			.25	3.75
22			x		1446	907.25		910.00					(2.75)	1.00
23				x	1455	908.00	x					903.25	4.75	5.75
24														

DATE 12-18-08a **GAP** +0.00 UP IN UPTREND **DISTANCE TO:** T/L 0.00 **BIG PIC EXT**

TRADE TYPE — ENTRY — EXIT

#	B/S	C1	C2	C3	TIME	ENTRY	PT	Initial Stop	Adj Stop	BE+1	Vol Div	Mom/ Exten.	+/-	Cu
1	Sell			x	833	905.00	x	907.25					(2.25)	(2.
2				x	842	906.00	x				899.50		6.50	4.2
3		x			900	900.50		903.00					(2.50)	1.7
4				x	924	901.75		904.50					(2.75)	(1.
5	Buy	x			1001	908.00			907.75				(.25)	(1.
6				x	1045	904.50	x			904.75			.25	(1.
7				x	1119	905.75		903.75					(2.00)	(3.
8	Sell	x			1150	903.00	x		907.75				(1.75)	(4.
9		x			1239	901.00	x		898.00				3.00	(1.
10		x			1308	896.50	x					889.50	7.00	5.2
11		x			1328	889.00	x			888.75			.25	5.5
12			x		1345	888.00		889.75					(1.75)	3.7
13			x		1400	890.50	x			890.25			.25	4.0
14		x			1405	889.25	x					884.75	4.50	8.5
15		x			1418	884.25	x					876.75	7.50	16.
16		x			1429	875.50		877.25					(1.75)	14.
17			x		1434	877.00		879.50					(2.50)	11.
18				x	1457	879.75		883.00					(3.25)	8.5
19														

Professional Day Trader

DATE 12-19-08a   GAP +0.00 UP IN UPTREND   DISTANCE TO: T/L 0.00   BIG PIC EXT

TRADE TYPE				ENTRY					EXIT				

#	B/S	C1	C2	C3	TIME	ENTRY	PT	Initial Stop	Adj Stop	BE+1	Vol Div	Mom/ Exten.	+/-	Cu
1	Buy		x		830	891.00	x			891.25			.25	.25
2				x	858	892.25	x	889.25					(3.00)	(2.
3			x		903	892.25	x				900.25		8.00	5.2
4		x			932	900.25	x	899.00					(1.25)	4.0
5		x			935	899.75	x				901.75		2.00	6.0
6			x		952	901.75	x		901.00				(.75)	5.2
7	Sell	x			1114	886.50		887.75					(1.25)	4.0
8			x		1141	884.75		886.75					(2.00)	2.0
9			x		1150	886.25		889.25					(3.00)	(1.
10				x	1251	889.50	x		889.25				.25	(.7
11				x	1309	888.50	x		888.25				.25	(.5
12		x			1334	887.75	x	889.75					(2.00)	(2.
13		x			1405	885.25	x				881.50		3.75	1.2
14		x			1425	882.75		885.00					(2.25)	(1.
15			x		1428	884.00	x		883.75				.25	(.7
16			x		1459	882.50	x		881.00				1.50	.75

DATE 12-22-08a   GAP +0.00 UP IN UPTREND   DISTANCE TO: T/L 0.00   BIG PIC EXT

TRADE TYPE				ENTRY					EXIT				

#	B/S	C1	C2	C3	TIME	ENTRY	PT	Initial Stop	Adj Stop	BE+1	Vol Div	Mom/ Exten.	+/-	Cu
1	Sell			x	833	882.75	x		879.25				3.50	3.5
2		x			850	880.00	x				875.00		5.00	8.5
3		x			921	876.50			877.50				(1.00)	7.5
4		x			936	877.25		878.50					(1.25)	6.2
5			x		1014	874.50	x				869.00		5.50	11.
6		x			1052	870.75		872.00					(1.25)	10.
7		x			1100	870.75	x			870.50			.25	10.
8			x		1130	869.00		870.75					(1.75)	9.0
9			x		1210	870.75		873.25					(2.50)	6.5
10			x		1233	871.25	x		869.25				2.00	8.5
11		x			1308	868.50	x					861.00	7.50	16.
12		x			1343	861.50	x	863.00					(1.50)	14.
13			x		1358	861.25	x		859.50				1.75	16.
14		x			1408	857.50					853.75		3.75	20.
15														

248

DATE 12-30-08a **GAP** +0.00 UP IN UPTREND **DISTANCE TO:** T/L 0.00 **BIG PIC EXT**

	TRADE TYPE					ENTRY						EXIT		
#	B/S	C1	C2	C3	TIME	ENTRY	PT	Initial Stop	Adj Stop	BE+1	Vol Div	Mom/ Exten.	+/-	Cum
1	Buy	x			830	873.75		871.25					(2.50)	(2.50)
2			x		845	873.75		871.00					(2.75)	(5.25)
3			x		920	873.75	x		874.00				.25	(5.00)
4		x			1012	874.50	x					880.75	6.25	1.25
5		x			1118	880.50			879.25				(1.25)	0
6			x		1145	880.25		877.50					(2.75)	(2.75)
7			x		1315	878.50	x			878.75			.25	(2.50)
8		x			1342	879.00	x	877.50					(1.50)	(4.00)
9			x		1426	878.25						886.50	8.25	4.25
10														
11														

DATE 12-31-08a **GAP** +0.00 UP IN UPTREND **DISTANCE TO:** T/L 0.00 **BIG PIC EXT**

	TRADE TYPE					ENTRY						EXIT		
#	B/S	C1	C2	C3	TIME	ENTRY	PT	Initial Stop	Adj Stop	BE+1	Vol Div	Mom/ Exten.	+/-	Cum
1	Buy		x		841	891.50	x		894.00				2.50	2.50
2		x			936	894.50	x		896.50				2.00	4.50
3		x			1047	897.50	x		898.50				1.00	5.50
4			x		1256	897.75	x		902.25				4.50	10.0
5			x		1359	902.50	x		903.75				1.25	11.2
6			x		1424	903.75		901.50					(2.25)	9.00
7			x		1433	904.25					906.75		2.50	11.5
8			x		1457	904.75		903.00					(1.75)	9.75
9														

RETURN ON INVESTMENT

TANGIBLE ROI - Here Is a bottom-line look at ROI analysis that realistically views $E=MC^2$ as a "Business Venture," complete with a plan for calculating real-time performance expectations.

The premise is as follows: Apply a filter to the $E=MC^2$ track record that conservatively takes into account the fact you cannot execute every $E=MC^2$ trade in perfect fashion. Maybe you will miss a trade, maybe you will make trading mistakes, maybe you just are not available to trade all day long, etc. If such scrutiny continues to produce a positive ROI, than you can feel very comfortable about your chances for trading success.

THE E=MC2 TRACK RECORD SHOULD BE VIEWED AS YOUR "*BLUEPRINT*" FOR TRADING SUCCESS- NOT SOMETHING TO DUPLICATE!

ROI Filter Example - Reduce average Track Record results by 50% to adjust for inefficiencies such as trading errors, missed trades, days off, and trade executions that are less than ideal, and costs such as commission costs, slippage, monthly chart and price data costs, etc.

I recognize a 1/2 reduction sounds extreme. The point is, if you can indeed benefit from only 1/2 of the listed track record performance, then you know you don't have to be perfect in your trading.

Note- All calculations presented are for a small trading account, involving minimum contract set, and a recommended minimum account size of $5,000. You can always increase account and trading size in accordance with your individual risk/reward preferences. For instance, if you prefer to trade an equivalent to the full S&P contract (vs. the E-Mini), you can multiply all results by 5.

Assume track record results shows an average daily gain of 5-pts (all trades)

ROI Filter- 5 X .50 (50% reduction)=2.5

If you can average 2.5- pts a day for 20 trading days a month:

50 x 2.5 x 20 = $2,500/month gross.
$2,500/mo - $1,000/commissions (10 trades/day) = $1,500/mo net, or
$18,000/yr on $5,000 margin

$18,000/$5,000 = 360% return!

Now, take the inefficiency factor one step further. Assume you cannot trade all day long, and some days you will take trades that end up losing money. Assume that you win 15 days of the month, and lose 5 days of the month.

15(2.5) - 5(2.5) =37.5 -12.5 =25 pts/month
25x 50 = $1250/month gross
$1,250/mo - $600/commissions (6 trades/day) = $650/mo net, or
$7,800/yr on $5,000 margin

$7,800/$5,000 = 156% return!

So, I think you can see, from very conservative estimates, E=MC^2 offers tremendous potential from a "real rate of return" standpoint, if you stay the course!

The main point is that hypothetical results often sound very nice, but in actual trading you cannot, and should not expect to match hypothetical performance exactly. Be careful of this fact as you explore any method to trade.

Sometimes you are only able to trade for part of the trading day. Sometimes you will fail to execute trades for other reasons.

Also, you must always take into account commission costs, slippage, and trading errors. Sometimes trading errors, slippage, can even work in your favor, but in general, you should factor a trading *"inefficiency"* multiplier into your trading plan. Start with something extreme (i.e. - 1/2) and see if you can still come out ahead- if not, understand you will have to be virtually perfect in all your trading efforts, and this is very hard to do.

You must have a trading plan, and a trading method, that accounts for trading inefficiencies and still provides a good chance to come out ahead from a return on investment standpoint based upon an overall trading philosophy that takes into account the actual costs and obstacles you will always face in a real time environment.

The philosophy of trying to capture "big" price moves with high probability setups in the S&P E-Mini market, allows E=MC^2 to overcome many of the trading inefficiencies you will always face when you trade for real.

As you consider the potential for the E=MC^2 Method, always keep in mind that the listed Track Record represents the maximum return for a minimum account of $5000. A $20,000 account can result in 4X the listed maximum return for the Track Record, etc.

From this benchmark, you must keep in mind the "Real Rate of Return" for E=MC^2, or for any other method.

A real rate of return must apply an "inefficiency multiplier" to "hypothetical" results.

Start with a very conservative multiplier so you know you can only move up, and not down, in terms of performance.

We started with a 50% inefficiency multiplier for the sake of example.

With E=MC2, A CONSERVATIVE MULTIPLIER CALCULATION STILL RESULTS IN A POTENTIAL 156% RETURN ON INVESTMENT FOR WHATEVER INVESTMENT SIZE YOU CHOOSE TO MAKE!

The potential of E=MC^2 is enormous if you are simply willing to put in the time and effort, day after day, and apply the E=MC^2 Method to the S&P E-Mini Market.

THE MASTER E=MC2 TRADER

I wish there was an easy way to snap my fingers and have everyone understand the following statement very clearly:

"THE E-MC2 METHOD IS DESIGNED TO TAKE ADVANTAGE OF BIG PICTURE AND INTRA-DAY PRICE DEVELOPMENTS, AND IS NOT SIMPLY A MECHANICAL APPROACH THROWN TOGETHER USING PRICE ACTION, VOLUME AND MOVING AVERAGES!"

We have mentioned that E=MC2 is as much a total trading framework as it is a series of mechanically based buy and sell signals.

We have mentioned that you only need to take a few trades each day to be successful with this approach.

We have mentioned that everyone should take this information and strive to turn it into his or her own in some way.

Finally, we have mentioned everyone should look at the big picture first, intra-day structure second, and mechanical trading signals third.

This simply means, "Always think about what seems to going on in the market relative to the developing structure, and how intra-day C1, C2, C3, C1-C structure relates to big picture price moves from Point A to Point B."

For instance, if you look at the big picture first, and you see the market is opening with a gap up near yesterdays high, does it really make sense to take a C1 buy trade on a gap up right at the open before the market really settles in for the trading session?

Unless you have a very good indication of what is taking place pre-market, the open, especially prior to any volume confirmation etc. is often a very aggressive, speculative trade. Therefore, when in doubt about momentum, stand aside with C1 setups early.

Or, let's say you have a choppy day in force with an obvious wide high-low range in place with price moving back and forth inside this range.

Do you really want to take C1 trades near the high or low of this range "after" price explosions to the edges?

If you can get a C1 to set up with good volume reversal confirmation, with room to run to the edge of the high or low of the range then fine, but can you see how taking C1 continuation trades right at the edge of a intra-day trading range without obvious momentum is not the intention of the method, even if it "sets up" on the charts.

Or, what if you see a major big picture breakout with heavy volume. This can be a consolidation breakout on the 5-minute chart, or a 5000 18/89-trend change in the middle of the day.

Can you see how you will want to look to be very aggressive with the first C1 pullback as soon as a 5000-price pullback "comes close" to the 18-ma.

I want you to think about what a C1 and C2/C3 setup is really all about (I will explain in a moment), and then I want to provide a diary of several trading days to show you how all this thinking comes together, and how this thinking should be applied to the market every day, <u>especially to be selective to uncover the best trading opportunities.</u>

<u>I simply want you to start thinking about bigger picture, and developing intra-day structure as you begin to explore the E=MC2 method!</u>

The biggest decision with E=MC2 is do you want to trade every signal mechanically without regard to the big picture, developing intra-day structure, etc. or do you want to take fewer trades and be a more selective with this approach according to unfolding market conditions.

I advocate the fewer trade/selective approach, which means you try to read intra-day structure as it unfolds from beginning to end from a very basic common sense directional standpoint, and then you decide when you want to be most aggressive with the mechanical signals or not, relative to the big picture.

This means at the open, you will have to use prior day(s) information to see where support/resistance is located in accordance with noting how overnight price action is developing.

Support or Resistance almost always starts out with the overnight high and low, and then yesterdays high or low, and then can be further determined by obvious high-lows that develop during the trading session.

As the current trading session unfolds, you need to monitor intra-day structure to see if you have a (1) Trend day (2) Narrow Range day or (3) A likely day in-between where obvious highs and lows and pullbacks develop during the day, accompanied by volume ratio flows. See if intra-day high and lows are also new daily high and lows which often helps dictate the overall bias for the day.

You must keep in mind that the best C1 trades are designed to go with intra-day momentum, and developing C1 intra-day momentum usually occurs (a) With a resumption of 5-minute trend after a 5-minute pullback when 1500 price rolls back over with trend, or (b) Counter-trend 5 minute moves that start from reversals off big picture support/resistance areas.

Therefore, anytime you see an 5000 18/89 C1 setup you should immediately ask a simple question: "Does this C1 setup align with the 5-minute chart as outlined above, or is this setup nothing more than a "chart pattern" pull back within a range without big picture support (i.e. Gap Open near support/resistance, Setup opposite a trend day, Choppy price action etc.?)

The next part about intra-day price trends is that once you have a few 5-minute swings during the day, (i.e. -successive C1 and C2 swings) that's usually it for the intra-day trend <u>unless you have a strong trend day</u>.

In other words, unless you have a strong trend day with continuing 5-minute swings in the trend direction, be aware that the 5-minute trend can change with either a new 5-minute swing high/low, and/or a strong overall 5-minute pullback past 50-60 percent of the days' range etc. **<u>THIS 5-MINUTE TREND CHANGE WILL BE ACCOMPANIED WITH A 1500-CHART THAT ROLLS OVER WITH A NEW VOLUME BIAS!</u>**

So, on non-trend days, look for successive C1 setups to only make small probes of the recent 5000 extreme (and know that the best trade is the first one), and look for C2/C3 setups to test recent highs or lows just once, or perhaps twice. The exception as mentioned is on a clear trend day, and these days are always the same with (1) Intra-day price structure in one direction all day, Strong/Weak Dow, and an A/D line holding beyond +/-1200 etc.

I do realize the integration of big picture and 5000 18/89 intra-day trend takes some experience and time to get used to, but it's really very simple too.

For instance, C2/C3 trades are simply designed to test a high or low in place for the day aligning with 5-minute price swings.

Therefore, the logic of C2/C3 is one or two tests of a high or low per day is probably all you are going to get as the day unfolds, and then maybe one in the opposite direction after an intra-day trend change.

The first 5-minute extreme that forms after a new 5-minute trend change is very likely to be tested again after a C2/C3 pullback. This is always an excellent trade!

Then after that, you need to key on volume ratio, overall intra-day structure, and bigger picture S/R levels to see if new 5-minute extremes will be tested again, and finally if you see a pullback from an extreme that is just too deep, or too late in the day, or after a 1500-volume divergence, or right after a big picture support/resistance area has already been reached, etc., then it's not worth taking C2/C3 setups anymore, because you are asking for the high or low of the day to be tested one too many times when on most days (other than trend days) these extreme levels are just probed once or twice, rather than being broken with sustainable follow through time and time again.

So again, with every C2/C3 setup, look at the high or low that needs to be tested and ask: "Is this the first or second high or low to be tested with the 5-minute trend (If so, a very good trade). Is 1500-volume and price structure still holding up nicely so another test is likely? Is there any big picture support or resistance in the way that makes another test unlikely? Is the pullback in price just too deep in overall range conditions, or too late in the day, where another test of the high or low is very unlikely?"

To conclude, you first must master the mechanical flow C1/C2/C3/C1C structure as it develops in order. You need to be able to do this no matter what, but I really hope you will take to heart that you can read the market (big picture/developing intra-day structure), and know when these signals make the most sense or not.

Zoom out the charts (5-minute, 1500w/volume) to include a lot of data during non-trading moments. Always know what the daily charts are "trying" to do" from a simple higher/high, lower/low, swing standpoint.

Next, categorize intra-day structure as it develops. Do you have a Trend Day, Range day, or Someday in-between? If in-between, note if price is 1500-price and Volume are flowing in accordance with the current 5-minute trend. **IF 1500-PRICE ROLLS OVER WITH A NEW VOLUME BIAS, SEE IF THIS IS CONFIRMATION OF A NEW 5-MINUTE TREND CHANGE.**

Finally, after you have a clear understanding of all of this, make sure every C1 setup is accompanied by either good volume ratio action in line with the big picture 5-miute trend, or opposite a trend after key support /resistance has been reached. Make sure every C2/C3 setup has a likely chance to test the most recent 5-minute high/low swing in place.

It really all comes together this easy, and you will gain so much more out of E=MC2 if you view trading in this complete manner rather than just a random series of mechanical buy and sell setups.

Remember, this method was designed to take advantage of the best big picture conditions to trade, and not just mechanically thrown together with price patterns, volume patterns, and moving averages.

Here is an example of a how to analyze the flow of several trading days and recognize the key trading opportunities as they unfold. This is the type of thinking you should try to incorporate every day.

I HOPE YOU COMPLETELY UNDERSTAND THIS SECTION BEFORE YOU START YOUR E=MC2 JOURNEY.

---

4 DAYS OF TRADING LOGIC

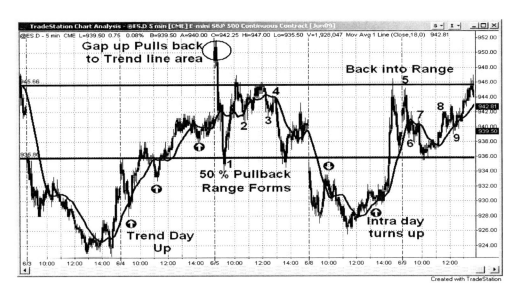

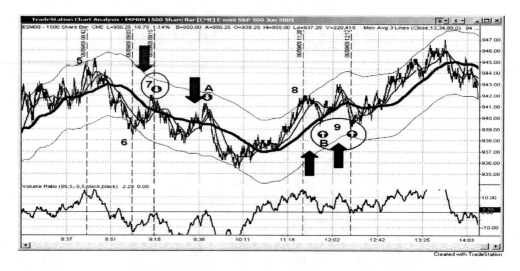

Above is the 5-minute chart for 4 trading days (Chart1), and the corresponding 1500 price-volume charts (Charts 2, 3) with sections labeled 1-9. We always want to view the big picture nature of the 5-minute chart, and tie this together with developing intra-day structure using the 5-minute and 1500 charts together.

In this example, looking at the 5-minute chart left to right, we see the following 4 days (1) Trend day up (2) Pullback day after a gap up that forms a range (3) Break below range that fails to continue down (4) A move back to original range.

Let's explore the key ways this flow develops on an intra-day basis and the corresponding trading opportunities that develop using E=MC2 structure.

Day 1- Monitoring Dow, Advance/Decline line, this was a <u>Trend day up</u> all day with one directional 5-minute price structure (broad 5 minute retrace moves hold 50-60%). Arrows 1 (Open fade to support) and 2 (Trend day pullback) represented excellent opportunities to get in with the trend and ride to new intra-day swing highs. Arrow 3 was late in the trend, but still offered small gains. Any mechanical short trades set-ups that developed at 5-minute trend line pullback areas should be avoided.

Day 2- Gap up offered great C1-C counter trade short back to 5-minute pullback area. If you look at 1500 chart (left side, before 1), you see a 1500-pullback to 89-ma with volume holding below zero for entry. 5-minute pullback is deep (1) but moves in normal retrace fashion to 50% of move of prior trend day. Expect range action to develop between gap up and 50% pullback low and watch for intra-day developments. Two arrows between 1 and 2 represent 1500-long trades back to 89-ma with volume confirmation as range develops. At point 2, volume ratio breaks down and 1500 pullback to 89-ma at 4 represents a great short trade coinciding with 5-minute pullback after 5-minute chart starts lower. Next arrow down (B) is one more aggressive C1 pullback short trade to test range lows, and a single push past the 5000 extreme is all that develops.

Day 3 – This day presented two excellent intra-day/big picture opportunities. Market first gaps down below range setting bias down, and a pullback develops to 5-minute trend line area. Excellent short (5 min chart, down arrow) for move to new 5-minute swing lows. Follow thru past lows never develops and eventually intra-day trend turns up (higher 5-minute swing highs, retrace of more than 50-60% of days range etc, confirmed by 1500-price and volume ratio (not shown), and a nice long trade develops at pullback to 5-minute trend line area (5 min, arrow 2).

Day 4 – End of day 3 takes price back into range (5 min, horizontal lines). Day 4 open takes price to top of range (1500 chart, #5), and C1 entries up here are very aggressive so be ready to exit quickly if upside follow-thru never develops. New intra-day low from top of range with volume confirmation (6) sets up a great short at (7). Between 7 and 8 is another 1500-89-ma pullback short opportunity to range lows. Range lows hold, and 5-minute intra-day structure turns up at 8 (volume confirm, retrace 50-60% days range, etc). This sets up two nice 1500 to 89-ma pullback longs in 9 area as volume holds zero area on pullback.

ACTUAL TRADING - 09-21-09 - 12 TRADES

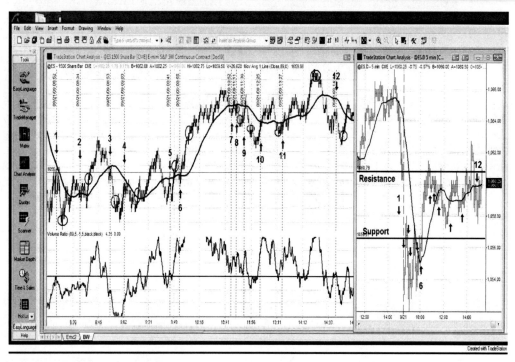

THE FOLLOWING TRADES HAVE BEEN MADE THIS DAY FOR YOUR ACCOUNT AND RISK.

9/21/9 F1 2 DEC 09 EMINI S&P 500 16 1054.00 US
9/21/9 F1 1 DEC 09 EMINI S&P 500 16 1054.00 US
9/21/9 F1 1 DEC 09 EMINI S&P 500 16 1054.25 US
9/21/9 F1 1 DEC 09 EMINI S&P 500 16 1054.50 US
9/21/9 F1 2 DEC 09 EMINI S&P 500 16 1055.00 US
9/21/9 F1 1 DEC 09 EMINI S&P 500 16 1055.25 US
9/21/9 F1 1 DEC 09 EMINI S&P 500 16 1055.75 US
9/21/9 F1 1 DEC 09 EMINI S&P 500 16 1056.00 US
9/21/9 F1 1 DEC 09 EMINI S&P 500 16 1058.25 US
9/21/9 F1 1 DEC 09 EMINI S&P 500 16 1058.25 US
9/21/9 F1 2 DEC 09 EMINI S&P 500 16 1058.50 US
9/21/9 F1 1 DEC 09 EMINI S&P 500 16 1058.75 US
9/21/9 F1 1 DEC 09 EMINI S&P 500 16 1059.25 US
9/21/9 F1 1 DEC 09 EMINI S&P 500 16 1059.25 US
9/21/9 F1 1 DEC 09 EMINI S&P 500 16 1059.50 US
9/21/9 F1 1 DEC 09 EMINI S&P 500 16 1059.75 US
9/21/9 F1 3 DEC 09 EMINI S&P 500 16 1060.00 US
9/21/9 F1 1 DEC 09 EMINI S&P 500 16 1062.25 US

        F1 12* 12* GROSS PROFIT/LOSS FROM TRADES US 337.50

9/21/9 F1 1 DEC 09 EMINI S&P 500 16 1052.75 US
ELECTRONIC TRADE
9/21/9 F1 2 DEC 09 EMINI S&P 500 16 1054.00 US
ELECTRONIC TRADE
9/21/9 F1 1 DEC 09 EMINI S&P 500 16 1054.00 US
ELECTRONIC TRADE
9/21/9 F1 1 DEC 09 EMINI S&P 500 16 1054.25 US
ELECTRONIC TRADE
9/21/9 F1 1 DEC 09 EMINI S&P 500 16 1054.50 US
ELECTRONIC TRADE

9/21/9 F1 2 DEC 09 EMINI S&P 500 16 1055.00 US
ELECTRONIC TRADE
9/21/9 F1 1 DEC 09 EMINI S&P 500 16 1055.25 US
ELECTRONIC TRADE
9/21/9 F1 1 DEC 09 EMINI S&P 500 16 1055.75 US
ELECTRONIC TRADE
9/21/9 F1 1 DEC 09 EMINI S&P 500 16 1056.00 US
ELECTRONIC TRADE
9/21/9 F1 1 DEC 09 EMINI S&P 500 16 1058.25 US
ELECTRONIC TRADE
9/21/9 F1 1 DEC 09 EMINI S&P 500 16 1058.25 US
ELECTRONIC TRADE
9/21/9 F1 2 DEC 09 EMINI S&P 500 16 1058.50 US
ELECTRONIC TRADE
9/21/9 F1 1 DEC 09 EMINI S&P 500 16 1058.75 US
ELECTRONIC TRADE
9/21/9 F1 1 DEC 09 EMINI S&P 500 16 1059.25 US
ELECTRONIC TRADE
9/21/9 F1 1 DEC 09 EMINI S&P 500 16 1059.25 US
ELECTRONIC TRADE
9/21/9 F1 1 DEC 09 EMINI S&P 500 16 1059.50 US
ELECTRONIC TRADE
9/21/9 F1 1 DEC 09 EMINI S&P 500 16 1059.75 US
ELECTRONIC TRADE
9/21/9 F1 3 DEC 09 EMINI S&P 500 16 1060.00 US
ELECTRONIC TRADE
9/21/9 F1 1 DEC 09 EMINI S&P 500 16 1062.25 US
ELECTRONIC TRADE
F1 12* 12* COMMISSION US 28.80DR
F1 EXCHANGE & CLEARING FEE US 27.36DR
F1 NFA FEE US .24DR

F1 TOTAL COMMISSION & FEES US 56.40DR

09-21-09 / 12 TRADES / +6.75 CUMULATIVE POINTS

#	B/S	Gap C/F	Rev CT	Rev S/R	Trd mom	Trd std	Trd deep	TIME	ENTRY	WIN	LOSS	+/-	CUMM
1	Sell					x		647	1055.75	1052.75		3.00	3.00
2		c						834	1054.00		1055.00	(1.00)	2.00
3				x				853	1055.25	1054.00		1.25	3.25
4					x			903	1054.25	1054.00		.25	3.50
5						x		946	1054.50		1056.00	(1.50)	2.00
6	Buy					x		955	1055.00	1058.25		3.25	5.25
7					x			1054	1060.00		1059.75	(.25)	5.00
8					x			1109	1060.00		1059.25	(.75)	4.25
9							x	1138	1060.00		1058.50	(1.50)	2.75
10							x	1225	1058.75		1058.50	(.25)	2.50
11						x		1332	1059.25	1062.25		3.00	5.50
12	Sell					x		1440	1059.50	1058.25		1.25	6.75

HIGHLIGHTS: Single contract per trade, all/in-all/out to highlight what typical trading activity looks like for a small account.

$337.50 Gross - $56.40 Commission = $281.10 Net, or "**5.62 Net Points for Day**."

BIG PICTURE - Overall daily Big Picture is up seeking a daily bracket high. Yesterday was a daily pause day inside the previous day's range, which alerts to either overlapping daily action developing, or a strong breakout soon. Overnight action was significantly lower, and a large gap down was forming. If you look at the 5-minute chart (Chart2, right) you see Support/Resistance highlighted from Yesterday (Horizontal lines)

GAP DOWN OPENING way below support. Watch for continuation lower (breakout), or failure (fade), and more overlapping daily price action.

(TRADE 1) A classic pre-opening trade developed after price had been sharply and steadily down all night long and pulled back to the 1500-89ma as volume pulled back to zero at the same time. Exit into extension and take 3-point gain before the market even opens at 8:30 because you don't know if the open will provide a gap down continuation, or fade.

(TRADE 2) This was not a very clear trade on 1500 chart. With price gapping down below support, the 1500-trend line still down, volume holding zero, a decision was made to try a gap down open/continuation trade with a very tight stop that resulted in a small loss.

(TRADE 3) After being stopped out of gap continuation short trade 2, this **ended up being a standard fade the gap C1-C long trade but volume ratio didn't confirm holding zero. You miss certain trades from time to time.** 1500-price moved up to pullback to swing resistance at the bracket low, and by the time it pulled back to the 89-ma, volume ratio was way below zero, which alerted us to take a first reversal short with a turn back down in the big picture direction from a bracket resistance area. Expectation was for price to test 1053 intra-day low. When price tested this low and didn't immediately continue lower, decision was made to play it safe and exit at 1054 for a 1.25 gain. (Example of cautious exit early in day).

(TRADE 4) Classic short set up with pullback to 1500 89-ma with Volume at zero, however, this was an aggressive pullback entry early in the session because the lows for the day were just tested and may have failed. Price spent quite a bit of time not following through to new lows (See 2 swing attempts lower on 1500 chart), and decision was made to again play it safe, tighten stops immediately, and breakeven plus a tick on the trade

(TRADE 5) An hour had gone by in the session, so at this point it was time to focus on the 5-minute trend which was clearly down and all you could do was wait for either (1) Price to roll back over to the downside in line with the big picture, or (2) Start a new 5-minute trend up. 5-minute price pulled back right to the 18-ma, in line with resistance on the day, and then rolled over to set up a short entry, Again, this was somewhat aggressive because it was still possible there was earlier reversal failure at the lows, but it was a good setup (1500 price and volume pullback), that hopefully would at least move down to the test the lows again and allow you to move your stop to breakeven plus a tick. Instead the trade moved back up, stopping you out for a small loss.

(TRADE 6) Volume ratio exploded past zero on the prior trade stop out, and the 5-minute chart was now moving above the 18-ma, setting up a <u>long pullback entry</u>, that also aligned with a bigger picture view of a failure at the lows from the beginning of the session. Price exploded through bracket low, which signaled a move to bracket high, and frankly a conservative decision was made to exit on the first extension for a 3.25 point gain. An explosive move through a dual resistance (support low from yesterday coupled with intra-day high resistance from today), signaled a move to the next big picture resistance point above near the 1060 area, so 2 more points were likely during this move. As stated, trading is an art, and there are times you will remain aggressive and other times you won't, however, you will always be fine if you stick with a basic exit plan to logical extensions.

(TRADE 7, 8) Price worked its way to big picture resistance near 1060, and pullback long setups developed at point 7 and point 8. These were classified as aggressive setups because 5-minute price was way above the 18-ma in the main trend direction and a resistance area had just been reached. Both trades produced small losses. A decision was made to jump right back into trade 8 immediately after being stopped out of trade 7 because it looked like trade 7 was just a one tick probe on the stop out which happens from time to time. Again, looking at the art side of trading, I hope you can see that these were setups in tricky big picture scenario. There will be times you will take these trades, and other times you will bypass these trades. At the time, I felt this was the first pullback after the a big momentum move higher, and therefore the intra-day highs would at least be tested again. This never happened.

(TRADE 9, 10) The next two trades were taken after a big picture decision was made that this was a non-classic trend day in force. The reasons were as follows. Price failed at the gap down lows earlier in the session. Price exploded higher into a prior consolidation area edge. A wide high-low range developed with a clear new intra-day high that looked like it would be tested again as long as a normal intra-day structure pullback (i.e. 40-50 percent), or pullback to consolidation low, held. Trade 9 was a long entry on a thrust in the trend direction after price pulled back right to the 5-minute 18-ma trend line area. This trade was stopped out at the pivot lows for a loss. Trade 10 was a long entry on another thrust in the trend direction after 5000 price pulled back to the 89-ma trend line area in line with all big picture trend day price/volume pullback scenarios holding. Targets for both trades was the intra-day high in place on the day, and trades were trailed using the flow of 1500-pivots that formed along the way back up. Trade 10 was stopped out on a trailing pivot that formed as price was swinging higher.

(TRADE 11) Trade 10 was stopped out by one tick in a normal uptrend pullback area on the 1500-chart while volume ratio was holding above zero. A decision was made to immediately re-enter a standard 1-2-3 that formed after being stopped out. Expectation was still for new intra-day high on the day, and Trade 11 pullback provided another entry opportunity for this scenario and was eventually exited into a new intra-day high extension/pause.

(TRADE 12) Price sharply fell after trade 11 was exited which represented a failure at high of the day. (Look for C1-C). It was late in the day, but price moving back below the 1500 89-ma, volume below zero, and 5-minute price below the 18-ma, to set up one more C1-C short trade after a failure swing at resistance for another small gain when price made an extension swing to new lows right at the end of the trading session.

Conclusion - This is a typical trading day. Some trades are clear, others required interpretation. Some trades were aggressively taken, other trades were missed.

On this day, the key was a failure breakout move to the downside early.

Therefore, once the intra-day highs were strongly penetrated after this failure, it was decided that this day represented a non-classic trend day up, until a failure swing developed during an attempt to move past intra-day high resistance near the end of the trading session.

There were some good decisions to tighten stops early in trading session because price was failing at the lows.

There were some conservative decisions to exit winning trades early.

There were aggressive trade entry decisions near upper resistance that resulted in small losses. There was one missed trade that would have provided big gains.

In the end, however, all decisions put together resulted in an overall good trading day (+6.75 points), which is a nice piece in the monthly goal trading puzzle.

FINAL THOUGHTS

The master E=MC2 trader moves from a single state of mind that E=MC2 is just an endless set of individual mechanical signals to a complete state of understanding that there are clearly better times to trade than others, and that intuition and flexibility have a big role to play in terms of trading decisions, and outcomes.

Let's explore just the mechanical side for a moment. E=MC2 is clearly a "take a piece of the wave" approach.

C1's are shallow pullback waves and C2's are deeper pullback waves and in each case we wait for price to start back in the direction of the wave before entering, and then try to ride these wave to extensions, doing our best to hold on for the big winners that develop when significant wave extensions take place.

Does this mean you always have to wait for the "wave to turn" before entering to trade successfully? Of course not. Does this mean you always have to "try to hold trades way beyond extensions for big winners" to trade successfully? Of course not.

Catching a piece of the wave is a solid way to trade, and provides a great benchmark to monitor going forward as you explore making trading adjustments when conditions are right to do so.

The master E=MC2 trader moves beyond the notion that every trading signal is exactly the same and begins to add intuition to the trading equation.

For example you can look to hold certain trades longer according to developing 5-minute structure. You can exit trades with gains early if you are already up on the day, or have a good idea of price symmetry in place. You can enter trades aggressively (before the wave turns) if you see clear 5-minute pullback developments forming on trend days. You can exit aggressive trades very quickly if they don't immediately go your way as most good trades almost always go your way right from the start. You can stop trading when you sense the makeup of intra-day structure offers little additional opportunity, unless clear developments unfold. I can go on and on with examples.

Does this mean you are not "following the system?" Absolutely not! The E=MC2 framework still totally guides everything that you do, but over time you can become pretty good about tying together many things to know when there are good times to be aggressive and when there are times to be more cautious.

There are many, many times you will follow the rules exactly, and if not, then you still know how you are trading relative to what the rules should be doing (which is still maintaining a following of the rules).

Also, you will never be perfect. You will always make mistakes. You will always take losses you will kick yourself for, but you will also learn to do many things right, and in the end, as long as you never take a large loss (i.e.- more than 3-points, and try to reduce to 1.5 points as soon as reasonable), and continue to follow your instincts, I can almost assure you that you will end up fine.

BUILDING INTUITION – Here are the building blocks to becoming a master intuitive E=MC2 trader, which begins with an understanding of the "very best times to trade."

The best times to trade combine: (1) An understanding of big picture support/resistance (2) An understanding of how intra-day structure evolves from opening price action relative to yesterdays price range, to morphing into today's current intra-day structure formation.

Keep in mind what C1, C2, C3 and C1C trades are all about, and then tie this all together to understand how this blends into the flow of big picture and developing intra-day structure analysis.

C1 - When you see a **clear 5-minute trend in place that pulls back to the 18 ma and then starts back in the 5-minute direction,** look for classic C1 setups on pullbacks to the 1500 89-ma for a swing push to new 1500 highs or lows. **Also look for aggressive C1's after a breakout from consolidation or chop**. Be cautious of C1 setups where 1500-price has already made several C1 swing moves, as a deeper C2 pullback is likely soon. Look to take C1 profits into new 1500-swing highs or lows.

The key to the best C1's is that a 5-minute trend is in place, or a breakout has just occurred! Then you watch for pullbacks back to 1500 89-ma where volume holds zero area, get in, and look to get out into new 1500-swing highs or lows. It's that simple, and the 5-minute chart flow leads the way.

C2/C3 - These are deep 5-minute pullback to the 18-ma trend line area, which is also a deep 1500 pullback past the 89-ma. Here the master E=MC2 trader has choices. (1) You can watch for signs to enter "before" the 1500-turns in the 5-minute 18-ma pullback area (Trend days, First 5 minute pullback). (2) You can enter as usual with 1500 1-2-3/ trend line patterns back in the trend direction. (3) If you miss an entry you can enter when price moves beyond the 1500 89-ma and then pulls back to the 89-ma. I mention the more aggressive, "before the turn entry" because sometimes it is very clear that a new 5-minute trend has formed (intra-day trend change/breakout of consolidation), and 5-minute price is making the first pullback to 18-ma area, with a good volume bias, and you can get excellent entry location by entering before turn. If not, then wait 1500-price to turn and cross back beyond the LT 89-ma before entering.

C1-C - This is a volume ratio leads the way counter-trade that best occurs at 3 times - (1) Fading a Gap when the 5-minute chart opens way beyond a previous close, and will retrace back. (2) When "overall 5000 intra-day structure" is over-extended and due for a retrace (i.e. - after a series of C1, C2 moves to support/resistance area). (3) After a double top/bottom failure at key big picture support/resistance area. Volume moving past and holding zero opposite the current trend leads the C1-C set up every time. Don't go looking for a C1-C at every moment, just the clear moments relative to a gap fade, over-extended intra-day structure, or failure at a key high or low. Target 5-minute 18-ma pullback areas, and/or a logical percentage retraces/extension of intra-day structure.

Other aggressive "before the turn" entries can develop when 1500-price makes a volume divergence swing in the 5-minute 18-ma pullback area.

If you take aggressive entries, <u>set a 3-point maximum risk stop and start watching 1500-price action very closely to reduce this stop as soon as possible</u>.

1500-price might consolidate in the pullback area a bit after entry, but it should begin to start back your way fairly quickly, and if not, either just get out, or tighten your stop to a new pivot that forms. When you are right about the timing of these aggressive entries, ride these trades with 5-minute price flow for new 5-minute price swings, and very nice gains.

If you enter with normal 1-2-3 patterns, or after the pullback and turn, you can also use intuition to ride 5-minute swings. Also, as a master trader, when you have a profitable trade, always look to move stop to <u>break even plus a tick</u> when you can sense price is on the way to make a new 5-minute swing extensions as expected. You simply don't want to lose money on the trade if it doesn't follow through as expected. You can always re-enter if price continues to hold in your trade direction.

Finally as a master trader, on <u>trend days</u>, look for deep 5-minute pullbacks to enter, and hold on for big gains to new intra-day highs and lows.

Trend days are often slow moving/choppy and you must consider the flexibility to adjust from normal E=MC2 mechanical setups and play big picture structure instead.

That's all there is to it!

This is what Master E=MC2 trading is all about. You have so many ways to make this all work for you as you remain patient and only wait for the best opportunities and conditions to trade!

The great strength of $E=MC^2$ is that it offers a **definitive, complete trading plan** – from the big picture of an overall trading philosophy right down to the details for methods of execution and trading goals. Any method you chose to trade must make a complete trading plan very clear. If not, beware.

There are many traders who attempt to trade without a solid foundation, or trading plan of any kind. This is very dangerous. Also, many traders apply trading methods without a clear sense of realistic trading goals or expectations.

$E=MC^2$ provides a consistent flow of trade opportunities day after day. **In the end, this is the single most important part of a trading method– consistent trade opportunity and consistent execution.**

You should follow the trades and results of $E=MC^2$ until you are absolutely comfortable that this approach performs as suggested before you ever decide to trade for real.

This is the only way you will develop the confidence necessary to trade this method without hesitation, or fear.

If you are already a successful trader, $E=MC^2$ will add a whole new dimension to your trading arsenal.

If you are new to trading, or searching for a method that takes a new approach from the one you are currently using, $E=MC^2$ represents an overall approach that has originated from years of actual trading experience - applying just about every type of trading approach there is.

The value of this trading experience cannot be overstated, and the benefit that it brings to the $E=MC^2$ approach is enormous.

In the end, however, it is simply up to you. You must have the discipline to follow, and execute the rules, and make this work for you in your own way. If you do, the rewards of $E=MC^2$ will last you a lifetime!

<u>GOOD LUCK IN YOUR TRADING!!</u>

Remember there is no Holy Grail in trading and nothing works perfect all of the time.

Learn to "Dance with the Market" and always remember that the market leads the way and you need to follow. The market is telling you where it wants to go most of the time.

The E=MC2 framework as a whole allows you to listen to what the market is saying, and also provides you with a host of logical ways to take high probability trades over and over again!

NOW AVAILABLE

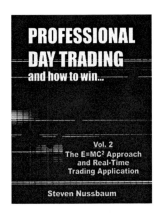

PROFESSIONAL DAY TRADING
and how to win....
Vol. 2 - The E=MC2 Approach
and Real-Time Trading Application

E=MC2 Vol. 2 is the highly anticipated follow up to E=MC2 Vol. 1 that takes you deep inside the mind of the E=MC2 trader by presenting a 1-month running diary of Real-Time E=MC2 Trading Application - including live trading examples - verified by account statements, while also providing an updated, and alternative approach to original E=MC2 trade entry, and trade management execution.

E=MC2 Vol. 1. lays the foundation for day trading success, and E=MC2 Vol. 2 takes this foundation a major step forward by utilizing a format that feels like you have a **"E=MC2 TRADING COACH SITTING BY YOUR SIDE AS YOU LEARN TO TRADE!"**

For an entire month, you are taken inside the mind of the E=MC2 trader with a detailed explanation of the way you need to look at the market each and every day- from before trading session begins, to reading the opening gap/first move of the day, to uncovering the best trade opportunities that unfold each trading session according to developing intra-day structure within the context of big picture support and resistance.

Live trading results are included within the diary format (verified by account statements) so you can see how day-to-day E=MC2 analysis translates into real-world results as you work to attain realistic E=MC2 trading goals.

In addition, E=MC2 Vol. 2 presents an alternative "scalping" approach for ***entering and exiting trades*** that remains under the umbrella of the standard entry and exit rules found in E=MC2 Vol. 1, but in many cases is easier and clearer to apply.

Therefore, for readers of E=MC2 Vol. 1, E=MC2 Vol. 2 is designed to take E=MC2 trading education to a new and exciting level by offering an alternative trade management approach within the context of original E=MC2 structure, and most important, compliments E=MC2 Vol. 1 material by providing a wide range of real-time trading application examples in an effort to speed up the E=MC2 learning curve tremendously.

The real-world trading information found in EMC2 Vol. 2 is designed to show you how to put E=MC2 "theory into practice," and brings E=MC2 education to another level when it comes to "How to Succeed at Trading!"

LaVergne, TN USA
06 January 2011
211355LV00003B/90/P